# Building the Bonds
# of Attachment

# Building the Bonds of Attachment

## Second Edition

## Awakening Love in Deeply Troubled Children

Daniel A. Hughes

JASON ARONSON
Lanham • Boulder • New York • Toronto • Oxford

Published in the United States of America
by Jason Aronson
An imprint of Rowman & Littlefield Publishers, Inc.

A wholly owned subsidiary of
The Rowman & Littlefield Publishing Group, Inc.
4501 Forbes Boulevard, Suite 200, Lanham, Maryland 20706
www.rowmanlittlefield.com

PO Box 317
Oxford
OX2 9RU, UK

British Library Cataloguing in Publication Information Available

**Library of Congress Cataloging-in-Publication Data**

Hughes, Daniel A.
  Building the bonds of attachment : awakening love in deeply troubled children /
Daniel A. Hughes.— 2nd ed.
    p. cm.
  Includes bibliographical references.
  ISBN-13: 978-0-7657-0404-7 (pbk. : alk. paper)
  ISBN-10: 0-7657-0404-8 (pbk. : alk. paper)
  1. Attachment behavior in children. 2. Adopted children—Family relationships. 3.
Foster children—Family relationships. I. Title.
  RJ507.A77H837 2006
  155.4'18—dc22                                                      2005028651

Printed in the United States of America

♾️™ The paper used in this publication meets the minimum requirements of American
National Standard for Information Sciences—Permanence of Paper for Printed Library
Materials, ANSI/NISO Z39.48-1992.

# Contents

# Acknowledgments

I wish to begin by acknowledging my debt to many foster and adoptive parents, throughout the State of Maine and other states, who have challenged, taught, and supported me in my efforts to understand and assist them and their children. I have frequently learned from them and I have constantly drawn inspiration from them.

I also wish to recognize the cooperative and creative contributions to this work made by many other therapists, caseworkers, and various other professionals who are themselves dedicated to finding ways to assist the unattached child become a full member of his or her family and community. There is not yet enough professional understanding as to the pervasive problems that these children manifest, nor with regard to the comprehensive interventions that are required to assist them. Professionals working with these children need to face their responsibility with humility, dedication, care, and creativity if they are to make a difference. I know many who are now doing that. We need to support each other in our work, recognizing that we are all searching for ways to be of help.

My understanding of attachment certainly originated in my family of origin. My mother, Marie, and deceased father, William, as well as my delightful and interesting siblings, Jim, Mary Pat, Kathy, Bill, John, and Mike, remain embedded in my sense of self-and-other. Finally, my wife, Barbara, who has been on her journey, which has interwoven with mine, for the past 35 years, has been a part of every insight that I have attained regarding facilitating attachment among children who have difficulty trusting their caregivers. With Barbara, I have truly learned a great deal about attachment through our continuing bonds with our children, Megan, Kristin, and Madeline, who are at varying stages of their own unique and interesting journeys.

# Preface

In healthy families, a baby forms a secure attachment with her parents as naturally as she breathes, eats, smiles and cries. This occurs easily because of her parents' attuned interactions with her. Her parents notice her physiological/affective states and they respond to her sensitively and fully. Beyond simply meeting her unique needs, however, her parents "dance" with her. Hundreds of times, day after day, they dance with her.

There are other families where the baby neither dances nor even hears the sound of any music. In these families she does not form such secure attachments. Rather, her task—her continuous ordeal—is to learn to live with parents who are little more than strangers. Babies who live with strangers do not live well or grow well.

This work attempts to describe the difficult journey needed to understand and help children who experienced severe abuse and neglect and who do not develop attachment security with their foster and adoptive parents. I chose a composite case study for this work to convey the story of many such individual children and families. Each child is unique and presents with a constellation of factors relevant to his or her life. The interventions that one child needs may be less valuable to another. I hope to be able to present the general principles of intervention, both at home and in therapy, with traumatized children who do not manifest attachment security. At the same time I hope that both therapists and parents can immediately recognize and identify with this story. I believe that the narrative format is best able to convey the affective tone and communications needed to make the interventions effective. I hope that the reader will find the basic principles of intervention that are relevant in this composite case study to be helpful in living and working with countless similar children and their families.

Katie, an abused, neglected, and poorly attached child, exists only in these pages. The same is true for her caseworker, Steven, her primary foster parent, Jackie, her therapist, Allison, and the various secondary characters. But the great majority of events, experiences, relationships, thoughts, feelings, and behaviors described in this book has occurred, do occur, and will continue to occur in Maine, the nation, and throughout the world. They will occur wherever there are traumatized children who do not know how to develop attachment security with their new parents. In my work as a psychologist, they have occurred countless times. Katie and Jackie are telling the stories of these living individuals because their stories must be heard, understood, and addressed. These children need our attention, our guidance, our love, and our help. They need to begin to live safely within the human community.

Katie's story represents the arduous journey faced by most traumatized children with impaired abilities to develop attachment security with their caregivers. Many have continuing histories that prove to be far less successful than does Katie's. Many disrupt from placements throughout their childhood and adolescence and enter adulthood without any relationships that provide them with a sense of being "at home." Many then enter into further unsatisfactory relationships that lead to deceptions, divorces, domestic violence, substance abuse, and ultimately to the abuse and neglect of their own children. The cycle of abuse is greatest among those adults and children who do not know how to form meaningful attachments.

The character Katie Harrison is followed from birth until after her eighth birthday. Over her first five years she is repeatedly abused emotionally and physically. She also experiences profound emotional neglect from parents who ignore her, are indifferent to her, and who have no place for her in their hearts. Over the following three years Katie experiences a series of foster homes. The damage done to her by her parents remains alive within her affective core and greatly impedes her readiness and ability to develop attachment security with her new caregivers.

# 1

## Introduction

It is not often that one can go back in time and change the events that shape one's life story. Actually, it is impossible to do so. We are able to change our experience of past events—how we think and feel about them, what meaning they have in the context of our life story—but not the events themselves. Yet, in this second edition of *Building the Bonds of Attachment*, I am doing just that. Katie's early life is unchanged and her behaviors as she came to live with Jackie are also the same. However, in this edition Jackie and Allison relate with her somewhat differently than they did originally. Since Katie's story first appeared in 1998, I have continued to develop in my ways of understanding children like Katie. I have continued to refine my interventions with such children, both in the treatment sessions as well as in the home. My recommendations to parents continue to evolve. For Katie's story to reflect these changes, a second edition is required.

Since 1998, there has been continuing research toward both understanding and providing interventions to children such as Katie who have experienced attachment-related traumas, neglect, and loss. I hope to incorporate aspects of this developing body of knowledge into this edition. Also, over the past eight years I have become more familiar with the extensive body of research knowledge that had been present even before I first wrote Katie's story. I hope that this edition is more congruent with the very comprehensive body of theory and research regarding child development with respect to attachment. Finally, as a clinician, practicing in an area for which there are not yet well-established "best practice guidelines," I have continuously reflected upon the interventions employed. I reduced or eliminated some as being not relevant, or even counterproductive to the treatment process. I added or increased emphasis on others as I found them to be quite beneficial to the goals of treatment and parenting that were established. My primary goal has been to remain faithful to the empirical knowledge that has emerged from academic centers as well as from experienced clinicians and parents who are engaged in the "real-life" stories of so many children and youths. I will now describe both areas of our understanding as they have affected this edition of Katie's story.

## SELECTED THEORIES AND RESEARCH

Fundamental to attachment security is personal safety. The central purpose for developing attachments for young children is to ensure their safety. Once safety is guaranteed, other aspects of childhood can proceed. The mind works the best under conditions of perceived safety. Without safety, the mind's almost exclusive function is to reduce threat and create safety through variations of "fight, flight or freeze." In making the split-second decision to reduce risk, the mind does not involve the later forming parts of the brain—the prefrontal cortex and the more verbal/associative functions of the brain. Once safety is insured, the infant or young child is now able to explore her world, involving all aspects of the brain in an integrative fashion. This central role of perceived safety as the foundation of all subsequent development is made explicit by those at the more abstract levels of neuropsychological theory and research (Schore, 2001; Siegel, 1999) as well as the applied research that rests on attachment theory (Dozier et al., 2001; Marvin et al., 2002).

When the infant and young child begins to explore her world, her first interest is the interpersonal world. A central characteristic of such exploration—optimized in circumstances of attachment security—involves **primary and secondary intersubjectivity** (Trevarthern, 2001; Trevarthen & Aitken, 2001). By **primary intersubjectivity**, I am referring to the infant and parent's discovery of each other, and also to the self in relation to the other. The infant discovers who she is—her original sense of self—in the eyes, face, voice, gestures and touch of her mother and father. Her self-discovery involves the discovery of the impact that she is having on her attachment figures. The parent discovers who he or she is—with respect to identity as parent—in the infant's response to him or her. Primary intersubjectivity involves this here-and-now **person-to-person** relationship.

By **secondary intersubjectivity**, I am referring to the infant's discovery of the features of the world—people, objects, and events—through experiencing the impact of the world on both her and her parents. When the parent responds to a stranger or to an event, the parent gives meaning to it and provides the template for the meaning that the child will associate with the stranger or event. Secondary intersubjectivity involves a here-and-now **person-to-person-to-object** relationship.

**Affect attunement**—shared affect—is only one aspect of intersubjectivity. Two other features involve shared *attention* as well as shared *intentions*. Not only are the parent and infant involved in a congruent state of vitality affect, also their attention has a similar focus on who/what is important to them both at that moment, and their intentions are compatible (to notice, discover, and enjoy each other or an event/object of the world). By focusing broadly on intersubjectivity rather than the more specific feature of affect attunement, one is able to comprehend how the parent-child dyad affects both the mind and the heart of each other. Through attunement, the infant feels receptive to and connected to his parent, and also is able to begin to regulate his affective states through first co-regulating his affect with his parent's affective state. Through the addition of joint attention and intention, the infant is also able to begin to reflect on her inner life of thought, affect, and intentions, as well as the inner lives of her parents. She is able to co-create the meaning of the people, objects, and events of her life.

To be intersubjective, this process must affect *both* the infant and parent. Just as the infant is engaged in a process of discovery of self-and-other through the joint experience with his attachment figure, so too does the parent discover aspects of self-and-other through being engaged in this process. It is inherently reciprocal. If the parent is not affected by his or her infant, the infant will be less affected by her parent. It is likely that in that situation—analogous to neglect—the infant's experience of self includes a core sense that "I am not interesting, not special, and not loveable to my parent." If the infant is not affected by her parent, the parent's sense of self-as-parent will be damaged. When a child has significant difficulty engaging in behaviors consistent with attachment security, her parents are at risk to begin to doubt their parenting abilities and to react negatively to their perception of their child's "rejection" of them.

When the parent's reaction to the child is one of anger, fear, or rejection, the child is very likely to avoid intersubjective experiences since they are likely to elicit a great deal of terror and shame. She will not be safe in intersubjective states. Her resultant sense of self is likely to be very negative as well as very incoherent, with large gaps and inconsistencies. She is not likely to be able to utilize the primary means of learning about herself, others, events, and objects—the mind and heart of her parent.

I have made the argument that for a child to develop well, she needs to have a positive impact on the key people in her life—her parents—and in Katie's case, her foster parents and therapist as well. Given the pervasive emotional/behavioral problems of a child similar to Katie, the danger for the foster/adoptive parents of this child is that she will have a negative impact on them. Her anger, rejection, withdrawal, defiance, and indifference may activate within the parents doubts about their parenting abilities. Sensing that they are failing as parents, these parents are not likely to feel safe while with their child. Their worth, value and abilities are being questioned continuously. These parents will be at risk to withdraw from intersubjective experiences with their child. They are at risk to become angry, tense, withdrawn, discouraged, and indifferent to their child.

For this reason, *each parent's own* **attachment history** is an important factor in whether or not the parent will be able to successfully raise a child who is very resistant to having parents who will raise her (Dozier et al., 2001; Steele et al., 2003). If the child's behavior activates within her aspects of her own relationships with her parents that were unresolved and poorly integrated, she is likely to react with anger or anxiety in response to her child. Not feeling safe herself, she will not be able to provide a sense of safety for her child that will be necessary if her child is to learn new emotional/behavioral patterns. A parent who has attained her own attachment security in the important relationships in her life will be able to remain affectively present—sensitive, responsive and available—to her child, when her child is becoming affectively/cognitively/behaviorally dysregulated. She will not react to her child's extremely angry and anxious behaviors but rather will respond to the aspects of the child that lie underneath those behaviors (loneliness, fear, shame, despair) and initiate intersubjective experiences that can facilitate resolution and integration of those states.

Nonverbal communication represents both the source of the initial decision as to whether or not to initiate an intersubjective experience as well as a central feature of intersubjectivity itself. When the young child perceives anger or rejection in the face or voice of his parent, he is unlikely to enter an intersubjective state with his parent. He will be unwilling to learn about self-and-other at those moments since he knows that what he learns will not be pleasant. Similarly, when the parent perceives her child to be angry or anxious, she may avoid entering an intersubjective state with her child if her child's affect is making her uncomfortable. She will avoid that connection if it activates unresolved experiences from her attachment history and if it makes her vulnerable to thoughts that she is failing as a parent.

The parent needs to be aware of the impact of her nonverbal communication upon her child and attempt to regulate and direct it in a manner that facilitates—and does not impede—intersubjective learning. Habitual annoyance, routinely avoiding interactions, and remaining ambiguous about the meaning of negative affective states, all make the child who lacks attachment security more guarded and avoidant with respect to entering intersubjective states. Without such states the child will remain lacking in safety and trust as well as in the interpersonal skills necessary to develop a more positive and integrated sense of self. This child is likely to see anger when it is not there and to perceive negative motives in both the self (shame) and the parent (negative attributions) (Feiring et al., 2002). This child is less likely to be able to perceive her parents as being both the source of safety as well as the way to understand important qualities of self, other, and the world (Pears & Fisher, 2005).

## MODIFICATIONS IN TREATMENT/PARENTING

There are a number of changes in the presentation of parenting and treatment as compared to the first edition of this work. The primary changes are the following:

1. The therapist must understand the attachment history of the foster or adoptive parent before the onset of the child's treatment. The therapist needs to have confidence that the parent is able and willing to explore how her history may impact her child-rearing. The parent needs to have confidence that the therapist is not blaming the parent for the child's problems. Rather, the parent understands that most adults are likely to have some aspects of their own attachment histories that are not fully resolved and integrated and which might make it difficult to raise a child with attachment problems of her own. During the course of treatment, when the parent's response to the child's behavior appears to reflect factors separate from the behavior itself, the parties involved must address and resolve these issues.

   Certainly all parents, at times, become angry, anxious, discouraged, or ashamed in response to their daily interactions with their children. When these affective states are dysregulating—when they make it difficult to remain sensitive to the child or to repair a disrupted relationship with the child—then the parties must address these states. When the parent is able to remain affectively present when their child is in such states of anger, anxiety, sadness, or shame, then the parent will be able to co-regulate the negative affect and co-create new meanings of self-other that the child can integrate.

   The second edition explores Jackie's relationship with her mother. Features of that relationship have increased the difficulty of consistently being a safe attachment figure for Katie. The same is true regarding Mark—and Allison—though the story does not recount these others.

2. In the first edition, Allison frequently held Katie throughout the treatment session. When she was not holding her, Jackie often was. In this
   edition, Jackie holds Katie during times of heightened enjoyment, nurturing, comforting, or distress, but Allison does not. This change is due
   to the need to facilitate the child's relationship with the parent at every
   opportunity. Circumstances that involve safely holding a willing child
   during moments of heightened affect provide excellent opportunities.

   Much more often now in treatment, no one is holding the child,
   though the parent or therapist is touching her frequently in a comforting, supportive, playful, affectionate, or validating manner. Touch remains an excellent means of communicating interest, empathy, reciprocal enjoyment, trust, and compassion for all of us. It is also a valuable
   means of co-regulating affect. The research of Tiffany Field (2002) and
   others demonstrates the crucial role of touch in human development and
   healing.

   I hope to make it more clear in this edition that touch is never used to
   intimidate, force compliance, intimidate, or cause any discomfort.
   Adults do not coerce it against the child's wishes. The child needs to
   feel safe when being touched or it will only increase fear and place the
   child at risk to experience it as traumatic. Children who have been traumatized by touch need to learn that they are "touchable" in a way that
   helps to build their sense of worth. Children who resist being touched
   by their parents need to discover the value of appropriate touch in their
   lives. If parents wait "until she is ready," the child may never be
   touched. The parents need to accept their child's resistance to touch,
   while at the same time gently encouraging her to address the underlying fear and in small, safe, steps to integrate touch with attachment figures into her life.

   Upon reflection, my early efforts to have the therapist rather than the
   parent hold the child represented an uncertainty as to whether or not
   the parent would feel confident, be able to co-regulate the child's affect, communicate safety and comfort, and reassure the child that no
   one is angry with her. I now believe that if the therapist is uncertain
   about the parents' abilities to co-regulate the child's negative affect,
   then the therapist's first goal is to address this uncertainty rather than
   work with the child in the presence of this doubt. The therapist—and
   more importantly, the child—needs to have confidence that the parent
   is able to remain present for the child, with empathy and strength,
   when the child is in acute distress. It is not appropriate to invite the
   child to become open and vulnerable in treatment—to the degree that
   the child might not fully integrate it by the end of the session—unless

the therapist is confident that the parent can appropriately contain this distress at home if necessary.

Another reason that Allison held Katie in the first edition was to facilitate her readiness to attend and respond to difficult themes. There is some danger, however, that the child might experience being held as being forced to address issues that the child does not want to address. A comparable danger is that the therapist and parent might begin to pressure the child to explore his behavior or trauma in a manner that elicits dysregulating fear or shame. I now believe that the therapist can achieve such attentional focus on the themes through both structure and also by setting a slower pace which incorporates taking breaks from the difficult themes. With an attitude of acceptance, curiosity, and empathy, children often will gradually begin to address events and behaviors that need to be resolved, at a rate that they can integrate. It is better not to associate holding with structuring, which might diminish the value of holding as nurturing, comforting, co-regulating affect, providing compassion and reciprocal relaxation and joy.

Many young children with intense symptoms secondary to trauma, loss and poorly developed frustration tolerance and affect regulation abilities, become aggressive and destructive frequently in their foster or adoptive homes. This may occur regardless of the quality of care that they are receiving in the home. With such children, the parent needs to be able to safely restrain the child until she can manifest sufficient self-control to not pose a danger to self or other. With such children, the slightest limit or frustration may elicit an intense rage outburst. At times, there is no apparent precipitant.

When restraint is necessary it needs to occur with maximum concern for the child's physical and psychological safety along with concern for the safety of the parent. With such children, therapy is likely to periodically elicit similar rage outbursts, if only because of the structure imposed or the stressful themes explored—regardless of how cautiously these themes are introduced. In such situations, it again is the primary responsibility of the parent, not the therapist, to restrain the child, until she is able to manifest sufficient self-control to no longer pose a risk to self or other.

When the child is being restrained frequently at home, and if they are not decreasing in spite of the parents maximizing the structure and interactions needed to minimize the need for restraints, then medication needs to be considered. Once safety becomes difficult to insure, then a more restrictive out-of-home placement may be necessary. For the sake of attachment security and the child's long-term development, this option needs to be avoided whenever possible.

3. In the first edition, Allison often told Katie to "say it louder" in an effort to generate more intense affect with each repetition. With an increase in affect, Katie would be more likely to experience the meaning of the event at a deeper level and then to respond in a way that genuinely reflected this deepening experience. I have since found that the better results can be attained through elaborations on the experience with curiosity and empathy. Through placing herself affectively within the child's experience, the therapist is able to intersubjectively deepen its meaning to the child. If the meaning does not seem to change, or there is no affect associated with an event that one would anticipate intense affect, then the therapist is able to be curious about this, rather than trying to induce it by having the child "say it louder."

4. In the first edition, I emphasized affect attunement and the co-regulation of affect. In this edition, I am focusing on the entire intersubjective experience (attunement, joint attention and complimentary intentions), not simply attunement. The intersubjective experience is central to the development and coherence of the sense of self. Therapy frequently provides this experience—the child experiences the impact that she is having on the therapist (playfulness, acceptance, curiosity, and empathy) in response to any memory, experience, or affective state, so that the child clarifies and deepens her subjective experience through the co-creation of meaning, and welcomes the experience into the sense of self.

5. In the first edition, a central feature of Jackie's care of Katie involved providing her with a high level of structure and supervision in order to assist Katie in regulating her affect, achieving successes, learning to rely on Jackie, and developing routines. Over time, these skills become habitual and there is less need for structure and supervision.

   In this edition, I hope to make it more clear that these levels of structure and supervision do not imply providing Katie with continuous chores. Structure and supervision are never a punishment. Rather they are a gift of child-care that a parent provides when a child lacks the developmental skills necessary to achieve successes in managing the events of his day. Parents routinely give this gift to toddlers and the same gift is often necessary for children like Katie.

   Within the context of structure and supervision, Jackie presents Katie with a routine that involves active and quiet activities, interactive and solitary activities, as well as opportunities for both play and doing age-appropriate chores. When given, the child often does chores best in tandem with the parent, much as pre-school children do. Parents may also give chores as a consequence for certain acts of destruction, aggression, or cruelty in order to "do something for" the one who was hurt by the action—never to force compliance and submission.

Hopefully this second edition of *Building the Bonds of Attachment* will prove to be as beneficial as the first edition to the therapists and parents who become part of the lives of children like Katie. Experimental, empirical, and experiential endeavors, occurring in academic settings, clinical offices, and homes need to constantly learn from each other the best ways of assisting each child. I believe that we do now know that at the core of such assistance will always be the parent-child relationship. More than anything else, the child needs his parent to assist him in discovering who he is and who he can become.

# 2

## The Abuse and Neglect of Katie

On Tuesday, August 4, 1987, in Augusta, Maine, Katie Harrison was born and Steven Fields spent his first day working as a child protective worker with the Department of Human Services (DHS), State of Maine. While Steven was beginning to work with the abused and neglected children of Maine, Katie was becoming an abused and neglected child. Eventually she would be placed in the legal custody of the State of Maine. That day would not come for five years, one month, and nine days.

It's an unusual reality—a child in the custody of a state. In the abstract, one might think that such a life would not be too bad for a child. Every adult citizen of Maine is responsible for Katie. If her parents will not raise her well, then we, all of the adults of Maine, will do it. But in reality, Katie's reality, all of the adults of Maine are not what she needs to resolve her traumas and develop into a healthy child. Rather, she needs one family. She needs to have this family provide her with safety, teach her to trust and to love, and help her to heal and resolve her countless traumas and develop an integrated self. Without such a family, she will not begin to feel worthwhile and she will not feel connected to others in the human community. All of the adults of Maine are not capable of raising Katie. Their responsibility is to insure that she receives such a family, and receives professionals such as Steven who provide for her various needs. Often many of the adults of Maine do not take their responsibility seriously enough. Possibly this failing is due to not knowing Katie. Her story, which is similar to countless others throughout the world, might help us all to understand our various responsibilities for all children.

On November 10, 1987, Katie was in her crib where she had spent much of her first three months. It was getting colder in Maine and she was now almost habitually cold since her thin blanket was not sufficient for the weather. Being cold was unpleasant, as was the common soreness that she felt because her diaper was changed infrequently and she was bathed even less frequently. More acute and irregular discomfort came from her hunger. At times, her cries brought food fairly quickly while at other times she cried for long periods of time before being fed. Actually, sometimes she cried until she fell asleep, exhausted and still in pain. At other times, she heard frightening noises that made her cry harder. On those occasions, her mother Sally, or her father Mike, were not patient with her crying and they screamed at her as if that would calm her.

This day proved to be worse than average for Katie. She had not been fed and she probably was crying louder that usual. Mike screamed at her and then shook her by the shoulders and slapped her across the head. The pain was sudden, unexpected, and acute. Katie knew no other response but to cry louder. Mike slapped her again and put his face inches above her and screamed. Katie's world became total pain and chaos. Her arms and legs shook and flailed out, her back arched and her cries made it difficult for her to breath. Her eyes were wide and unfocused.

Sally came into the room and screamed at Mike to leave Katie alone and to never hit her again. She picked Katie up, spoke quietly, and rocked her. Sally continued to yell at Mike and her tension made it even harder for Katie to relax. Finally, Katie began to drink from her bottle, but she fell asleep before drinking what she needed. After two hours of restless sleep, she awoke and cried for more milk. Sally was now sleeping and did not respond so eventually Katie fell asleep again, still hungry, troubled, and frightened.

Sally Thomas was nineteen when Katie was born. She and Mike Harrison, who was four years older than she, had been together for eighteen months in spite of frequent conflicts and periodic separations. Sally wanted Mike to "settle down" and when she brought her wishes to him, he generally left in anger. Over time, Sally kept to herself the resentment she felt about his lack of interest in working or getting married. He did get odd jobs but she generally found that he drank more and stayed out more with his friends when he was working. As a result, she had mixed feelings about him having a job. Usually it just caused more fights.

Sally was initially excited to have Katie. Her own mother, Helen, and her older sisters seemed to be pleased that she was a mother and she enjoyed her new status as an adult. She also had hoped that Mike would take an interest in Katie and want to help out with her and maybe even provide for her. When the opposite proved to be the case and Mike became more withdrawn and irritable than ever before, Sally began to resent Katie's constant demands. She found herself becoming increasingly impatient with her. She initially resisted this change in her attitude toward Katie since she had always told herself that she would do a better job raising her children than did her own mother in raising her. It seemed to Sally that during her own childhood her mother either yelled at her or ignored her. There seemed to have been little else. She had been sure that she and Katie would be different.

Sally knew that now she did not enjoy Katie very much. Katie might look at her and Sally would look away. She felt at times that Katie just wanted too much from her! Katie never seemed to be satisfied. Sally tried not to think about it. In some ways Katie seemed to be dissatisfied with her just like her mother always was. She couldn't please her mother and now she couldn't even please her own kid! Sally was confused over Katie's reaction to her. At times, she did not think that Katie liked her. She would play with her but Katie would not seem to be interested. She would feed and bathe her but Katie might cry 30 minutes later. She might cry when Sally held her or cry when she put her down. She did not feel that she knew Katie and she did not feel much pleasure from caring for her. Being a mother wasn't what she had expected.

Sally thought about telling the nurse at the pediatrician's office that she really didn't think that she knew what to do when Katie cried. She wanted to tell her how hard it was and how tired she often felt. She wanted to tell her that being a mother wasn't what she had hoped it would be. But how could she say those things? How could she admit that she couldn't even raise a kid? Maybe she could ask for some help. Maybe someone could give her something to read. She had heard of a parenting class at Adult Ed at Cony High. Maybe she should take that. But who would watch Katie? Mike wouldn't. Instead, Mike would be annoyed with her for going off and doing something on her own. Sally ended up not thinking about her doubts. It seemed to be easier to just do what she had to do and then try to relax in front of the TV. She felt too tired to do anything else.

Katie, at three months of age, was actually not rejecting her mother. Her energies were going toward feeling safe and warm, being full, and making sense of her world. Inner feeling states led her toward food, sleep, removing some discomfort, or noticing something new. She was especially interested in human faces. "Sally" was a significant part of her feeling states that best served to meet her various needs. "Sally" did not have meaning for Katie apart from those needs. At times, Katie fussed and cried and "Sally" was there and Katie would feel better. But sometimes "Sally" was not there. Katie would fuss and cry over some discomfort and the "Sally" part of herself was not there to bring comfort. The discomfort continued and intensified and still "Sally" was absent. Katie could not bring comfort to herself because "Sally" was absent. She did not have confidence in herself because she did not trust a response from that part of herself, "Sally," that should bring comfort. She did not have confidence in her "world" since for so long it provided her with nothing but varying forms of discomfort which were driven by hunger, sudden, loud sounds, water that was too hot or too cold, or a habitual soreness that was developing under her diaper.

On February 14, 1988, Sally may have made her last extended effort to raise Katie "right." Her father, Sam, who spent much of his life in the Portland bars and fishing boats, was coming to visit Sally with his new girlfriend, Tammy. If Sam held true to form, he was likely to "settle down" for a few months until he lost interest in Tammy. His trip to Augusta to visit his daughter and granddaughter was most likely to impress Tammy, but Sally didn't mind. She would show her father that she was a good mother who was making something of herself. He might come again, enjoy her and her family, and even want to be a part of her life.

When Sally began the day with Katie, she felt happy and capable. She fed Katie her bottle and then bathed her. Katie seemed glad to be with her. She smiled and splashed and seemed to respond when Sally played and laughed and acted silly with her. Katie did like her! She was doing a good job and her father would be proud of her. She put Katie down to sleep and got everything ready.

Katie was now six months old and on most days Sally wished that Katie could begin to take care of herself more. Mike never helped and he even resented Katie when she took Sally's attention away from him. Sally didn't often enjoy Katie anymore, but she did what she knew she was supposed to do, at least most of the time. She took some consolation in knowing that she was probably doing a better job with Katie than her mother ever did for her or her sisters.

Katie was increasingly confused because a subtle need that had been gradually increasing over the past three or four months was not being adequately met. Katie had one magical and pleasurable feeling state whenever Sally and Katie interacted in a playful and affectionate way. Katie would feel drawn toward Sally's eyes, her smile, and the musical sound of her voice. When Sally was dancing in front of Katie's eyes, Katie would feel arms around her and her body would rock and dance. At these times too, Katie would feel hands on her head and face and body. Those touches brought such pleasure when they accompanied Sally's face and voice! Katie more and more sought those feeling states that were deeply connected to her experience of Sally. But they were not happening often. Katie would search for those eyes, and smiles, and hands, and arms, and very often not find them. At times, they came along with the milk feeling state. But even then, more often than not, when Sally brought the milk she did not bring with it the playful and affectionate feeling state that would invite the reciprocal state in her that Katie wanted desperately to feel.

Katie awoke crying 30 minutes before Sally's father arrived. Sally carried her, sang to her, fed her, and changed her diaper. Sally was calm and hopeful initially, but when Katie did not stop fussing, she became tense. Mike could not stand her crying and she needed to have Mike stay calm. If her father were not coming, Katie would be back in the crib to cry herself to sleep and Mike would take off and she'd turn on the TV. That's the only way they could get through the crying. But her father arrived and she had to get Katie to stop.

As usual, Sam and Sally were awkward together after not having seen each other for a year or so. Initially Katie was a distraction as her father and Tammy laughed at how loud she screamed and they praised Sally for being able to raise her. Tammy, who wasn't much older than Sally, made it clear that she never planned to have a kid. Hearing Katie cry convinced her that she was right.

Eventually Sam gave Sally some suggestions about how to quiet Katie. She was not sure if he wanted to be helpful or if he had enough of the noise. Regardless, she didn't want his help. She knew Katie better than anyone did and if she could not get her to stop crying then no one could. She took Katie into her bedroom and placed her in the crib.

Sam followed her and told Sally that she shouldn't leave Katie in bed when she was crying. Their interchange flared and the focus moved from Sally raising Katie to how Sam had failed to raise Sally. Finally, Sam exploded,

"Instead of talking to me that way you should be taking care of your kid!"

"I do take care of her. It's more than you ever did for me!"

"If you don't want us here, we're leaving! What's your problem?"

"I'm a good mother. It's not my fault that she's crying."

"Why don't you go feed her then? We're OK here."

"No! No!" cried Sally. "I'll take care of her the way I damn well please! Leave it alone!"

"That noise is driving me crazy," yelled Sam.

"Then leave. That's what you've always done," said Sally.

Sam and Tammy left. Mike said that Sally had not handled that well. Sally didn't hear him. She could only hear Katie. She ran into her room.

"Shut up! Shut up!" she screamed as she pulled her from the crib and threw her toward the bed. Katie hit the side of the bed and bounced to the floor, with her leg awkwardly bent beneath her. Katie cried in acute pain. Sally screamed, shook, and covered her face. Mike swore and yelled and paced. Finally, Sally was able to call an ambulance. Mike told Sally to tell the people at the hospital that Katie rolled off the bed while Sally was getting her milk.

At the hospital, Sally seemed to be in shock. She tried to care for her daughter appropriately but she was emotionally withdrawn. She refused help when offered it by the hospital social worker. The hospital staff had reservations about the injury and the overall family situation but decided that there were not enough questions to warrant an investigation by DHS. There were no previous accidents or signs of significant neglect. They offered to make an appointment for Sally to see their mental health consultant but Sally declined.

When she brought Katie home, Sally seemed to be calmer with Katie than Mike had ever seen her be. But she could not forget how Katie had ruined her visit with her father. Katie would not hurt her again. What little pleasure Sally had felt when she was caring for Katie now became even less. At some level, Sally knew that Katie wanted her to hold her, laugh with her and play with her. She knew that her six-month-old found nothing to be better than having her mother act silly with her, sing and dance, fuss over her and run her fingers over her belly, arms and neck but Sally couldn't get herself to do those things very often. Katie was ruining her life and Sally wasn't going to go out of her way for her. Sally wasn't aware of this decision. It was the way it was. Actually, it now was the way it had been with her and her own mother. But Sally wasn't aware of that either.

Sally was right. Katie's entire being wanted to play and laugh and gaze at her mother. Katie's emotional life was developing rapidly at six months and it needed those experiences of reciprocal pleasure with her mother to fully emerge. If they were to develop, Katie's feelings of curiosity and joy and excitement were dependent on Sally having reciprocal experiences with her. Her emotional and neurological developments were interwoven and needed activation by Sally's loving and sensitive frequent involvement with her. When Sally was absent, both physically and psychologically, Katie was lost and unable to proceed with her emotional and interpersonal development. Katie could not trigger these internal processes alone. She needed Sally to do it for her and with her. Increasingly, Sally did not.

Katie would often lie in her crib, fussing and crying. More often, she would simply stare or engage in some repetitive hand and leg movements. She might fixate on some object in the crib or on the nearby wall, as if she were inviting it to interact with her. She wanted her world to respond to her feeling states and to share them. Getting little response, she began to overlook those states and to more often simply be tense, isolated, and desperate.

When Sally was present, Katie had some awareness of wanting this special interaction with her. Anticipating that she would not get it, Katie would often look away from Sally or become more restless, as if she were trying to hide from herself what she was missing. Or she might become frantic, not being able to integrate the intense affect that Sally's presence was eliciting. At other times when Sally was particularly tense herself, such as after a fight with Mike, Katie would feel her mother's distress and she would fuss even more.

At those times, Katie would actually feel calmer when Sally would leave. A profoundly sad reality for Katie was now developing. Unlike most infants who experience total delight in the presence of their mothers, Katie was very often anxious and ambivalent when Sally was present. She hoped for something from her mother, but she anticipated not getting it. Unlike most infants whose emotional and neurological developments were driven by reciprocal enjoyment with their mothers, such developments within Katie were occurring slowly, with significant gaps, and lacking in adequate differentiation and integration.

On July 19, 1989, Katie was almost two years old. Months before, Sally noticed that Katie never cried. She and Mike had thought that it was strange but they really didn't mind much. Katie whined a lot now and followed Sally around bugging her, but that was a lot better than her crying.

It had been almost 18 months since Sally broke Katie's leg. For the most part, Sally was able to feed, wash, and clothe Katie on a fairly regular basis. When Katie began to crawl and then walk, Sally generally managed to keep an eye on her, prevent accidents, and keep her from bothering Mike. Sometimes she really did not care if Mike were bothered. Then Mike would scream at Katie and push her away with as much force as was necessary. Mostly though, Katie followed Sally wherever she went. She clung to her and whined when she learned some words. For a time Sally made a small effort to respond, even with a degree of enjoyment, but gradually she lost her sense of obligation to Katie and to motherhood. The seemingly constant barrage of demands led Sally to almost complete withdrawal from her daughter. Katie never seemed to be satisfied. She always wanted more from Sally. Sally had no more to give.

If there were any minimal benefit to this situation it was that Sally learned to emotionally deaden herself in a way that left her feeling little rage toward Katie. Mike could not do that. Katie could get him screaming at her in 30 seconds. Sally learned to ignore her whining and clinging and go on with her reading, eating, talking on the phone, or watching TV. Once in a while, Sally might push her away when she clung to her leg and whined too loudly, but for the most part Sally went about her life without feeling much of anything toward Katie. She knew that she would not abuse her again. She also knew that she would do her job so that no one would criticize her mothering. Katie would be fed, clean, and well dressed. That would have to be enough.

That day in July started the way most days did. Sally got up with Katie, changed her, got her something to eat, and put her on the living room floor with a few toys while she got her coffee and toast and turned on the TV. Since Mike was sleeping and Sally did not want him yelling, she held Katie in her lap and made some effort to play with her puzzles and blocks while she watched her show. She explained to Katie how the puzzle went and she picked up the pieces that kept falling to the floor. Eventually she noticed that Katie was deliberately throwing the pieces on the floor. Sally became angry and she threw the remaining pieces and blocks across the room and spoke harshly to Katie as she roughly put her down.

Katie then asked for crackers and Sally gave her some and returned to her TV. When Katie asked for more, her mother continued to watch her show. After being ignored again, Katie threw a puzzle piece that hit Sally's arm. She screamed at Katie and threatened to hit her. Katie threw another piece and this one hit her face. Sally leaped from the chair and slapped her daughter hard across the face. Katie then screamed and bit Sally's arm. Sally swore, and hit Katie again. Katie ran to the other side of the room, screamed and stared at her mother with hatred. Katie would no longer be afraid of her mother, or sad at what was lacking between them. No, she felt only rage toward this woman who hated her.

Katie would soon begin to have frequent aggressive tantrums. Nothing that Sally or even Mike could do would stop them. She often got what she wanted when her anger was loud or destructive enough. She sensed that her rage would gain her some control over Sally. She liked seeing Sally get upset when she screamed at her. When Sally seemed frustrated and upset over her tantrums, Katie experienced a sense of power that felt good. She could have an impact on Sally! Any impact, even a negative one, was much better than having no impact. She no longer looked for enjoyment or nurturance from Sally. At some level, she sensed that she was bad and could not expect such a relationship. Besides, she concluded that Sally was bad too. Sally was mean and Katie was becoming good in finding ways to pay her back.

At the same time, Katie's wishes seemed to change. She did not want attention or affection nearly as much as she wanted food or toys or other objects that she saw. If not objects, then she wanted Sally to do something for her. When she got what she wanted, she seemed to be content. If Sally did not give her what she wanted, Katie could get her upset, and that brought some contentment too. Having fun with Sally was no longer important to her. Life was simpler this way. And there was no reason, and little time, for tears.

On September 13, 1992, Katie entered protective custody in Augusta, Maine. She was now over five years of age. She had continued to change a great deal since she had begun her tantrums at 23 months. Before that, when Sally and Mike noticed that she didn't cry much, they didn't give it much thought. When they noticed that she didn't try to cling to them very much, they were pleased. Not that it was easier to raise her now. She always seemed to be angry and complaining and to throw herself on the floor for—what seemed to them—little reason.

They really had to yell and punish Katie if they expected her to be quiet. But that strategy had its price. Often Katie got even with Sally for punishing her or for not giving her what she wanted. She was less likely to pay Mike back for his treatment of her. He slapped her hard when he was angry. For Katie, it was more fun to get Sally upset. Once, Sally refused to allow Katie to have any dessert. The next morning all of the chips and candy were gone. Another time Sally made her sit on the couch while Sally and Mike ate dinner. Later that evening Sally sat on the cushion to discover that Katie had urinated on it. Sally's hairbrushes were missing, the toilet was stuffed up, the shampoo was spilled in the tub, and her favorite CDs were broken. Sally could not catch Katie being destructive or stealing something, but she knew that she was responsible and she would spank her often. What upset Sally the most was that Katie didn't seem to care. She would punish her more and more severely and Katie would look at her with resentment, indifference, or even pleasure. Somehow Katie seemed to be getting what she wanted no matter what Sally did. Somehow Katie was in control.

Mike would get tired of Katie and Sally yelling and fighting. Sometimes he would grab Katie, push her into her room, and slam the door. At times, she would be in her room for hours or even the whole day. At other times, he would blame Sally for Katie's behavior. Mike would find whatever Sally did to be lacking. Then they would scream and Katie would seem to be pleased. Often Mike would just leave. He might come back late at night drunk and the next day have a hangover. Katie would be quiet then. She knew Mike's unpredictable rage after drinking. Sally had trouble keeping quiet. Often Mike would hit her and she might hit him back. But that made him worse and Sally would get beaten. Katie would actually feel safer when her parents were fighting. If she stayed in her bedroom, she'd be left alone. Also, on the next day one of them might do something nice for her, if only to upset the other one.

Katie's mistake on September 13 was in allowing herself to get even with Mike rather than focusing her anger at Sally. That morning Katie spilled her cereal and Mike was in a particularly bad mood.

"You stupid ass," he said. "Can't you do anything right? Well, you're going to lick it up. Put your face on the table and start licking."

Katie yelled "No!" and tried to run from the kitchen. Mike grabbed her by her shirt, pulled her back to the table, and pushed her face down onto the milk. "I said lick it up!"

He held her face in the milk and Katie screamed and fought. He held her more tightly, pushing her even harder against the tabletop. Then he began to wipe her face in the milk. "There, now you look like a pig, you little shit. Get out of here or I'll mop the floor with your hair."

Katie ran to her room where she screamed and threw her toys. When she heard Mike leave, she was still enraged. She went back to the kitchen, took a carton of milk, brought it into his bedroom, and dumped it over his clothes in his bureau. She did show tears then, tears of anger and bitterness, not sadness or fear. Back in her room, however, she became frightened. She realized what she had done. Sally was not home. She knew that there was nothing that she could do if Mike returned.

Ten minutes later she heard Mike return home with a man, Kirk, who lived nearby. From her room she could hear them talking about his stereo system which Kirk wanted to buy. Then she heard Mike walking into his bedroom.

She heard Mike scream, "That god damn little bitch! That little fucking asshole! Where is she?"

He ran into her room and she hid on the floor behind her bed. He kicked her. He then dragged her by her hair into his bedroom and he threw his wet clothes on her. He kicked her again, spit on her, and began to urinate on her. She could not remember anything else happening but could hear Kirk yelling at Mike and then Mike slamming the door.

Kirk left and told a neighbor who called the police. When they arrived, Katie was alone. From her appearance and Kirk's report, they took her to the hospital. They returned later and arrested Mike.

That night, Margaret Davis, a child protective worker, brought Katie to her first foster home. Two months later, after a court hearing that Sally minimally contested, Katie entered permanent custody. The next day, November 9, 1992, she was assigned a Children's Services worker, Steven Fields, who had transferred from Child Protective Services the week before.

## COMMENTARY

Katie's first five years of life featured specific incidents of physical abuse, verbal and emotional abuse, and long periods of emotional neglect. The endless acts of emotional violation to Katie's heart and soul through looks of disgust, screams of rejection, and the deadly silence of indifference were what led to her losing her desire to form a secure attachment with her parents. The trauma of sexual and physical violence attracts well-deserved documentation. The "trauma of absence" which characterizes neglect is less obvious to many. The cycle of abuse that leads inexorably from one generation to the next is powered most forcefully by the inability to enter and maintain meaningful attachments (see Egeland & Erickson, 1987; Cicchetti, 1989; Schore, 1994). Regretfully, our society often overlooks the absence of crucial affective interactions between parent and child as insufficient justification to forceful intervention in the life of a young child. As incredible as it may seem, there are reasons to be thankful that a child like Katie was abused by her parents, since that justifies such intervention. The legal system minimizes emotional abuse and neglect despite their profound long-term effects.

Schore (1994), Greenspan & Lieberman (1988), Stern (1985), Sroufe (1995), Siegel (1999, 2001), Cassidy & Shaver (1999), and others describe the crucial role of attachment in the psychological development of the young child. Affective attunement, defined as the intersubjective sharing of affect, is central to the development of a secure attachment during the first year of life (Stern, 1985). Intersubjective experiences of attunement, joint attention and shared intentions, were not present very often for Katie and their absence severely damaged her ability to have a secure attachment with her parents. Katie's attachment suffered severe damage by the lack of ongoing intersubjective experiences with her parents. These experiences, the original dance of humanity, are the reciprocal interactions between the mother and infant that serve to regulate the infant's early affective life, develop deep interests, and begin to create the meaning of self/other as well as the events and objects of the world (Stern, 1985, 2004; Trevarthen & Aitken, 2001). For there to be intersubjective experiences, Sally's affect would mirror Katie's, they would be attending to the same object or event, and they would engage so for similar reasons. These interactions center crucially on eye contact, facial smiles and expressions, voice prosody, bodily movements, and gestures. Through intersubjective experiences, the infant discovers her mother, and in so doing, discovers herself. Katie discovered a mother who took little notice of her. Through her use of Sally as a mirror, Katie could only conclude that she, herself, was not "noticeable." She was worthless and of no special interest or value. She would further conclude that Sally held little pleasure and joy for her. Katie's subjective experience held little interest to Sally. Katie was becoming an object to Sally. For Katie, Sally would gradually become an object to manipulate in order to get things, or to attack when she became the source of discomfort. Any felt wish that Katie originally had to be a star in her mother's eyes or to snuggle closely to her magical warmth slowly faded during the thousands of times that Sally refused to dance.

Between the ages of nine and eighteen months, Katie would have been ready to enter into the world of social expectations. The toddler's behaviors organize increasingly as she integrates her own initiatives with her mother's socialization limits and directives. During socialization, the toddler experiences shame, which is healthy and necessary for further stages of her development. The act of the mother saying "No" and limiting her toddler causes a healthy experience of shame during which the infant hangs her head, avoids eye contact, loses her smile, and is briefly motionless. During this experience, the toddler is in distress because she does not experience attunement with her mother, she is confused over the uncertainty of her mother's intentions, and her expanding sense of self feels diminished. Within a secure mother-toddler attachment, the mother quickly reestablishes, or repairs, the intersubjective state with her child and this enables the toddler to integrate this socialization experience, to regulate her experience of shame, and to remain in a secure, and even stronger, attachment with her mother. Early impulse control emerges and gradually the toddler is increasingly able to resolve the conflict between her own wishes and the limits placed on her behaviors by her mother. Because her mother is able to maintain empathy for her subjective experience even while she presents an expectation and limit, the toddler is able associate the limit with her behavior, not with the self. Shame experiences are contained. Feeling empathy for self, the child begins to feel empathy for others.

In conjunction with socialization and repair experiences, the toddler is engaged in increasingly complex cognitive developments. With language, the young child gradually is able to identify and give expression to her inner life of affect and thought and she is beginning to reflect on herself. At the same time, she is aware of her parents' wishes, affect, intentions, and behaviors and her own inner life begins to resemble that of her parents. She is able to notice the effects of her behavior on others and when she causes another distress she is often likely to feel guilt, not shame. This movement from shame to guilt is an extremely important aspect of psychological development (Tangney & Dearing, 2002). Guilt correlates to empathy, whereas shame does not. Shame correlates to various symptoms of psychopathology, whereas guilt does not. Schore (1994) regards pervasive shame as the greatest impediment to the full development of a conscience. Sometime during the child's third year of life, she is able to enter into truly reciprocal, intentional, interactions with her parents, and this skill continues to develop during the remaining years of her early childhood. This child has formed both a coherently developing sense of self, as well as a secure, differentiated, attachment to her mother. Katie was not such a child.

In Katie's first 18 months, she experienced many fewer intersubjective experiences than are necessary for the development of her early sense of self, her affect and neurological development and regulation, and her attachment security with her mother. With an insufficiently developed sense of attachment security, she was ill-prepared for routine shaming experiences and their effects on these early intrapersonal and interpersonal processes. However, her shaming experiences were far from routine. The extensive rejection, contempt, and disgust that she experienced when "socialized," greatly damaged her few early positive self-experiences. These pervasive shame experiences were made even more traumatic to her development because they were not followed by quick repair experiences that would bring her the reassurance needed to maintain any possibility of maintaining a stable and positive sense of self and a secure attachment. As a result, she denied the behavioral events associated with shame and she increasingly reacted with rage in response to these hostile and self-negating realities. She stopped seeking or responding to any intersubjective experiences that might become available. Rather, her life became one of increasing emotional isolation from her parents, along with behavioral patterns meant to defensively control her environment, and early cognitive constructs that conveyed a sense that she was bad and that her parents did not value her and were not to be trusted. According to Schore (1994, 458–59), the severe pathological shame experienced by Katie greatly limited her capacity for internalization that enables a differentiated attachment, and greatly compromised her early schema of herself. Katie's shame was a cancer that extended throughout her psychological self. It permeated every perception, experience and behavior and left no air or light for her growth. For good reason, J. S. Grotstein refers to pervasive shame as the "black hole" of one's psychic life (quoted by Schore, 1994, 421). Kaufman's excellent work, *The Psychology of Shame* (1996), demonstrates the devastating effects of pervasive shame on the development of first one's affective life and eventually one's very identity.

Katie's path cut through a harsh and barren land. It began in terror, an infant lying among noise, cold, and pain. As she began to comprehend this land, she moved into despair, a sadness that acknowledged what the core of her self screamed for and did not find. Terror and despair created her tears, tears that parched and cracked her heart but which caused nothing to grow in her land. She was not soothed by any presence and affection from her parents and she did not develop the ability to soothe herself. She did not seek to please her parents, to learn about the world from them, or to become like them. She embarked on an isolated journey in which manipulation, anger, avoidance, and control—not love and autonomy—are crucial for survival. When this journey has become irreversible, it represents the death of the soul. At two years of age, Katie's path was following that direction. It was not irreversible. In fact, professionals do not have the ability to predict when a person's functioning becomes impossible to change. We can only continue to develop our knowledge and skills, get to know the person and her life, and then get busy.

Shame accompanied Katie along her path. Shame permeated her sense of self and it left its scent on every initiative and interaction that defined her young life. Shame is not a warm companion. It turns her away from moments of joy as well as feelings of worth and contentment, holding her head down and away from the disgusted gazes of her parents. Shame etches its message into her muscles, her heart, and her mind: You are flawed. You bring no joy to others. You are bad and without merit.

But Katie's shame, as is often the case, does not lie quietly, seeking not to disturb. Rather, it erupts in rage again and again. Denied a place in the sun, it screams to blot it out for all. Near the sun, for those who have no place, there is pain. It screams, "Yes, I have no worth. I am worthless. And so are you! I am hateful. And I hate you! I will not feel the pain that never leaves. I will give it to you!"

Such was Katie, as she arrived at her first foster home. She could not, and would not, dance. She felt only the rage that she used to medicate her shame, her terror, and her despair.

# 3

---

## Ruth Daley (Foster Home #1)

When Katie entered foster care, she was placed in the home of Ruth Daley. Ruth lived in Sydney with her husband, Bill, two children of their own, and another foster child, three-year-old Dustin. Ruth had been a foster mother for a number of years, following a tradition started by her own mother a generation before her.

Katie's Children's Services caseworker, Steven Fields, had recently transferred from the child protective services of the department. Steven brimmed with excitement about the transfer. He would no longer be investigating reports of abuse and determining the initial service plan. He tired of trying to convince parents that abusing their child was wrong. He wearied of confronting their lies and absorbing their rage when he wanted to scream at them for violating their own children. He could not face more excuses, more blame flowing in every direction, and more indifference to the terrible physical, emotional, and mental scars that they left on their children. He could not muster much empathy for those parents, although intellectually he knew that they most likely had been abused themselves and had not received any help. Finally, he could no longer face the extreme doubt and fear that he felt whenever he decided to allow a child to remain in his home with the possibility that there might be further abuse.

Now Steven would be working with the foster children who had been placed in protective custody. They would be in safe homes while he worked with their parents to see if they would reunite. If the parents were unable or unwilling to work, he would be able to insure that the child received an alternative that could ultimately lead to his or her adoption into a stable and loving home.

Today, Steven would obtain his first case assignments from his supervisor, Kathy English. He didn't endure the anxiety that he felt when he started in child protective services. He felt confidence in his skills. He hoped that he would now have increased opportunities to use these skills to make a real difference in the lives of the foster children assigned to him. He liked Kathy, who seemed to be very thorough and professional while at the same time being sensitive and responsive to the foster care workers and the children. Two coworkers, Al Fortin and Barbara Stevens, also seemed to be good people to work with.

Kathy brought Steven into her "office" with an actual window, which was simply a space half as large as that of her three workers combined, surrounded by panels that went within two feet of the ceiling. She gave him five cases that day, suggesting that he read their records, discuss them with her, and then visit each child at his or her foster home over the next week.

The first case that Steven reviewed was Katie Harrison. He noted her birth date and looked at his curling, yellow paper, now pinned above his new desk, acknowledging his first day at DHS, August 4, 1987. They had something in common already. He felt drawn to her even more when he saw her big brown eyes, short straight black hair, and her wide smile in the photo under her name. What a delightful looking five-year-old girl. He remembered her immediately as the little girl covered with bruises who had won Margaret Davis' heart when she picked her up at the hospital. Margaret was determined that she would not get hurt again. She had worked overtime to get the case to court quickly.

Steven quickly reviewed her file. She lived with Ruth Daley who had been a foster parent for 10 years. Other workers found her to be competent and committed to the children in her care. Katie was now in a Head Start program. She had a therapist, Jan Temple, at the Mid-Maine Mental Health Center.

He discovered that Katie's parents, Mike and Sally, were still together. Although he tried not to be judgmental, he still couldn't understand how Sally could stay with Mike after what he had done to Katie. Sally had weekly one-hour visits with Katie that were supervised by a homemaker from Catholic Charities. She had completed a psychological evaluation that expressed some concerns about her functioning and general parenting. Sally agreed to begin individual counseling at the mental health center as well as to sign up for a parenting course. Mike faced pending criminal charges and his attorney advised him not to talk to a psychologist until after his case was heard.

Steven called the mental health center and was fortunate to get through to Jan Temple. Jan indicated that she really didn't know Katie very well yet, having seen her only twice so far. She would be spending some time getting to know her and establishing a relationship. Right now, she allowed Katie to choose whatever she wanted to do in her play therapy sessions. So far, Jan found her to be a delight to work with. Katie hadn't said much of anything about her life with her parents.

Steven called Ruth Daley and arranged to go to her home and take Katie to McDonald's for lunch. It was about a 20-minute drive from his office. Ruth and her family lived in an old farmhouse surrounded by large fields that were still being worked by a neighboring farmer. Steven saw two dogs as he pulled into the driveway. He decided that Katie couldn't have asked for a better home.

Ruth was a friendly, down-to-earth woman who had lived in Sydney most of her life. She met Steven at his car and she showed him their small barn with a pony and two pigs.

"How are things going with Katie?" asked Steven.

"She's quite a handful so far. We're hoping that she'll settle in as she gets more used to living here. She's a strong-willed kid, probably had to be to survive. She does not like to be told what to do! She's also plenty rough on Dustin, my three-year-old. I got to watch her a lot."

"How is she about the visits with her mother?"

"She goes OK but doesn't talk about them much. She never mentions her mother at other times, either. She's also likely to be a lot angrier and more easily upset for a day or so after the visits."

Just then, Katie came running outside yelling "McDonald's!" Steven laughed and immediately liked this lively and direct child. Ruth introduced him to her and without pause Katie asked Steven if he would take her to McDonald's right then. He smiled and said that he could. He walked and she ran to his car. Steven saw this as an excellent beginning. No worries now that she might be afraid of him. He even thought that she already liked him and was happy that he was her caseworker. He'd not let her down.

At McDonald's Steven discovered the amount of energy that was required to supervise this five-year-old child. She did not hesitate to tell him what she wanted to eat, where she wanted to sit, when she wanted to play in the play area, and when she wanted her apple pie. He was only too eager to please her; she was so appreciative and enjoyable. She did fuss and complain when it was time to leave, but what kid wouldn't? Steven tried to explain to her what his job was on their way back to Sydney. She wasn't interested. Nor was she interested in leaving on her seat belt. He had to tell her twice to put it back on. She paused and looked at him, but did what she was told. That wasn't too hard. She just needed some time to listen to what she was told to do. One shouldn't push her too hard; she'd eventually do it. He thought of making this suggestion to Ruth but forgot about it when he was meeting Dustin and her own older kids. When he left, he heard her hollering to Katie to put down Dustin's truck. She kept yelling, a little louder each time, as Steven walked to his car. He would have to talk with her about other ways to approach Katie.

Over the next few months, Steven had gotten to know his first 5 children and he had been given 15 more. Kathy indicated that he could expect 5 more in a few weeks so that he would have a full caseload of 25. He was beginning to sense that Al might have a point. The paperwork! The visitations between parents and children that he had to arrange and often supervise if there was no homemaker or aide available! The preparation for court! So many written documents to review, organize, and prepare for the assistant attorney general who would be representing DHS in court. The requests from foster parents also took much time and energy. Then there were the frantic phone calls from a foster parent indicating that a child's behavior was intolerable and that she would have to move within a few weeks. Steven would try to resolve the problem, but his efforts were too often unsuccessful and he spent hours finding another home.

It was after his second failure to maintain a child's placement that he got a call from Ruth Daley saying that Katie's behavior was getting worse.

"It seems like every day she does something that I have to get on her about," said Ruth. "Yesterday she threw Dustin's little bike into the pig pen and we didn't find it until this morning. What a sorry mess it was! The day before she stuffed up the toilet with some wash cloths and a few days before that she stole my bracelet that Bill had given me for Christmas. We still haven't found it. And those are only the *big* things that she's done."

"How do you know that she took your bracelet?" asked Steven.

"She's the only one who was upstairs alone that morning when I missed it. Plus she had shown a lot of interest in it."

"Is anything bothering her now?" wondered Steven.

"Nothing I can think of. The visits are hard but they've always been."

"Have you talked with her therapist?"

"Not about these most recent things. I usually fill her in on things before the therapy session. We'll be seeing her tomorrow."

"If it's OK with you I'd like to sit in on the meeting," said Steven.

"That's fine," said Ruth. "I'll see you there."

The next day, January 15, 1993, was busy but Steven arranged his schedule to be at Jan Temple's office by 10:00 a.m. He did not want to lose this placement.

Ruth told Jan about the bike, toilet, and bracelet and added a few more incidents that involved Katie swearing at Ruth, breaking her 15-year-old son's tape recorder, and putting a nail in the pig feed.

"I've tried everything," Ruth said. "I tell her not to do something and she listens fine and then does it anyway. When I catch her, she lies about it even if I'm right there when she does it! If I tell her to stop doing something she wants to do, that's when she'll swear and try to hit me. And when she gets mad at someone, that's when she'll find a way to pay him back. She was mad at Jack for telling me about her hitting Dustin and two hours later his tape recorder was broken. Nothing seems to work, time out, losing privileges, talking to her. We don't know what to try next."

Jan was an experienced therapist who had treated a number of foster children over the past 10 years. She liked Ruth and had agreed with Steven that this was a good placement and needed to be saved.

"Katie has only lived with you now for about four months," Jan said. "She's still showing the signs of abuse that she probably received for four years. She's still a very mad little girl and she doesn't trust anyone much. I know that she's really hard to raise now, Ruth, but I'm hoping that if we can keep working with her, she eventually will begin to trust more and not be so hard. It will take a lot of patience but I think that she can make it."

"Have you seen progress in therapy yet?" asked Steven.

"Nothing significant. She's an easy kid to work with. In therapy with me, she doesn't present any of the problems that she's showing at home. She is showing some of her anger in her dollhouse play. She can be quite aggressive in her play with the parent dolls often hurting the children. I'm hoping that she can work through some of her fear and rage for how she was treated."

Turning to Ruth, Jan added, "Catch her being good and let her know how pleased you are. Pick your battles, overlooking some of her less extreme behaviors. Use time outs but only one minute for each year of her life. Use a timer and only start it when she is sitting in time out without screaming at you."

"What should I do when she breaks or steals something?" asked Ruth.

"If you're sure she did it, give her a time out and make her say she's sorry. Try to get your kids to not leave important things around where she can get them. Make their rooms off-limits to her."

"I'm afraid she'll find a way to break something," Ruth replied. "We can only watch her so much. She can be out of my sight for one minute and be into something."

"Maybe you'll have to put locks on the bedroom doors up high so that she can't reach them. Only your kids or you could open the door then," Jan suggested.

Steven took notes of Jan's recommendations. Her early suggestion that Katie needed patience seemed important and he emphasized that to Ruth. He added that Ruth was important to Katie.

Ruth thought for a moment and then said, "So far I'm not so sure what I mean to her. If she left tomorrow I don't think that she'd give me or anyone else in the family another thought."

Steven was not sure what to say. Jan broke the silence by suggesting that they meet again in a month and review Katie's progress. Steven and Ruth left for the waiting room and Jan went to get Katie for her session.

"Do you really think that Katie wouldn't care if I moved her tomorrow?" asked Steven.

"I'm afraid I do," replied Ruth quietly.

On January 27, 1993, Steven's wife Jenny gave birth to Rebecca at home on their king-sized bed. The midwife, Tina, had been there for three hours prior to the birth. Steven was busy coaching Jenny in her breathing, as well as running around the house for blankets, music, water and anything else that he thought might justify his value. Every 15 minutes he asked Tina if everything was going well. Finally, Jenny had enough.

"Steven if you need to do something why not go out to the wood shed and split enough wood for next winter. We'll call you when the baby arrives."

Tina smiled and said, "In some ways waiting is harder for you than for Jenny since you're not doing the work. You can help Jenny the most by setting a relaxed atmosphere. Focus on your own breathing and listen to the music. I'll let you know if there is something more practical that you can do."

As Rebecca was being born, Steven sat behind Jenny, held her hand, and held a wet cloth to her forehead.

"A girl!" said Tina with delight, "and so much energy! She's going to be a fighter." Tina checked her, weighed her, and placed her in Jenny's arms.

"What beautiful brown eyes," said Jenny. Steven too could only see her eyes as she gazed at Jenny.

"She's really ours, isn't she?" whispered Jenny. "She's home now, she's safe. Hi, Rebecca. What a cute baby you are. We're so happy to meet you."

Jenny was lost in wonder, "She's so beautiful, so precious. She's our daughter."

Jenny looked over Rebecca's body from her tiny toenails to her dark brown hair. She touched her and pulled her closer and slowly rocked her and spoke to her, welcoming her into the family. Steven could not make out what Jenny was saying to Rebecca but whatever it was, it was right.

For the next week, Rebecca could not say or do anything that did not get a response from Jenny or Steven. Jenny's mom had come and Steven was happy to have her. Alice did most of the cooking and laundering and she managed to keep the house fairly neat. She also brought an air of confidence. Her approval of how Jenny and Steven were caring for the baby was important to them. She knew kids in ways that they didn't. She and Jenny talked more than Steven could ever recall. So far, she was becoming a great grandmother.

Since Alice would be staying with them for one more week, Steven was able to go back to work without too much anxiety. He was welcomed with streamers and balloons over his desk and a large mug with the word "dad" on top. Betty, Barbara, and Kathy smiled and fussed and asked more questions that Steven could not answer. He finally agreed to make a list of questions to ask Jenny if he wanted to be accepted at work the next day.

Steven spent most of the day catching up on his cases. A message from Jan Temple needed a response.

"Hi, Jan, I just got back. What's up?" Steven asked Jan.

"The last three weeks with Katie in her foster home have been as difficult as ever. Ruth seems to be wearing out. I've begun to talk with Katie about her behaviors at home but she wants none of it."

"Has Katie done anything serious?" he asked.

"No, unless you would call her constant defiance, anger, and destructiveness serious. We have a behavioral specialist here who could consult with us about developing a behavioral management plan for Ruth. That might give her some tools that would be more effective than what she's now doing. Do you want me to set up a meeting with him?"

Steven replied that it probably would be a good idea to develop a more effective way to get through to Katie. "Set it set up and let me know. I'll make sure I can attend. I'll give Ruth a call and offer her my support."

When Ruth answered the phone, she spoke with Steven for 10 minutes about Rebecca before he was able to ask about Katie.

"I just don't know how to get through to her," said Ruth. "She's a great kid but she does not want to be told what to do. If things are going her way, she does fine. But my goodness, that's not the way life is all the time! She will not tolerate not getting her way."

"Why don't I talk with her," said Steven.

"That would be great," Ruth replied. "When I talk to her I get nowhere. In fact, she seems to be thinking that she's somehow winning."

Steven told Ruth about the meeting with the behavioral specialist and he arranged to see Katie the next day.

On February 6, 1993, Steven picked up Katie for their third trip to McDonald's. He would let her buy what she wanted, and then they would go into the play area for a while. After having fun, she would be more likely to cooperate when he talked with her about her problems. As they headed back home, Steven told Katie about Ruth's concerns. He asked her why she thought she was getting into trouble so much. Katie's manner changed immediately. She seemed to be sullen and tense. He repeated his question and she replied, "Ruth isn't fair to me! She's always yelling at me but she never yells at Dustin. She likes him!"

Steven suggested to her that Ruth did like her. He suggested further that Ruth might get angry at her behaviors but not at her.

"Yes, she does!" said Katie. "She never lets me do anything. She's mean to me!"

Steven did not know what to say. He did not think that arguing with her would change her mind. Maybe if he told Ruth about Katie's feelings Ruth could reassure her and try not to get angry with her so much.

"You're in a good home, Katie," said Steven. "I'll try to help you and Ruth get along better. I want you to be happier with your mom."

"She's not my mom! I don't like her anyway," said Katie.

When Steven got back to Ruth's home, she asked how it went.

"She thinks that you like Dustin more than her," said Steven. "She seems to need reassurance that you do care about her."

"I don't know what else I could do to show her I care about her and want to help her," said Ruth.

"When she does something wrong could you tell her you do care about her and only are correcting her to teach her what is right?" suggested Steven.

"I'll try to be more careful when I scold her," replied Ruth. She did not seem too optimistic that Steven's suggestion would help.

Back at the office, Steven asked Barbara for ideas, "She's in a good home but I don't think that she believes it. How can we get through to her?"

"She probably doesn't know how to be 'good,'" replied Barbara. "It can take a long time before it gets better. Some kids just never do."

"Why not?" asked Steven.

"I wish we knew," said Barbara. "If Ruth can hang in there maybe Katie will begin to trust her. But if Ruth gives up on her, she may never trust anyone."

Steven was troubled. What could he do? "It seems to me that Rebecca in one week trusts me and Jenny more than Katie trusts Ruth after five months. Why can't Katie get it?"

"Rebecca was never abused and neglected. Katie has a lot of reasons not to trust. She needs more time. Your job is to help Ruth to give Katie more time so that she won't have another reason not to trust."

"Ruth isn't sure that Katie really cares about staying with her," said Steven.

"She must care. She probably doesn't know how to show it."

"Well," said Steven, "she had better learn how soon or we may have a big problem."

On February 11, Steven and Ruth met Bill Jenkins, the behavioral specialist, at Jan's office. Steven liked Bill. He seemed to be a reasonable man who wanted to help Ruth and Katie. They all presented him with Katie's behaviors over the past five months.

"I think we have to begin finding ways for Katie to experience some success," said Bill. "She's in trouble so often that she probably has given up all expectations that she can do better. We should start with a reward system that is easy for her to succeed in and gradually build up the demands. Why don't we start by developing a list of behaviors that we want her to increase, behaviors we want her to decrease, as well as things that she likes that we can use as rewards."

For the next 45 minutes, Bill helped Ruth to identify very specific behaviors that needed to change in one direction or the other. He also determined from her what Katie really liked to do so that he could make these privileges contingent upon appropriate behaviors. He identified three behaviors—no physical aggression, following directions, and asking for permission—that they would focus on first. He broke each day into blocks of time and suggested that Katie receive one play coin for each of the three behavioral goals that she attained in every block of time. She could trade in her coins for rewards each day and she could save her coins for larger rewards available each week. Bill suggested that Ruth start by making it fairly easy to get the rewards so that Katie would "buy into the program" through having early successes. They would review the success of the program in two weeks. Ruth seemed to be very motivated to try the plan. She would explain it to Katie that evening and start the next day. Steven felt some cautious optimism that this plan would help.

Three days later Steven called Ruth to find out how the plan was working. "So far so good," said Ruth. "Katie seems to be interested in getting the coins. In fact, she is quick to remind me if I owe her some. She's not so often aggressive and she is more willing to do what I tell her. She's not spending them so far. She's saving them to buy a doll next week."

When they met with Bill, Ruth was not as pleased as she was initially. She said that Katie got her doll, but after two days she broke it, "Now she's working to go to McDonald's. She's not getting the coins as fast as she did earlier but she's still doing better."

Bill made some modifications in the program. Katie would have to spend some of her coins each day, rather than be able to save them all.

They met again in two more weeks and Ruth was becoming somewhat discouraged. She indicated that Katie would still get coins, but again, not as frequently as she once did. She seemed to take some pleasure in the fact that she had discovered how to earn rewards while at the same time maintain many of her previous problem behaviors.

"Yesterday she hit Dustin and knocked him down. Ten minutes later, she gave me five coins to watch a video. She had a smile that seemed to be saying 'ha, ha, you have to let me watch it even if I did hit Dustin.' I wanted to take her coins and throw them away, but I didn't. She got her movie."

Bill suggested that Ruth modify the program again, but not make it harder to earn rewards. He was reluctant to have Katie lose coins for certain behaviors out of fear that a negative cycle would emerge again. Katie also would get a special reward at the end of each day if she was not aggressive the entire day.

In March, they met again with Bill. Ruth was now even more frustrated.

"If she wants something a lot, she will follow the program perfectly. As soon as she gets it, she'll be as aggressive and oppositional as ever. Or if for some reason she doesn't particularly want any reward, she'll do whatever she wants that day and not try to follow the plan at all. Then if she changes her mind and wants the reward, she's as mad as ever at me for not giving it to her."

Bill suggested that Katie was learning that she did have to follow the plan if she wanted rewards. She was testing it now and once she realized that Ruth would follow through with the plan and not reward her, she would be more likely to comply. He then suggested changing the value of the coins in order to increase their reinforcement for Katie's behavior, which was of greatest concern to Ruth.

By the end of March, Bill acknowledged that Katie's behavior was not significantly different from how it was when the program began seven weeks earlier. When she wanted something, she easily did what it took to get what she wanted. Nothing carried over after she got it. Bill still feared that if Ruth made it harder to get the coins or if Katie lost coins that she earned already, her motivation would be even less.

In April and May 1993, Steven and Ruth spoke three times each week about Katie. Mostly their conversation consisted in Ruth reporting something new that Katie had done. Steven initially would ask various questions, trying to understand her motives so that they would know how to prevent it from recurring. But why would she scratch the paint on the minister's car when he came one afternoon for a visit? Why would she destroy her own mattress with a fork? He could begin to understand why she took crackers and cookies. But why would she take dirt and put it in the toaster? Why did she scream and swear and kick at Ruth for telling her to put her clothes in the drawer? Why did she hide behind the door and jump out at Ruth or Dustin as they walked past? Once Ruth became frightened, jumped and lost her balance and twisted her ankle. Katie seemed to like *Aladdin*. Why did she put the videotape in five inches of water in the sink?

Steven met with Kathy, Al, Barbara, and Betty to discuss what he could do to improve the situation.

"Why not try to be sure that Ruth gets respite from Katie one weekend a month?" Al suggested.

"She'll be six in August," said Barbara. "She might be able to attend a summer recreation program that would help this summer."

"There's a parenting program at the mental health center that might be helpful to Ruth," said Kathy. "You might offer it to her. She'd probably appreciate the offer even if she doesn't want to enroll."

"You mentioned that Katie's behavior is somewhat worse after visits with her mother. Ask Jan if she'd be willing to write a letter recommending that the visits be discontinued until Katie has begun to stabilize in her functioning."

"But how do we get Katie to stop acting like she's the worst kid in the world or like she's in the worst home in the world?" asked Steven.

"Steven, if there was something that you haven't tried that might help, Jan, Bill, Ruth, or one of us would have suggested it by now," said Kathy. "I know how hard you want this to work. You're doing the best you can. So is Ruth. She needs your support now. Just listen and reassure her that this is not her fault."

Steven replied, after a long pause, "You're right, Kathy, thanks. But she's just a little five-year-old. She can be so cute and friendly and helpful. Why won't she stop the rest? I know she was abused, but it's been eight months. Ruth has been so good to her. Jan's a good therapist. When will it end?"

On June 17, 1993, Katie's placement with Ruth ended. Katie and Dustin were outside playing at the swing set with Ruth watching them closely from the open kitchen window while she relaxed after lunch. They were chasing each other around the slide, laughing together more than Ruth could recall them ever doing. Katie could have caught Dustin but she was careful not to and he laughed harder. Katie looked at Ruth, seemingly for approval that she was playing so nicely with Dustin. Ruth smiled and yelled that she'd get them each a Popsicle since they were playing so well together.

As Ruth opened the freezer, she heard a scream. She hurried to the window to see Dustin on the ground with Katie standing over him. In horror, Ruth watched Katie pull back her foot and kick Dustin in the head. Ruth yelled, "Katie, no!" and ran outside. As she approached, she saw Katie kick him again and then run behind the swing. Ruth went to Dustin, who was screaming and crying on the ground. She held him and tried to calm him. She looked toward Katie and she lost her breath. Katie was watching her and Dustin, with a smile that Ruth had never seen before. Katie seemed excited and pleased, not frightened or angry. Katie seemed happy!

Ruth took Dustin inside to tend to his bruises. She checked him over and held him until he stopped crying. Katie then came in and demanded her Popsicle!

"You hurt Dustin, Katie," said Ruth. "You're not getting a Popsicle. Tell him that you're sorry."

"You said I could have a Popsicle!" screamed Katie. "I want it, get it for me!"

"No, Katie!" said Ruth. "Not after what you did to Dustin. Say you're sorry."

"I hate you!" said Katie. "I'm not sorry! I'm glad I hurt him! I hate you!"

Katie ran outside again, while Ruth continued to try to comfort Dustin. Finally, she went looking for Katie. She found that Katie had begun to throw rocks at the pony in the pasture. As Ruth approached, Katie ran toward the road. Ruth hesitated, not knowing if it would make matters worse if she ran after her. She decided to return to the house and watch her from the windows. Her decision worked and Katie slowly returned to home in about 30 minutes. She walked past the kitchen where Ruth and Dustin were and looked angrily at them both. She was mad at them! Didn't she have any awareness of what she had just done?

That evening Ruth and Bill decided that Katie would have to be placed elsewhere. The next day, Ruth called Steven and, with both sorrow and guilt, informed him that Katie would have to leave soon. Steven could say nothing. He knew that Ruth was right. He would have to find a home for Katie that had no small children. He finally reassured Ruth that he knew that she had done the best that she could.

## COMMENTARY

What motivates a child like Katie often does not resemble the more normal motivations of childhood. For this reason, the usual reinforcers are not likely to be effective for any period of time. Concrete reinforcements and activities may work briefly, but most such external objects have little inherent motivation. Generalization from such objects to relationships is unlikely to occur since relationships themselves have little reinforcing value. The typical reinforcers of the child with trauma/attachment problems are not common to most kids. They include being in control of the feelings and behaviors of others and winning every power struggle. These children also love saying "No!" They strive to maintain their negative view of themselves and others. They also find it reinforcing to be able to need no one, and to avoid experiences of reciprocal fun and love. Being praised and asking for help makes them vulnerable so they avoid those experiences. Most often the stickers and M&M's selected to direct the child into more socially appropriate behaviors are no match for these very powerful reinforcers that developed within them during the first two years of life. I often think that when parents present such children with clear and specific behavioral plans, they are making a mistake. They have told the child what is important to them and thus he is now more able to know how to gain control and cause them distress. It is similar to having the coach of a football team presenting the opposing team with his game plan prior to the contest!

I do not want to suggest that cognitive-behavioral interventions have nothing to offer in the daily care and treatment of the child with attachment/trauma difficulties. Rather, I am suggesting that "cognitive-behavioral" needs a broader definition to include features of intersubjectivity including reciprocal affective experiences, and that the manner in which those processes are developed and maintained needs to be understood and incorporated into the interventions. Also, I believe that one needs to initially focus on affect identification and regulation, relationship factors involving reciprocity, conflict resolution, emotional communication, seeking comfort, and attachment security. Once there is progress in these areas, more traditional cognitive-behavioral interventions are likely to be more effective.

Traditional play therapy often is not sufficiently effective in facilitating the development of attachment between a child and his parents. While play therapy stresses nonverbal interventions, these interventions tend not to be preverbal but rather involve nonverbal symbolic processes that really do not emerge within the securely attached child until he is 18 months old. With many children who manifest significant attachment problems, they are not able to endow the play objects with sufficient symbolic meaning through which to resolve past traumatic events. While play therapists stress that the therapeutic relationship is the vehicle for therapeutic progress, children who have significant attachment problems are not likely to be able to form a relationship in an hour a week that will have an impact on these profound deficiencies. Also, much play therapy tends to be fairly nondirective. Since children with attachment disorganization compulsively need to maintain control, they are often unlikely to relinquish that control when they have a choice. They will then be able to avoid indefinitely experiences of both intersubjectivity and shame. Finally, play therapists tend to leave the parent out of the therapeutic process with the exception of providing parent counseling in separate sessions. When we want the child to develop attachment security with her new parent, we should seriously consider bringing that parent into the treatment sessions. At the same time, I consider principles of empathy, acceptance, and meaning-making that I first learned in play therapy training to be crucial aspects of the intervention model that I will present. Play therapy interventions can easily integrate into the model of treatment that I will propose in this work, though they are likely to remain in a secondary role, especially initially.

The symptom complex that Katie is beginning to manifest within Ruth's home is common among foster children, though hers is more severe than many. The complexity of the behaviors makes formal diagnosis difficult. However the overall pattern is consistent, I believe, with attachment disorganization, a risk factor for the development of psychological problems (Lyons-Ruth & Jacobvitz, 1999). When the majority of children enter foster care, they are likely to manifest attachment disorganization (Lyons-Ruth & Jacobvitz, 1999). They are likely to manifest a high need to control the people and events of their daily lives. Their affect regulation is likely to be poor. They are at risk for manifesting problems of both externalization and internalization. They likely lack behaviors that are congruent with attachment security. Establishing and maintaining a secure attachment seems to be of low priority, if it is even considered. Ruth's worry that Katie would not miss her if the placement were to disrupt is well-founded. That does not mean that Katie would not suffer psychological harm by the disruption. It most likely would increase the risk that she would miss her subsequent "attachment figures" even less.

Many foster parents resemble Ruth. They are very committed to providing the foster children in their care with a family experience similar to what they provide their birth children. They often work for weeks and months with a foster child who is presenting severe problems that disrupt their family life. Most are eager for information, suggestions, and support. When they finally "give up" on an extremely difficult child, they often feel considerable guilt and distress over that child's future.

For the foster care system to be adequate in provided stable and therapeutic homes for children with significant attachment problems, it needs to develop and maintain foster homes that are provided with highly specific recommendations that have some probability of success in assisting the child to learn to form a secure attachment. Foster parents quickly know that if they raise the child with serious attachment problems in a manner similar to how they raised their birth children, the results will not be the same. Principles and strategies needed for raising these children are often difficult to incorporate into a parent's routine child-rearing initiatives and responses.

When Katie's first placement ended in failure, it certainly confirmed in her mind that she was a bad girl and that no one would ever really love her. Ruth might have been nicer than Sally to her, but Katie would have to conclude that Ruth ultimately saw her as Sally did. Namely, she was a child who was not worth the effort.

One of the possible preconditions of the diagnosis of Reactive Attachment Disorder is multiple placements. In our foster care system, many children experience multiple placements. Thus, our system, developed to safeguard, protect, and nourish these vulnerable children, often can fail to meet their psychological and developmental needs in ways profoundly similar to the effects of the original family of abuse and neglect.

For the foster care system to be more responsive to the needs of our children, it must be able to respond quickly and appropriately to these children's placement needs for security and continuity. Each child should have only one temporary placement prior to moving to a permanent home, either back with the birth parents or into an adoptive home. The foster parents critically need sufficient training to be able to begin to understand the effects of abuse and neglect on the daily functioning of their child. They need to know how to most effectively raise this child, who may well have significant deficits in his affective, cognitive, and behavioral development. Ruth, a competent and committed foster parent, did not have the knowledge, support, and intervention strategies that she needed if she was going to effectively engage a child as damaged as Katie, and lead her into the realities of attachment security and healthy family relationships.

Steven quickly found that he had monumental responsibilities in trying to provide his foster children with the comprehensive services that they needed. These children often require various psychological, medical, educational, and social services, all of which need to be coordinated if their various needs are to be adequately met. At the same time, Steven needs to be working on the reunification plans with Katie's parents. He has to monitor the services that they are receiving and insure that the visitation arrangements are in place. He has to constantly communicate with lawyers and prepare reports for the court. If he fails to maintain adequate paperwork, he might hurt Katie in court much more than he might help her by spending time with her.

To provide truly effective services for children in foster care requires a great amount of time, money, training, and commitment from significant members of our society. If Katie could have been maintained in her home with Sally and Mike, through teaching her parents how to notice and respond to her developmental needs, and providing them with other psychological services, she would have had an easier time. Prevention services initiated at birth, early childhood education, and family support services all should be in place in order to prevent the need for children like Katie to enter the foster care system. Given that, however, some parents like Sally and Mike either refuse or are unable to benefit from such services, we must have a strong and effective foster care system that is able to meet Katie's developmental needs. We cannot endlessly attempt "family preservation" programs while the children in such programs continue to experience emotional abuse and neglect and remain at risk for physical and sexual abuse. Living for months in circumstances of emotional abuse and neglect is causing significant psychological damage to the minds and hearts of these children. When mental health and social services providers refuse to recognize that reality, we all have little reason to hope that our society will ever take the developmental needs of these children seriously.

# 4

## Karen Miller (Foster Home #2)

On June 25, 1993, Steven went to Ruth's home to bring Katie to her new home. The most suitable home that he had been able to find was with Karen and Ken Miller, a fairly young couple who had become foster parents nine months earlier. They had a few short placements that seemed to go well. There were no children in the home. Karen would be home most of the time. She had a part time job with a local business and she had any necessary day-care arrangements in place. They were excited about taking Katie because of her age and the likelihood that she would be able to stay with them for a while. When Steven spoke with Karen, she even suggested that she and her husband might be interested in adopting Katie if that became possible. Steven informed her that the plan was for Katie to eventually be able to return to live with her parents, if they were able to meet the terms of the service agreement.

When Steven had told Katie that she would be moving to Karen and Ken's house, she immediately asked if she could bring the toys and clothes that Ruth had given her. In the most supportive way possible, Ruth explained to Katie the reasons for the move. Katie seemed indifferent to her support. She showed no emotion until later, when she became excited about moving and spoke about it as if it were an adventure.

During the drive to Karen and Ken's house Katie spoke constantly about nothing relevant. When she paused for breath, Steven said, "I'm sure you're sad about having to move."

"No, I'm not," she replied. "This is a better home because you said there are no other kids."

"But you'll miss Ruth and Bill. You've lived with them a long time. Maybe you can visit them after a while."

"I don't miss them. Ruth was mean to me. This is going to be more fun."

When they arrived, Karen and Ken were waiting on the porch. Steven introduced them and Katie gave them each a hug and called them "mom" and "dad." She began asking questions about their home and she was pleased over the tour, followed by a snack of cookies and milk. She immediately ignored Steven and spoke to her new parents. When Steven went to leave, she took no notice of him. Neither did Karen or Ken who were enthralled by this charming child.

Later that week Steven called Karen to check on Katie.

"She's such a good kid. We really enjoy having her," said Karen. "Once in a while she gets angry when we tell her to come for dinner or to get ready for bed, but it's nothing major. I think that she likes being here."

"I'm glad that it's working out so well," said Steven. "Any trouble with taking food or destroying things?"

"None at all," said Karen. "You know, I think that maybe Ruth was a little too hard on her about eating. We give her plenty of food at meals and snacks too and she doesn't take anything to her room at night."

"Well, again, I'm glad that she's off to such a good start."

"Maybe I shouldn't say this but I really think that Ruth just wasn't the right match for her. Katie tells me how much she was yelled at and how often she got punished. She needed more understanding and patience than Ruth was able to give."

Steven defended Ruth and indicated that Katie's behaviors had been very difficult. Later he shared Karen's comments with Barbara. They both agreed that Karen was minimizing Katie's responsibility for her difficulties. Barbara expressed the fear that Karen might have to learn the hard way how serious Katie's problems seemed to be.

Over the next few weeks, Karen continued to tell Steven how well things were going. He called Jan who indicated that in therapy Katie was somewhat more resistant. In fact, she seemed to be complaining about therapy and Karen had asked Jan if therapy might no longer be necessary. Jan suggested that they continue for another few months and then reevaluate it.

On August 4, Steven stopped by the Miller home to give Katie a birthday present. A big family party was underway and Katie had no interest in Steven or his present. Karen was busily enjoying the activity and Steven decided that things could not be going much better. He met Karen's mother, Anne, who spoke with pleasure about Katie. As he talked with Anne, he discovered that Katie apparently was demonstrating some behavioral problems that Karen had not told him about. The next day Steven called Karen to ask about the problems hinted at by her mother.

"Oh, mom worries too much," said Karen. "Sure, Katie is not perfect but we're managing well. She peed on the couch once and she was really sorry about it. She has had a few other problems like that but nothing major."

Steven began to wonder about Katie's placement but could not be sure if there were more problems than Karen was willing to acknowledge. With other kids on his caseload demanding his attention, he had little choice but to assume that Karen would tell him if she really had some problems with Katie.

On September 16, 1993, Steven decided that it was time to catch up on his paperwork. A day at the office with a large mug of coffee and the receptionist, Molly, holding his calls should help a lot.

At 10:30 a.m., Molly came with a note for him. This most likely would not help his paperwork. Jan was on the phone. She said that it was important.

"We have a problem, Steven," said Jan. "Katie is mad at Karen for not buying her some candy when they stopped at K-Mart before today's appointment. She seems to have decided to get Karen in trouble for not buying her some."

"Is she making up lies because she didn't get what she wanted?" asked Steven.

"I don't think they're lies," said Jan. "She said that Karen had tied her to a chair because she would not sit for a time out. There are marks on her wrists that look like rope marks. She also said that Karen slapped her and scratched her face. There is a scratch mark. She gave other examples that have a ring of truth to them. Then she asked me if I would yell at Karen and tell her to get Katie some candy."

"What other examples?" asked Steven.

"She said that Karen has called her a little bitch. She said that she was locked in a closet and also that Karen forced food into her mouth. But the scary thing for me is that Katie was really upset that I was going to call you. She does not want to move. She said that Karen is a great mother because she always buys her things and lets her do what she wants. She just wants that candy bar."

Steven indicated that he would be right over. Jan said that she would wait with Karen and Katie until he arrived.

At Jan's office, Steven asked her to tell Karen what Katie had said. As Jan talked, Karen became upset and tense. She quickly said that the rope marks were caused accidentally when Katie was playing with some rope. Karen had never tied her up. As Jan continued, giving one example after the next, Karen began to cry.

"Why isn't she ever satisfied?" Karen finally asked. "We have given her so much. Nothing is too good for her. But she still wants more. And when I finally say 'no' she screams at me and says that I'm mean to her. She's never satisfied with me!"

"Did you slap and scratch her?" asked Steven.

"Yes, yes, and I've spanked her, too," Karen replied. "It's just that sometimes I can't take it. She's always mad at me. She'll only do what I ask if I'll give her something. Sometimes I get so mad I just want to hurt her like she's hurting me. I couldn't stand it that day."

"You could have asked us for help," Steven said quietly.

"You would have thought it was my fault. I thought it would get better. I thought that someday she'd realize how much I love her. I just wanted her to be happy with us. I hated it when she told me that she didn't want to live with me."

"I'm sorry Karen that this has been so difficult. I wish that you had told us. Maybe we could have helped before it got to this point. I'm afraid with all that has happened that we'll have to move Katie."

"No!" screamed Karen. "I do love her and won't do any of those things again. Please give me another chance."

"Even if you were able to control your anger at Katie, and ask us for help, I'm afraid that so much has happened that Katie would not be able to change while living in your home. I don't think that it would be fair to you or Katie to keep her with you, Karen. I'm sorry."

Jan agreed with what Steven said and supported Karen. She then called in Katie and they told her that she would be moving.

"No!" screamed Katie. "I want to stay with Karen. I lied. She hasn't done anything wrong."

"Yes, I have," said Karen. "You don't have to lie for me. You weren't wrong Katie, I was."

"I want to stay with Karen. She buys me things and lets me watch TV. She lets me play more than Ruth did," said Katie.

As Karen cried, Katie stared at her but showed no emotion herself. She eventually went with Steven with no difficulty and when she got into his car she immediately told him that she wanted to go to another home "like Karen's."

At the office, Steven found some crayons and paper for Katie while he went to tell Kathy about the crisis. She supported his decision to move Katie and they began searching for a home. Kathy recalled a recent foster child who returned to his parent's custody and she asked Betty if that foster home would be appropriate for Katie.

"Susan Cummings is a good foster parent, Steven. From what you've said about Katie, I think that she could manage her. Why don't I give her a call?" said Betty. She was back in 10 minutes to say that Susan agreed to take Katie immediately and would consider keeping her indefinitely but wanted to learn more about her first before deciding.

Steven breathed easier as he drove Katie to Karen's to get her things and say goodbye. Katie would be going to her third home.

## COMMENTARY

Katie's response to the move from Ruth's to Karen's home is not unusual for children who have difficulty forming secure attachments. Such children show little grief when they leave a home that they may have lived in for months, if not years. Their lack of emotion seems to reflect how their relationships with their foster or adoptive parents lack depth. Their parents are there to be used. They are objects whose function is to meet their immediate concrete needs. Parents-as-objects are interchangeable. They do not become sources of inter-subjectivity. Their parental value is determined solely by the percentage of times that they gratify the child's wishes. Since these children are never satisfied for long, they inevitably became dissatisfied with their current foster parents. They are usually quite willing to move to another home.

One might speculate that Katie was hiding her feelings of grief from others. She might be pretending that her feelings were shallow in order to minimize the rejection that she felt. I do not believe that is an accurate account for what is occurring in the inner lives of children with features of attachment disorganization when they move to another home. Katie truly had not begun to trust and identify with either Ruth or Karen, processes that would have elicited significant feelings of loss and abandonment. Katie was an individual who focused almost exclusively on meeting her own needs. She had very little empathy for others and did not experience her parent as a separate person. She needed to be "selfish" because her sense of self was fragmented, filled with gaps, and covered with shame. She spent all of her psychic energy trying to find band-aids that would hold her self together, repair her wounds, and cover over her emptiness. Band-aids could not hold such a child together; she needed a mother, a mother who could "hold" her so that she would learn to develop her "self" in a differentiated and integrated manner. Katie's attachment security with such a mother would be the mold from which to fashion her self. The joy and interests that would emerge from such an attachment were prerequisites if she were to be likely to give up her "selfish" preoccupations.

One of the saddest comments that I have ever heard from a child emerged from a nine-year-old girl who had been in her most recent foster home for over two years. I stated that her words and behaviors made me think that she would like to move from one home to the next every three months. She thought about my comment for a moment and then hopefully asked, "Can I?" I could not think of anything to say.

Katie's immediate desire to call Karen and Ken "mom" and "dad" is not unusual either. Such comments do not reflect a favorable emotional response to her new parents. Rather, they are simply her efforts to establish control over these new parental objects. She is saying, "I really like you a lot. Now you have to be nice to me and give me what I want." Regretfully, she does not know how to "like" someone. But she knows that parents want to think that they are special to their child so she tells them that they are. Katie, and the actual children whom she represents, excel at manipulating adults in new relationships. They are able to be charming, polite, friendly, and helpful when they think that they will get something from such behaviors. Most adults assume that such behaviors, while being superficial now, will lead to something with deeper reciprocal affect. They are then likely to be extra nice to Katie, not wanting to jeopardize the "good" start. They want to "reinforce" their new child's appropriate behaviors. Karen waited quite a while for some reciprocity to Katie's interactions. When it failed to come, in spite of her "doing everything for her," she became enraged at Katie's rejection of her as a mother. When she did not know was that Katie never thought of her as a mother. To Katie, Karen was a servant, not a mother.

There is a danger that when the foster or adoptive parent begins to observe the "manipulation," the parent responds in anger at rejection. The parent views the child's associated actions as dishonest and immoral. It is crucial to understand that the child's utilization of "manipulation" developed as a necessary survival skill because she had never experienced an adult doing something for him or her from a parent's normal caregiving intentions. The child was responsible for meeting her needs. Since she could not rely on her parents to do so spontaneously, she had to develop means of inducing them to do so. Charm, manipulation, and intimidation are likely to be the best options available. These defenses should not be used against the child to induce even greater shame and need for even more pervasive defenses.

Many foster placements resemble Karen, although more resemble Ruth. These parents may or may not have the right motives in taking these children into their home. Children similar to Katie often elicit strong emotional responses from the adults who care for them. Foster children will often compulsively try to recreate the abusive situations that they experienced in their original home. They also often manifest extreme emotional and behavioral outbursts because of their poor affect regulation, self-control, and self-reflection. They often trigger emotional responses that reflect their foster parents' own unresolved issues from their own childhood. When foster parents have such unresolved significant problems, they eventually are at risk to maltreat the children in their care, often verbally or emotionally, though possibly physically or sexually as well. When that occurs, the severe problems that the child had when entering their home are made worse by the maltreatment that they subsequently receive by the adults chosen to keep them safe.

Caring for children with trauma/attachment difficulties is an extremely difficult 24-hour-per-day task. It requires a high degree of personal maturity, self-control, empathy for their child, and ability to tolerate long periods of stress. It requires that these foster parents manifest resolution in their own attachment histories. Excellent foster parenting requires a high level of screening, training, and support. Even then, there remains the risk that a given child will prove to be too difficult for the foster parents. When that occurs, our solution to the tragedy of the abuse and neglect of children only makes the problem worse. We must reduce these system failures as much as possible. Our commitment must begin with the selection, training, and support of the individual foster parent. Without a qualified parent, the overall system will fail the individual child.

# 5

## Susan Cummings (Foster Home #3)

Susan Cummings reminded Steven of Ruth Daley. She had a relaxed air of warmth and confidence. She clearly enjoyed her work and seemed pleased to meet Katie. Her husband, Richard, ran a local oil dealership and left her to run their home. She had two "grown" children—Beth, who was "away" at college, and Dick, who was living on his own and working for his dad. She had two other foster children, nine-year-old Jessica and twelve-year-old Dan. She was about to leave to pick up Dan at soccer practice and she invited Katie and Steven along for the ride.

Katie did not waste a minute getting Susan's attention. She jumped into the front seat of the car. Susan suggested that she get in the back with Jessica. She looked hurt, almost rejected. Still, she "bounced back" quickly. She was calling Susan "mom" as if she had known her for months. Susan enjoyed answering her questions about school, her room, and whether or not Susan liked McDonald's. Katie also wasted no time telling Susan how Karen, her last mother, had abused her in various ways. Susan reassured her that she would not do those things to her. Steven was glad that Katie had addressed that issue so directly with Susan. He was puzzled at how quickly she had begun to speak of Karen in such a negative manner. Steven interrupted their discussion to say that Karen had really tried to raise Katie but simply did not have enough practice taking care of kids to know what to do in hard situations. Katie turned to Steven and with a tone meant to end all debate, said, "She was mean to me and I don't like her."

Back home, Dan and Jessica offered to show Katie her room while Susan talked to Steven. Katie immediately replied, "I want Mommy to!"

"Why don't you go with Jessica, Katie? She'd love to show you around," Susan suggested.

"I want you to do it," Katie was almost tearful.

"OK, honey. You'll have to wait a few minutes while I talk to Steven."

Katie sat down to wait. Jessica and Dan left the room. Steven decided that he would call the next day to tell Susan more about Katie. When he left, Susan showed Katie her room.

Katie seemed to settle into Susan's home fairly well over the first few months. She wanted to be with Susan a great deal, talking to her about anything and wanting to know everything. Only when Richard came home from work would she give Susan a rest. Richard immediately liked her. She was so friendly and affectionate. She tried to be helpful and was disappointed when he was busy and could not do something with her.

Jessica and Dan were much less favorably impressed with Katie. She did not want their help. She seldom played with them unless she needed them to do something for her. Whenever they went to Susan to talk or relax, she would try to get between them and Susan. If they hugged Susan, she would stop whatever she was doing and hug Susan twice. She would interrupt their conversations and find things that she needed Susan for whenever they asked for help.

Susan initially asked Jessica and Dan to be patient. Katie simply needed extra attention until she felt comfortable with the family. Later, she would ask Katie to wait her turn, "I need to be with my other kids, too." She thought that Katie was beginning to accept her need to "share" Susan with the other two. Then she noticed that when she spent some close time with Jessica or Dan, Katie would take or break something of theirs. They would become enraged at Katie. Susan would calm them down and correct Katie. She thought that Katie would stop but the pattern seemed to become stronger. Jessica and Dan did not like their "new little sister."

On November 13, 1993, Dan was outside helping Richard finish raking up the leaves that they would later be spreading in the gardens. Dan hurried to keep up with his "dad," always looking for Richard to nod and say "good job." Never before had Dan had a father who wanted to be with him and appreciated his efforts and abilities. When Richard had managed to attend his last soccer game, Dan felt a degree of pride and joy that he could barely contain.

Richard enjoyed Dan. He was a good worker. He was quick to learn. In some ways, Richard was closer to Dan than he had been with his own son Dick when Dick was Dan's age—funny how that happened. Dick seemed to grow up so fast. They never seemed to have time to do much together. Richard was planning to go hunting with Dick for two days next week. That would be good. Dan wanted to go. In a year or two, Richard thought, the three of them might go together.

Katie and Jessica were playing at the swing set behind the house. That was unusual. They were together without fighting. Dan saw them, too. He also saw Katie, now sitting at the top of the slide, playing with his Gameboy.

"Katie, I told you not to play with that," Dan yelled. "Put it back in the house."

Katie ignored Dan. He yelled again. Katie looked up, stared at him, and then went back to the game.

"Katie!" Dan screamed as he threw down the rake and ran toward her. She still ignored him. "Give me that!" he yelled as he reached the swings.

"No!" she screamed back and then she suddenly threw it into the driveway.

"Katie, I hate you!" yelled Dan as he ran to his game. He picked it up and there was nothing on the screen. He tried to get it to operate but it would not.

Dan turned and ran at Katie, still sitting on the top of the slide. Richard yelled to Dan to let him handle it but Dan did not hear him. Katie tried to escape by sliding down but Dan arrived at the same time and pushed her as she was half way down. Katie fell over the side, landing on her back and letting out a piercing cry.

Richard watched Katie fall and he ran to her, pushing Dan aside.

"Get in the house!" he yelled at Dan.

"But she broke my Gameboy!"

"Shut up and get out of here. I don't want to see you!" Richard replied. He bent down and attended to Katie. She reached for him and he held her as she cried. Susan came out, they checked her to see that she was all right, and Richard went looking for Dan.

He went into Dan's room and shouted, "Don't you ever touch her again!"

"She's always breaking my stuff!" Dan shouted back through his tears.

"I don't care what she breaks of yours, she's just a little girl, and you will not hit her again if you want to live here!"

Dan became motionless as if he were hit. He stared at Richard. Finally, in an angry voice, he said, "Maybe I don't."

"Well, it's your choice. Let me know what you want." Richard left him alone.

Susan later went to Dan to quietly explain that he was much bigger than Katie was and could hurt her. She knew that Katie sometimes did not treat him well but he had to control himself around her. If he were patient with her, maybe she'd start to treat him better.

"Mom, I can't stand her. Ever since she came here, nothing is the same. Dad always takes her side and yells at me. Why does she have to live with us?"

"Dan, when you came here two years ago you had hard times, too. Remember Johnny who lived with us then? You were so jealous of him. He couldn't stand you, either."

"But that was different, Mom. I was never mean to him the way Katie is. And she just wants to get me and Jessica in trouble all the time. She doesn't try to get along at all, Mom."

"You just have to keep trying like we all do, Dan. Katie has had a hard life and she's still a little girl. She needs our patience," said Susan.

Dan stared long at Susan, "I had a hard life too, Mom."

On December 18, 1993, the Cummings family was beginning their Christmas preparations. This was the most enjoyable season for Susan. Decorating the house, baking special breads and pies, and selecting just the right gifts were the activities that she truly treasured.

Richard and Dan had just brought in the tree and they were standing it in the traditional spot in the dining room. The table was set in the corner so that there would be plenty of room for presents to be placed between now and Christmas with most of them mysteriously appearing on Christmas Eve.

Susan had become concerned that Katie really was not "settling in" as she had expected. It was now three months. She was still very mean to Jessica and Dan. She would pout and complain whenever she did not get something that she wanted. She had begun to take things from Susan. Just last week, her wedding band was missing from the sill above the kitchen sink. She found it in Katie's backpack. Katie's teacher had called to say that Katie was showing off her "new ring" at school. When she confronted Katie, she got no response. Katie seemed to "shut down" when confronted with something that she had done. Susan would say what needed to be said and Katie would wait until she was done and then walk off. Susan suspected that Katie was neither sorry nor committed to changing her behaviors.

Susan hoped that the Christmas season would help Katie to begin to relax and be a regular, happy kid. Jan Temple had said that it wasn't likely to happen that quickly. Jan thought that Katie wasn't likely to begin to trust for another year or two. Susan prayed that Jan was wrong.

Susan, Jessica, and Katie were unwrapping the ornaments and other tree decorations and placing them on the table, waiting until the tree was ready. Each year Susan would give each child a new ornament. This tradition was an important part of Susan's own childhood. She still had 15 ornaments that her parents had given her when she was a child. Each ornament held its own memories. She had shared these memories with her own children and they then treasured their own ornaments even more. Jessica received a lovely white ornament last year in the shape of a swan. Jessica loved it and had pleaded to keep it in her room rather than wrap it up with the other ornaments at the end of the season. Susan explained that not only would her special ornament be safer if kept in the box with the others but it also would retain its magical Christmas quality if she could see it only during this season.

Jessica was thrilled to see it again. She carefully unwrapped it and placed in the center of the table. She stared at it and gently touched it.

Eventually the tree was ready and they began the process of turning it into "The Tree." Susan gave each child the ornaments, one at a time, and they found the place on the tree that was "just right" for each one. Jessica and Katie each went to put an ornament on the same spot. Jessica got there first and Katie yelled. Susan told Katie to find another spot and she did, though only after her usual pout.

A few minutes later, Susan looked up to see Katie look toward Jessica, smile, and then drop a book on Jessica's white swan. Susan and Jessica both screamed and Dan and Richard looked up. Jessica ran to the table and lifted the book off her shattered ornament.

"Why did you do it?" Susan grabbed Katie's arms and yelled at her.

"It was an accident," Katie replied.

"I saw you do it. You did it on purpose. That was a very bad thing to do!" Susan continued to hold Katie by the arms and stare into her face.

"You're hurting me! Leave me alone!" Katie screamed at Susan.

"No I'm not! I'm not going to let you go until you tell me why you did such a mean thing!" Susan's anger continued.

"You better let her go, Susan," said Richard. "Maybe it was an accident."

"It was not! I saw her do it!" Susan turned to Richard. "She's going to tell me why!"

"You're hurting me!" Katie continued to scream.

"You better let her go," Richard said again. "You might be hurting her!"

"I am not!" Susan yelled at Richard. "Let me handle this."

"Now you go to your room, Katie. What you did to Jessica was very mean and you're not going to have a Christmas until we deal with this," Susan yelled. Katie screamed and ran to her room.

"Don't you think you're overreacting?" Richard asked. "Maybe she did do it on purpose but she didn't realize how important it was to Jessica."

"She did realize it. She knew what she was doing and she enjoyed hurting Jessica. I saw it and you didn't." Susan was becoming annoyed with her husband.

"Let's just drop it, Susan," said Richard.

"You can drop it but I'm not. She's going to face what she did."

Richard dropped the streamer that he had been attaching to the window and left the room. They heard him slam the door. Susan by now was holding a crying and shaking Jessica in her lap.

"I'll get you another ornament, Jessica," said Susan.

"I want my swan!" cried Jessica.

"I'll find another swan just like that one," promised Susan.

Dan stood for a time by the tree. "She always ruins everything!" He ran from the room and went outside, looking for Richard.

During the next two weeks, the Cummings family celebrated the Christmas season with the same activities and traditions that they had always done. Susan was not able to get Katie to "face" what she had done. Susan stopped trying and instead worked harder to have a good Christmas for the family. She and Richard did not feel as close as they usually did at this time of year. Susan felt sad often during that time. She had lost something special to her. Katie got her presents and she seemed content. In fact, she almost seemed to be peaceful. This may have been the best Christmas that she had ever had. If she noticed the mood of the rest of the family, it did not interfere with her own. Actually, it might have helped her own.

On the morning of January 27, 1994, Steven sat at his desk planning his lunch break. Jenny had given him a list of things to bring home for Rebecca's first birthday party later that day. Jenny's parents were visiting, with their camcorder, piles of presents, electric blankets, and lots of advice and concern. Steven wanted to bring something home for Rebecca's birthday that he picked out, something that would delight his daughter. Usually Rebecca's joy and excitement centered on her mother. Steven decided he needed a bit of help if he were to merit some attention from his daughter. He asked Barbara and Al for ideas. After hearing various suggestions, he decided that no one could compete with his in-laws for the newest presents. He would find something later.

Steven received a call from Susan. His anxiety rose just as it had done at every phone call over the past four weeks. Katie was not doing well at Susan's. Steven and Jan had met with Susan. Jan had seen Katie for extra sessions. So far, there were no signs of progress. During the last meeting, when Jan had told Susan that Katie had only been at her house for four months and that it took time for a child to begin to trust her new parents, Steven felt dread. He had heard that before and he had said it himself. Katie had been in foster care for 16 months and received therapy for 14 months. Ruth and Susan were excellent, experienced foster parents and Karen had really tried to give Katie a good home. What could he do next? What was going to happen next?

"Steven, I'm losing it with Katie," said Susan. "Lately she is getting up at 4:00 a.m. The alarm on her bedroom door has stopped her from roaming the house but she has discovered it to be a great way to get us. She deliberately sets it off when she awakens and the whole house wakes, too. She always has an excuse. Either she has to use the bathroom, or she falls out of bed, or she has a scary dream. I tell her those reasons are not acceptable but she does it anyway. It's hard for us all to get back to sleep. Even Richard is losing patience with her."

"She really is giving you guys a rough time lately. Any ideas yet why she might be doing so poorly?" asked Steven.

"I really don't. It seems like every day I'm trying to come up with a new explanation for her behaviors. I try everything. Maybe I'm too strict so I give her more attention and go easier on the consequences. Then I think that maybe I'm too easy and I tighten things up. Then I think I'm too inconsistent and I set up rules and routines to try to cover everything that happens. Whatever I do seems to have no impact on her."

"Has there been any effect from the antidepressant medication that Dr. Veilleux decided to try?"

"Not yet. He did say it would take a few weeks and she's only been on it for 10 days. It just gives her something else to complain about. 'Why do I have to take medicine when Jessica and Dan don't,'" Susan replied.

"Do you explain that it's not a punishment but simply a way to help her to be happier?" Steven asked.

"I do, but she doesn't listen. I think that she would take medicine cheerfully if it were her idea. She always wants to be in charge! She would argue if I gave her ice cream and the other kids celery. She'd want both the ice cream and the celery and she'd want to decide what to give them. There's nothing that happens that she doesn't want to control," Susan said wearily.

"I guess the honeymoon is over, Susan," Steven said, for nothing better to add.

"I'm beginning to think there never was a honeymoon, Steven. Her 'good' behavior over the first few months seems to have been an effort to charm me and Richard. I think that she even thought that we might get rid of Jessica and Dan. All of her negativity seemed to be directed at them. Now she is sending it toward us all, even Richard. Yesterday, Richard asked her to get his gloves for him when he was leaving for work. She refused to do it for him. He didn't say anything but he stared at me when he left. He seems to want me to fix her. Or he might be blaming me for her problems, I don't know. We don't seem to be able to talk about Katie without one of us getting upset."

"How are the other kids managing things?" Steven asked.

"They avoid her. If anything, they might be doing better, since she's been getting into trouble more with me and Richard. I think they might be relieved that we now see her for who she is. She's not the sad and troubled angel that she first seemed to be. I probably give them more understanding than I did before over their anger at her. I still worry about Richard and Dan though. They're not as close as they were before Katie came," Susan said.

"I'll try to stop by later in the week. I hope you can hang in there. She's bound to get better eventually," Steven suggested.

"I hope so. But it sure would be nice to know when," Susan replied.

As he had done many times, Steven updated Al and Barbara on Katie's current functioning. They both knew how important Katie was to him. She represented his hope that he could really make a difference with children who had been abused and neglected. He met her shortly after her fifth birthday. Certainly he could insure that she received a good life. He tried not to think of Betty's quote, "You can lead a horse to water . . . ."

On the way home that evening, he stopped in a local hardware store and glanced at their small toy section. There on the top shelf sat the largest, happiest, stuffed ladybug that he had ever seen. That bug must have been two and one-half feet round and eighteen inches high. It was bright red and had large black eyes. It seemed to watch Steven and smile. When Rebecca ripped off the paper covering his present later that evening she squealed with delight. She hugged that big happy bug and tried to pick it up. She couldn't, it was too big. So she lay on top of it with her arms wrapped tightly around it. Steven felt proud of his contribution to Rebecca's first party. She insisted that the ladybug share her crib and Jenny somehow found the space.

The first year for Jenny and Steven as parents had been busy, tiring, fulfilling, and challenging. They had never worried so much before about anyone or anything. At the same time, they both felt no regrets. Rebecca brought so much to their lives. She needed so much and they had to work out schedules so that they shared the responsibilities. But Rebecca had a way of making time vanish. Steven might play with her for an hour, making strange sounds and faces, crawling after her, showing delight and surprise at her countless gestures and movements. He would hold her and carry her. She would chase him and grab his feet. They would crawl around the dining room table, first one chasing and the other screeching, and then they would change directions and it was the other's turn to howl. Their fun and excitement were mutual. Steven gradually sensed that Rebecca was tiring and he intuitively slowed his pace and gestures and vocalizations. Soon Rebecca would fall into his lap, put her thumb in her mouth, and become quiet. He would wait for her cue that she rested enough. She would then get up and generally wander to some other activity.

Steven had initially sat in awe at Jenny's relationship with Rebecca. When they were together, nothing else seemed to exist. Jenny always seemed to sense Rebecca's moods and intentions as they were being expressed and she would respond in a way that meshed just right with her daughter's emerging inner state. They would stare at each other for endless minutes, with Rebecca on her back on Jenny's legs. They would smile and move their heads and squinch their eyes and nose in time with some unheard music. Steven didn't think that he could engage Rebecca as intimately as did Jenny. At the same time, he didn't think that Rebecca was as interested in engaging him as she was with Jenny. Those first 12 months seemed designed for Rebecca and her mother. Their union at birth still seemed to exist. Rebecca was becoming herself while dancing with Jenny.

On March 8, 1994, the principal at Katie's school called Susan. Katie had refused to return another child's snack that she had taken. When her teacher went to take it from her, she kicked the teacher and ran from the room. The teacher and her aide eventually were able to carry Katie to the principal's office, who promptly called Susan to come and take Katie home. The school suspended Katie for the next day as well. This was the principal's first experience with suspending a first grader.

When Susan brought Katie home, she noted that Katie acted as if nothing had happened. She ignored Susan's talk in the car about hitting her teacher. When they entered the house, Katie ran to the TV and turned it on. Susan turned off the TV and informed Katie that she needed to spend some time in her room before doing some schoolwork that the teacher had given her. She told Katie that since the other children were in school she would have her schoolwork at home.

"No, I won't. You can't make me!" Susan was not surprised at Katie's response. Katie's defiant attitude had become the norm.

"Katie, I want you to go to your room now," Susan said and prepared herself to take Katie to her bedroom.

Katie screamed at Susan "I'll kick you, too!" Given warning, Susan tried to protect herself, but as she reached for her arm, Katie still managed to kick her leg hard. She spun Katie around and pushed her toward her room. Katie reached up and grabbed onto Susan's hair. Susan's glasses fell and both she and Katie landed next to them on the carpet. Katie screamed that she hurt her leg. As Susan released her Katie leaped up and ran toward the kitchen. Susan followed, yelling for Katie to stop. Katie grabbed the portable phone and threw it through the bay window. Katie darted outside. Susan followed but Katie ignored her yells to return. She leaped in the car and locked the doors. She refused to let Susan in. Susan went for her keys and returned to see Katie's look of hatred from the front seat. Susan turned the key and the door release popped up. Before she could open the door, Katie had pushed the release down again. This must have happened 20 times before Susan retreated to the kitchen. It was cold outside and Katie did not have her coat on. After an hour of waiting, she tried to open the car door again. Katie again managed to keep the door closed. Finally, Susan became concerned about Katie's health in the cold so she called Richard from his office to come home. When he arrived, Katie remained locked in the car and refused to let them in. Richard and Susan had to open both front doors at the same time in order to get to Katie. Richard had to carry her to her room. She screamed and swore at him and managed to scratch his face. She then destroyed her bedroom.

Steven felt intense discouragement when he met with Susan at Jan's office before Katie's therapy on March 11. Katie had been with Susan for about six months and her problems were worse than ever. She had been in foster care for 18 months and what had they accomplished? He turned to Jan and asked what they might try next.

"I wish I knew," Jan replied. "We might consult with Bill again about another behavior plan. We need to try to get back a positive attitude toward Katie or I'm afraid we'll have a vicious circle that won't do her or anyone else any good."

"I haven't given up yet," Susan said. "What's a bay window as long as Steven will pay for a new one? But we have to find some way to get through to her. She's not like Jessica and Dan who seem to want to do better. When they mess up, they seem a little sorry anyway and are almost grateful to get some consequence so that it's over with. But Katie, she doesn't care. It's the rest of the family's fault. Give her a consequence and we'll pay for it as if we have no right to be so cruel to her."

"Did you ever see any effect from the medication?" Steven asked.

"No, Steven," Susan responded. "And Dr. Veilleux has tried another that he thought might reduce her rage outbursts. That hasn't helped either."

"Let's meet next week with Bill. A new behavior plan might give us all a fresh start," suggested Jan. Steven and Susan agreed and Jan suggested that she meet with Katie and try to understand what's going through her mind now.

In therapy, Katie would have nothing to do with processing her recent behaviors at school and at home. Jan knew that if she pressed too hard Katie would insist on ending therapy early that day and that they would lock in a power struggle over her need to stay until the session finally ended. Jan accepted her refusal and became hopeful when Katie chose to play with the dollhouse that she might nonverbally express her recent experiences. Katie's play had its usual intense, driven quality. The child figure was quite aggressive. On this occasion, the child went further. She took the furniture from the entire house and placed the pieces in a pile in the living room. She left the baby upstairs. She then pretended to set the furniture on fire and the entire house burned down. The baby, of course, died. Jan wondered if the baby represented Susan and her family or Katie herself. Probably both, she thought. When she suggested that to Katie, she received a "Shut up!" with more force than usual. Maybe she got through to Katie. If so, would it do any good?

During the next few weeks, Bill helped them to develop a behavioral program that focused heavily on the positive. Katie had various rewards available to her for maintaining fairly appropriate social behaviors. They overlooked misbehavior or simply told her that the rewards would be available to her as soon as her behavior was on target again. Katie learned the system very rapidly.

For a few days, she seemed to be responding favorably. Then Susan began to note that as soon as she got a reward her behavior would get worse. Susan received warning not to expect this to happen or Katie might act to meet the expectation. Susan tried to avoid anticipating anything after the reward but Katie's behavior still became more aggressive and defiant. Maybe she was communicating something negative to Katie without being aware of it. She tried harder, but nothing changed. She soon began to feel somewhat disappointed when Katie earned a reward. Somehow that wasn't what was supposed to be happening.

Early in April 1994, Susan again met with Steven, Jan, and Bill. Katie's behavior might be somewhat better, but for some reason she didn't feel better. She tried to explain it.

"I think that Katie might be doing a little better because she's able to get what she wants more now than before. She knows that when she does something wrong she really won't lose out on anything that she most wants to do. It's not hard for her to hold it together enough to get what she wants and then she doesn't care for a while and she does whatever she wants to annoy the rest of us. Then when she wants something again, she turns it on, and gets another reward."

"That's a start," suggested Bill. "She is aware of the connection between good behaviors and rewards. This is something to build on. If she does it enough, eventually she should start to take pleasure in doing good for its own sake. Be sure to verbally reinforce her good behaviors."

"I'm careful to do that, Bill," said Susan. "But so far I haven't seen any sign that she cares about anything I say. She does it to get the reward. But only when she wants the reward. When she doesn't care about it, she does what she feels like and it's often something that the rest of us don't like."

"But again, it's a start," said Jan. "Since things are better at home now maybe eventually she will begin to want to get along better with the family so that she is liked and praised for what she does."

"She never had these positive reinforcements when she was young, Susan," said Bill. "It will take some time before she begins to associate the concrete reinforcers and then the social reinforcers with her good behaviors. Once that happens, you'll begin to see that she is trying harder to please you and do what you're reinforcing."

On May 1, Susan was preparing for the annual early spring family cookout that had been a tradition in her home for a number of years. Dick and Beth would be home and Susan and Richard's parents would be over as well. Susan's brother Mike and his family were also planning to come.

Susan hoped that Katie would be OK for the family gathering. While she really had not seen any improvements over the past few months, there were no outrageous behaviors, either. She again thought that Katie was doing better because she was getting what she wanted more. She was still hurtful, oppositional, and selfish. Susan did not feel that Katie was any closer to her. Katie still lied almost constantly and tried to get away with whatever she could. Susan and Richard were pretty good at biting their tongues and not reacting to these behaviors. When Katie did what she was supposed to do, they were able to praise her and she got her reward.

Katie was in a good mood that morning and even offered to help prepare for the cookout. Susan thought that she might be competing with Jessica to see who could be the most helpful. If that was her motive, it was all right with Susan! She'd have enough jobs for them both. She'd simply make sure that they worked separately.

"Jessica, why don't you vacuum the living room and TV room? After that, you can make the lemonade. Katie, I'd like you to stay here and help me get the food ready."

Both girls readily agreed and Susan began preparing the food. She had Katie wash the vegetables for the salad while she prepared the ground beef for hamburgers that her husband would use on the outdoor grill. Katie quickly bored with washing the lettuce and Susan could see that she'd have to do it over herself. She suggested that they trade tasks and Katie again agreed. They worked for only a few minutes when Richard called Susan outside to inspect their garden.

Fifteen minutes later, Harold and Margaret Woods, Susan's parents, arrived and joined them in the garden.

"It's going to be a great summer. We figure we'll have enough food to feed half the town," Susan said to her parents. "Glad you're both feeling well today." Susan worried about her parents recent health problems. "Would you help me finish up in the kitchen, mom? Your salads are the reason we have this cookout every year."

"Sure. And if I believe that, I'd believe that Harold and I just won the lottery," Margaret replied as they walked toward the house. "How are all the kids doing?"

"So-so," Susan said. "I still don't think we're doing much for Katie. You just can't get through to her."

"Well, you can only do your best. And your best is good enough for most kids," said Margaret.

When they entered the kitchen, Jessica was making the lemonade and Katie was not there. "Where's Katie?" asked Susan.

"She went to her room," replied Jessica.

Susan went to check the hamburgers. She figured that she'd have to squeeze them harder than Katie could do. They looked like they'd fall apart before they got on the grill.

Susan took one in her hand and began to form it into a ball. Something was wrong. It didn't feel right. It didn't look right. She inspected it more closely. It smelled awful. Something was wrong with the meat. But she had just bought it fresh yesterday. She turned to Margaret. "Smell this, mom."

"Yuck!" Margaret replied, "that's not hamburger."

Susan had a bad feeling when she thought of Katie in her room. She took one of the hamburgers and walked through the house to her bedroom. She knocked on the door, entered and immediately knew that she was right. Katie had that look about her that meant that she had done something wrong.

"What did you do to the hamburger, Katie?"

"I didn't do anything!" Katie yelled.

"Katie, this smells awful, what did you put in here?"

Susan then became aware that the smell was much worse in Katie's room. Also, it was now more familiar. She walked in, and looked behind the bed. On the floor were Katie's soiled underpants and a towel smeared with feces.

"Katie, did you put your poop in the hamburger meat?" Susan screamed.

Katie's look removed all doubt. Katie was pleased! She had done something that would really upset Susan. She was enjoying Susan's look of horror.

"Katie, you did!" Susan continued to yell. "Why did you do that? What a mean and disgusting thing to do! Why did you do it?"

Katie did not answer. She only stared at Susan. She didn't appear to be frightened. If anything, she seemed to want Susan to yell at her and maybe even hit her. She wanted to get Susan to hate her!

Susan didn't know what to do or say. Tears came to her eyes. She felt like rubbing the meat in Katie's face. She wanted to drag her into the kitchen by her hair and make her clean it all up and tell everyone what she had done. Susan could not accept such feelings. She could not feel anything toward Katie. She was beaten. She did what she could for this child for eight months. Now she could only cry. She left Katie's room, saying nothing more to the child. Susan needed to be with her mother. She needed to grieve with her mother. Katie did not grieve. She was as content as she was capable of being.

When Susan called Steven to tell him that he would need to find another home for Katie, she did not feel anger or guilt. If she felt anything, it was sadness. She had failed. It didn't hurt as much as it first did. Her mother had helped her to come to terms with it. But she was still sad for Katie. She was not yet seven years old.

Steven took the news with resignation. He was as upset over the meat incident as Susan was initially. What was Katie thinking? Who could raise this child? What could he do with her?

He consulted with Kathy who arranged to consult with Dawn at the Central Office regarding placement options for Katie. Susan had said that she would be willing to keep her to the end of the school year, which gave them four or five weeks.

The next day, Steven summarized the past 21 months in Katie's life for the other workers and for Dawn. He had pulled together the various symptoms that she had manifested in all of her placements. The more he listed her problems, the worse they seemed. He questioned his own experiences of Katie, which, for the most part, went fairly well. He was impressed with her energy, initiative, and general expressiveness. While she did seem pushy at times and self-centered, her behavior showed little of the oppositional and aggressive behaviors shown in her homes. For whatever reason, she wasn't making it in the homes that they provided her.

Dawn asked if they had considered one of the therapeutic foster home programs in the area. Kathy indicated that she was thinking the same thing.

"What's different about these homes than our regular homes?" asked Steven.

"In general, the parents receive more training and support than the regular homes. They receive a higher board rating and are expected to be more actively involved in the child's treatment. While many of our regular foster parents are as skilled and committed as are these parents, they are a resource that you might consider if you cannot find the right home among the regular DHS homes," Dawn suggested.

"I'd support that, Steven," Kathy said. "We have to do everything we can to get the right placement for her. She can't afford anymore moves after this one."

"I just don't know what any home can give Katie that Susan and Ruth did not give," Steven said. "Somehow we're missing something."

"Would you say that Katie has difficulty forming attachments with her foster parents?" asked Dawn.

"She sure has difficulty getting along with them if that's what you mean," Steven replied.

"Does it seem to matter to her when she is moved or does it seem that one home is as good as the next to her?" Dawn asked.

"I don't think it matters. Ruth and Susan don't think so either. Her other parent, Karen, thought that she meant something to Katie, but the moment she left she seemed to forget her."

"Also, would you consider her to be manipulative and controlling? Will she always have an excuse, lie, and blame others?"

"That's Katie," Steven replied.

"Why don't you have her evaluated by Allison Kaplan in Farmingdale? She's done a lot of work with children who have difficulty forming an attachment to their foster or adoptive parents," Dawn suggested.

"Some of my kids have seen Allison in the past," Betty said. "She did a good job. Her therapy isn't like what many therapists offer."

"What's the difference?" Steven asked.

"Well, she's kind of pushy with them. She challenges their behaviors. But she also gets the foster mom involved and actually works on teaching the child how to accept nurturing from the mom. Why not ask her to evaluate Katie; she's a psychologist."

"You should know that there are some questions around Allison's work. I think that it relates to how direct she is with the children. She believes that they will avoid their difficulties unless she asks them to address them. I'm confident that she does not push them harder than she needs to do, but maybe others are not so sure," Dawn said.

"Well, why don't I call her and talk with her about Katie. At least maybe she can see her and give us some ideas about the most appropriate placement for her," Steven said.

"Sounds good. Let me know what you find out," Kathy said.

The next day, Steven was able to reach Allison Kaplan. She sounded interested in Katie and indicated that she would be willing to evaluate her. She asked for a summary of her history prior to and after she entered foster care. She also wanted to speak with her foster mother. Steven felt hopeful that she might help him to understand Katie. He was even more encouraged when Dr. Kaplan said that she knew of a foster family that might be suitable for Katie. She had just finished working with Jackie Keller, a foster mother, and her foster son, Gabe, who recently attained an adoptive home. Jackie was taking some time off now but had expressed interest in taking in another child soon.

## COMMENTARY

Children who manifest significant difficulty forming a selective attachment with their foster and adoptive parents tend to have a variety of symptoms that create moderate or extreme difficulties in the major areas of their life. These symptoms may often reflect their abilities for basic biological regulation, affect modulation and integration, behavioral organization, and the development of language and reflective thought. Katie definitely manifested such pervasive problems during her three foster placements. Her various symptoms reflected a significant inability to form a selective attachment with her caregiver. They represented unresolved trauma. The same symptoms also reflected a lack of continuity of the self from one experience and affective or ego state to the next. Such continuity of self depends a great deal on a continuous and secure attachment figure during the first two years of life.

Katie's behavior toward Jessica and Dan did not represent the normal jealousy among siblings or even the jealousy of a child who doubted that she was as special to her parents as were her siblings. Rather, Katie wanted affection from Susan only when she saw her siblings seeking affection. She had no interest in affection itself. As an infant, she wanted affection. Now the reminders of it that she saw in Jessica and Dan's actions toward Susan elicited distress which she wanted to avoid. She wanted to keep Susan as her servant and her's alone. If Susan were attending to the other children, she would not be available for Katie. She also may have wanted to hurt Jessica and Dan. She knew what they wanted and she worked to prevent them from getting it.

The same dynamic entered Katie's perception of Susan and Richard's marriage. She wanted each parent to attend to her and relate to her, not to each other. Nothing would make her happier than to be able to create a conflict between Susan and Richard. Since Susan was the primary caregiver, most often she perceived her as being the "bad" parent and Richard as the "good" parent. When she had a conflict with Susan, she would immediately seek out Richard for sympathy. When she was able to cause them to argue over her, she would become as happy as she was capable of being.

In general, children similar to Katie have many conflicts with their new mother and then turn on their charm the moment the father comes home. Many are quite accomplished at inducing the father into thinking that the mother might be too harsh, hoping that he will encourage her to "lighten up" a bit. Nothing will discourage and infuriate a mother as much as seeing her husband be so influenced and then turn to see her child smile at her behind her husband's back. She then finds herself competing with her child for her husband's heart and mind. I recall how in one family the adoptive father began to think that his wife was actually lying to him about their child.

Katie succeeded in causing conflict among the members of her foster family. Many foster children equally succeed in creating discord among all of the professionals with whom they relate. A foster child's cries for sympathy at school create disagreement between her teacher and parent. Her carefully placed comments make her therapist question the decisions and comments made by her caseworker. The caseworker, in turn, begins to second-guess the medication prescribed by the psychiatrist or the decisions made by the previous caseworker. When the child is really successful, most of the professionals eventually agree that the parent is probably the reason that the child has not made progress. Such divisiveness increases the difficulty in being able to successfully assist a child like Katie. The adults involved need to be aware of the risk that such conflict may occur. They need to have developed open communication with and confidence in each other's abilities, knowledge, and commitment to a particular child. If the adults differ, they need to openly work to resolve their differences, with respect for each other's views. Since the parent is the most important person in the child's treatment, the professionals should share their recommendations and concerns and then accept the decision of the parent, unless there are exceptional reasons. If parents receive respect, most often they will be very receptive to assistance and ideas when their own efforts are not effective. It is hard to fail when we want so desperately to make a difference in the lives of such troubled children. If we begin to blame and not support each other, we will have become like the children we are treating and will be of little help.

Generally, Katie's first motive in interacting with others was to be able to convince them to give her what she wanted. If she got her parents to do what she wanted she would be satisfied temporarily. However, the objects or activities that she wanted never brought her any inner satisfaction or enjoyment. She would then make her next demand and her satisfaction with her parents would depend primarily on whether they again did what she wanted. The 10 previous positive responses would be insignificant if they refused the present request. Sooner or later each parent realized that granting her request did not make her feel safer or more trusting. When they refused her requests, Katie began to respond with anger at how unfair and harsh they had become. In her mind, they caused her to be angry and it was their fault that she was destructive, aggressive, sneaky, and defiant.

Katie and those like her do not experience remorse for hurting others. They have little empathy for others and little guilt for their behaviors. Empathy and guilt emerge within aspects of attachment security, within which the child increasingly identifies with his parents. Her parent is a person, not an object, and the securely attached child experiences empathy for her parent's distress when she is responsible for it. Katie had not reached that developmental level. She remained lost in shame, an emotion that focuses on the self, not the other, and which—in well-functioning families—remains small, enabling the child to develop through socialization, identification, empathy and guilt (Tangney & Dearing, 2002). With Katie, shame led back to her own worthlessness and to her hatred toward others who did not take care of her and so were equally worthless. Feces in the hamburger was to her an amusing representation of her contempt for the efforts of others to enjoy themselves. Mutual enjoyment necessarily excluded her and she would not tolerate it.

As is often the case among those who try to live or work with children like Katie, Steven, Jan, and Susan would look at recent events in Katie's life to try to understand what might have precipitated her symptoms. Frequently, parents and professionals spend a lot of time trying to identify the "triggers" as if that would enable them to help the child to better manage those stressors. This is a reasonable strategy when the child has only a few triggers. When we are talking about children lacking in behaviors representing attachment security and manifesting unresolved trauma, they have many, many triggers that lie among the thousands of events that occurred during their first two years of life. We can work diligently on identifying and trying to limit every "trigger," only to eventually become discouraged and begin to blame the child or each other. Professionals and parents need to recognize the deeper effects of the pervasive experiences of intrafamilial abuse and neglect, and then provide the child with the therapeutic experiences at home and in the office that will address the developmental and attachment deficiencies that originated years before. We need to discover what lies under the symptoms, address those traumas and developmental deficiencies, and lead the child into restorative intersubjective experiences with his or her attachment figures.

# 6

## Allison Kaplan, Ph.D.

On May 12, 1994, Katie met Allison when Susan and Steven brought her to Allison's office. They had not yet told her that she would be leaving Susan's home sometime after the school year ended. Allison met them in the waiting room and directed Katie to remain there while she talked with Susan and Steven. There were various toys in the room and Katie didn't mind staying.

Steven immediately noticed Allison's capable, relaxed manner. She appeared to be a calm and comfortable person and he sensed that she enjoyed her work. She wore gray slacks and a dark red pullover. She reminded him of many successful business and professional women. She seemed to be in her early 40s and had an air of confidence about her with her graying, light brown hair, a few freckles, and lovely smile. Her office reminded him of someone's living room more than a professional space. There was a large couch that held a variety of pillows, some of which seemed to have fallen to the floor. There was a rocking chair near the center of the room and a large stuffed chair near the window. The drapes over the windows also made him feel that he had entered the warm home of one of his foster parents. A small desk was in the corner, as if to prove to the skeptical that she actually was a psychologist and this was her office. Two standard office chairs were by the desk, but if Steven were to sit in one of them, he would be quite removed from any conversation around the couch and comfortable chairs. After Susan and Allison sat, he was left with the rocking chair.

Allison questioned Susan in detail about the past eight months. Steven noted that she was clearly not blaming Susan for the disrupted placement. If anything, she was expressing admiration for how hard Susan had worked to help Katie.

"If only Katie had known how to respond to you, Susan, we wouldn't be talking about her having to move," Allison suggested.

"Let me summarize what you've told me about her. She's an angry and controlling child who always insists on getting her way. She often does mean and hurtful things, especially if someone 'crosses' her or if she has just had a lot of fun and excitement. She is affectionate when she wants something from you or if she has done something wrong. She's frequently lying and stealing and generally she seems like a 'dark cloud' in your house. Originally she was able to create conflict between you and the other kids somewhat and then between you and your husband, who thought that you were too hard on her. You tried a behavioral plan that she seemed to play with—using it or not depending on whether she wanted something at the time. You don't think that you or anyone else really means anything to her. You have to watch her around animals or younger kids. When you set a limit and consequence, you know that you'll either have a fight on your hands then or you'll pay later in some way. Does that about cover most things?"

"That's Katie, Dr. Kaplan. I don't mean to seem too negative about her but that's the way she really is," Susan said.

"My impression, Steven," Dr. Kaplan said, "is that her first foster mother had basically the same experience when Katie lived in her home."

"That's right," Steven replied, "And it's my impression that Ruth was as competent and committed to Katie as Susan has been."

"Why don't we bring her in now? You wait here Steven while Susan and I get Katie. I'd like you both to be present for the interview," Allison said.

Allison and Susan went to the waiting room. Steven heard some commotion from Katie but they all entered Allison's office in a few minutes. Katie stayed close to Susan and sat near her on the couch.

"Katie didn't want to stop playing with the toys," Allison said in a relaxed and mildly playful tone. "So I told her that she needed to come in here with us and she had a choice. She could walk in or we would carry her. Oh, she did not like to hear that! Having us carry her! And she doesn't even know me! Well, she decided to walk, which, I guess, was a good choice for her."

Susan hugged Katie, who was pouting somewhat while still leaning against her.

Steven noticed that Allison was fairly direct as Betty had said, but she did it in a nice way. He wondered if Katie would now give her the silent treatment as she did with him if he asked her to do something that she didn't want to do. Allison quickly shifted gears and made a fuss about Katie's shirt coloring. Katie responded rapidly and positively when Allison brought over a stuffed cat that had the same shade of tan as was on her shirt. Allison let her hold the cat and she told her that the cat could talk for her if she had trouble talking about something. Katie said that she'd like to play with the other stuffed animals and puppets too. Then Allison denied her request and Katie threw down the cat.

"You're mad at the cat because I said no?" Allison asked. "Or are you really mad at me but aren't sure if you want to tell me? No problem with telling me. Why don't you say, 'I'm mad because you won't let me play with the animals. I'm really mad at you'?"

Katie didn't respond and she squeezed Susan's arm.

"Since you don't want to say it, have the cat say it for you," Allison said.

Katie ignored her. Allison then took the cat and she spoke for Katie. This annoyed Katie and she put her fingers in her ears.

Allison turned to Susan and said quietly, "I see what you mean, Susan. It really is hard for Katie when she can't do what she wants to do. Then she *really* doesn't do what she's asked to do. She just seems to get madder and madder."

Allison then put the cat on Susan's other side and asked her to put her one arm around it just like her other arm was around Katie. Allison then began talking to Susan about Katie's hair. Steven noticed that very quickly Katie was talking with Allison again. Allison seemed to have a way to keep Katie relating positively even after there was a conflict.

After more small talk, Allison moved her chair closer to Katie and began to focus on Katie's past life, without changing anything about her manner of relating.

"Now, Katie, I'm going to be talking about some things that are probably hard for you to talk about. It's OK if it's hard for you. If you need to take a deep breath while we're talking let me know by putting up your hand. Let's practice, show me how you'll do it."

Katie smiled and took a deep breath. "Good job, Katie." Allison went on, "Now tell me what was hard about living with your mom and dad, Sally and Mike."

Katie immediately became tense and looked away. Just as suddenly she said, "They were mean to me. Mike hit me and kicked me. He even peed on me!"

"Oh, Katie, that must have hurt you so much! And you were so little! And they were your parents! And parents aren't supposed to hurt their kids that way!"

Katie struggled for something else to say. She was not comfortable with Allison's empathy for her pain. "And they didn't feed me! And they never played with me. They said I was bad!"

"They hurt you so much, Katie," Allison said more quietly than before. "I'll bet you were so sad you cried a lot."

"I didn't cry!" Katie exclaimed. "I hit them and was mean to them!"

"I can see why, Katie, since they were mean to you and they were your parents! But you were so little. I'll bet you wanted to cry a little bit once in a while."

"I didn't cry!" Katie said again.

"Well, it never should have happened, Katie. And they never taught you how to live in a good family. They didn't teach you how to play with your parents. They didn't teach you how to do things with them. They didn't teach you how to have fun with your parents. No wonder it's been hard for you to learn how to live in the good homes that you've been in since you moved away from Sally and Mike. They never taught you!"

Katie said nothing. Allison reached over and raised Katie's hand. "I thought that you might need some help remembering to take a deep breath. This talk has been hard for you." Allison then put her hand on Katie's chest and took a deep breath herself. Katie smiled and also breathed deeply. "That should be better now, Katie. Why don't you tell me some of the things that have been hard for you to do while living with Susan."

Katie hesitated and then said, "Sometimes Susan won't let me have dessert and she makes me sit in the time-out chair."

"But what is hard for *you* to be able to do, Katie? What don't *you* know how to do well?"

Katie again said nothing. She did not get the sympathy for losing her dessert that she had sought. She didn't know what Allison wanted her to say.

"You seem stuck, Katie. I'll help you," Allison said. "Is it hard for you to tell the truth when you have done something wrong and Susan asks you about it?"

"Yes," Katie replied quietly.

"Is it hard for you to put away your toys when Susan tells you to?"

Katie again said yes, with a smile now.

"Was it hard for you to be at Jessica's birthday party?"

"No, that wasn't hard," Katie said.

"But you started yelling and you knocked over your soda when you couldn't have the piece of cake that you wanted," Allison suggested.

"But it wasn't hard," Katie maintained.

"I'm a bit confused then, Katie. I would have guessed that if you were having a lot of fun you would not have cared what piece of cake you got."

Katie again was silent. Allison rested her hand on Katie's and slowly said, "Katie, my guess is there are many things that have been hard for you while you're living with Susan because she's a good mom and you don't know how to really relax and feel safe with a good mom."

Katie seemed somewhat sad. She looked down and was motionless for a moment. Then she saw the cat, suddenly grabbed it, and smiled at Allison and said, "I want to play with the other animals now."

Allison put her hand on the cat and said, "Not now, Katie, we need to finish our talk first."

Katie pulled the cat away and yelled, "I want to play with them *now*."

"*My*, Katie, how you got so mad at me again so quickly," Allison said. "You must not like some of the things I was saying and you want me to stop talking. Why don't you say that? 'Stop talking, Allison!'"

Katie looked out the window and yelled, "Stop talking, Allison."

"Good job saying it, Katie," Allison said, "but you forgot to look at me when you said it."

Katie quickly looked at Allison for a split second and screamed it again, more loudly than before.

"Yes, Katie! I knew you could do it!" Allison said with a smile. "I sure can understand why it is hard for you to live with a mom like Susan when your first mom, Sally, was so different. Susan never hurt you like Sally did. But you probably thought that Susan did hurt you sometimes when you were mad at her."

"Shut up!" Katie screamed.

Allison turned to Susan and said quietly, "Katie has such a hard time talking about these problems. She probably thinks that you hate her when you tell her to stop doing something. She's really mad at me now for not doing what she wants and talking about things that she'd rather not think about. She does get mad! And I think that she's probably kind of sad a lot, too."

"I am not!" Katie yelled at Allison again.

"Oh, Katie, there's nothing wrong with being sad. And I sure can understand why you might be sad when you've been hurt as much as you've been. Many other kids who have been hurt a lot are sad about it sometimes."

Katie quietly looked away. They all sat without talking for a moment.

Allison turned to Steven and Susan and said that she'd like to talk with Katie alone for a little while. They went to the waiting room.

"I'm glad that she got to see some of Katie's anger," Susan said. "Often Katie is so charming with adults that people look at me strangely after they meet her. They think that I'm too picky or too strict."

"Yes," Steven said, "Hopefully Dr. Kaplan will be able to give us some good ideas about helping her."

"She was firm with her and Katie didn't like that," said Susan. "Usually when teachers or doctors first meet her they try to be nice to her and give her what she wants so that she is happy and will cooperate. Dr. Kaplan didn't do that and Katie didn't expect it."

They talked quietly for 30 minutes until Dr. Kaplan returned with Katie and brought Susan and Steven back to her office. Katie again was content to play alone in the waiting area.

"She certainly is a child who is likely to be very difficult to raise," Allison said. "She really doesn't have any idea of how to become engaged with good parents and depend on them. She is very controlling because she had to depend on herself so much that she just can't trust enough to depend on you, Susan. She won't let herself begin to trust and rely on you and without developing a secure attachment with you she's not likely to settle into your home, learn from you, accept your authority or begin to enjoy herself, value herself, or feel good about having parents."

"Why won't she, Dr. Kaplan?" asked Steven. "Other foster kids do. She's been in foster care for 21 months and she hasn't seemed to change a bit."

"Probably her first few years did not meet her basic needs both for safety and also for learning how to become engaged in a reciprocal relationship. I know that she was abused when she was five, but I would bet that she was abused long before that, and at least as importantly, she probably was neglected a great deal too. When babies and toddlers are ignored and yelled at all day they never really learn what a wonderful source of safety, comfort, and enjoyment their parents can be. They eventually stop asking for any nurturance and enjoyable interaction with their parents. And just as importantly, they often don't develop in ways that children who are cherished do. They aren't comfortable with physical comfort, which is central in the infant's initial sense of self. Their affective development is poorly regulated and integrated. With rejection, anger, and abuse comes extreme shame that they are not able to integrate. Rather than routine feelings of brief shame being a vehicle for socialization, overwhelming pervasive shame destroys their self-worth. Such overwhelming shame is such a painful experience that it leads to denial and rage and the resultant behaviors tend to be extreme rather than becoming more moderate and self-regulated. And they really never learn to notice what they feel or think. If they were able to feel anything it would be shame and rage. Their inner life remains ignored and does not develop coherently. They don't know how then to engage others with mutual enjoyment and interest. They don't know how to assume the viewpoint of another; they cannot read their parents' motives and so they simply assume the worst. They can only manipulate, make demands, and scream or withdraw when their 'needs' are 'neglected' again. That's why you've been struggling so hard for eight months, Susan, with few, if any, changes in Katie."

"That's so sad," Susan said quietly. "I wish I could say that I'm willing to try again with her, Dr. Kaplan, but I just can't. The rest of the family can't stand her anymore, and that probably includes my husband, too. I don't have the patience anymore for her and she needs a lot of it."

"I certainly understand, Susan," Dr. Kaplan said, "You've been through a lot and you're the only one who can say if you think that you can meet her intense needs or are even able to try again."

"What would you suggest that we do now, Doctor?" Steven asked.

"Well, you first need to be very careful about selecting a new home. If the foster parents have not had successful experiences with children like Katie, they should get some training beforehand so that they're not surprised and discouraged when they get to know her. As I mentioned on the phone, I worked with a foster family and another child similar to Katie. The foster mom's name is Jackie Keller and she might be interested in working with her. Secondly, you should find a therapist who has some experience providing therapy that will get through to her. The more traditional therapies were really developed and are of benefit to children whose problems are not as severe as Katie's. Most traumatized kids are more able and willing to rely on their foster parents than Katie is. They also are more able to enter into a therapeutic relationship with their therapist. I work with kids with more severe problems similar to Katie and I can give you the names of a couple of other therapists who do, too. I can send you my report with recommendations. You probably should discuss them with her current therapist, and then decide how you want to proceed."

"Is there much hope that Katie will ever change?" Steven asked.

"Well, I don't know her very well. But her age is a plus. And I was able to elicit some positive engagements, no matter how brief, although I wouldn't make too much of them because right now Katie was taken off balance a bit. Also, there really isn't significant research available on both understanding her symptoms and knowing how to parent and treat her. So one should be cautiously hopeful, develop a comprehensive plan, and get to work. Her parents, therapist, and social worker need to have hope that she is able to change. They need to be able to see her strengths that lie under her problems, respond to her strengths, and then help Katie to recognize them. She needs to discover and accept assistance in developing parts of herself that she is not ashamed of. She also needs to reduce the shame associated with other parts of herself that now contain it."

"What is her disorder?" Steven asked.

"I wish I could say with confidence, Steven," Allison replied. "Some would say reactive attachment disorder, though there is still little consensus about how to make that diagnosis. Some would say posttraumatic stress disorder, though her symptoms are so pervasive and intense that her difficulties are likely to represent something more than PTSD as it is now understood with regard to children. For now I might say posttraumatic stress disorder, severe, and add that her symptoms might not be changing due to her history of trauma, probable neglect, and attachment behavioral patterns that are consistent with the attachment disorganization classification. Attachment disorganization is a research classification that is common among foster children and which is considered to be a risk factor for the development of significant psychological problems. She just does not know how to rely on and relate reciprocally with good parents and other caregivers. She only knows how to try to control everything and to avoid what she cannot control. If she receives the specialized forms of parenting and treatment that are developing for a child with her difficulties and did not respond after nine to twelve months, then I would be more likely to consider her to manifest reactive attachment disorder."

Steven left the office that night with more questions that he wished he had asked Dr. Kaplan. She seemed to make sense. She certainly described Katie when she listed the symptoms. But Steven really didn't have any idea what a parent or therapist would do differently that would make much difference. Two of Katie's foster parents were basically good parents in their previous work with troubled kids. And her therapist, Jan, also had a lot of experience with foster kids. Maybe different parenting would be a little better, but would the difference be that significant? Maybe if therapy pushed her a little harder, she couldn't avoid her problems. But if she really doesn't know anything about love from a parent, how could she learn that?

When Steven arrived home, Rebecca greeted him, running merrily toward the door, waving her arms, smiling, and shouting, "Dada!" He dropped his briefcase, swooped her into his arms, and shouted, "Becca!" They both giggled and he walked toward the couch in circles, holding her close to him and crying, "Weeeee!" until he flopped down with his daughter on top of him. She grabbed his ears and tried to bite his chin and he now cried, "Eeeeeee!" until her giggles made her lose her grip on his chin and he picked her up only to lay her on the couch and pretend to bite her chin. He blew on her chin and neck and her little fingers dug into his cheeks and pulled his face to hers. He hugged her tight and swung her back up into his lap and said, "Home to my Becca!" She settled in for a moment and then pulled back and began to get down. She had an idea! She grabbed his finger and began to pull him toward the doorway to the hall, while pointing and saying, "Phone!" Knowing her plan, he walked with her to the play area in the corner of the dining room and sat with her on the floor. She reached for her play phone, held it to her ear, and said, "Hi, Dada." He picked up a book to cover his face, "Hi, Becca." She paused for a moment as she usually did. Then she said, "Home, Dada." He replied, "I'm almost home, Becca. What's for supper?" She jumped up and ran into the kitchen. He heard Jenny whisper to her. She ran back and again grabbed the phone, "Scetti!" He yelled back, "Spaghetti! Great! I'll be home fast!" Her eyes grew wider as she watched and listened while Steven made loud "car" sounds from behind the book. Then he knocked on the book. She got up and pulled the book out of his hands. He exclaimed, "Becca, I'm home!" She smiled and grabbed him again. He picked her up and they went into the kitchen to greet Jenny.

"Hi sweetie, Becca tells me we're having spaghetti!" Steven and Rebecca both kissed Jenny. She gave them each a piece of celery from the salad she was making.

"What have you and Rebecca been up to today?" Steven asked.

"Well, Steven, we were in the garden and we saw . . . crawling on the ground . . . some tiny, tiny . . . ."

"Ants!" Rebecca said and smiled. As she remembered, she got excited and held out her hand to show her dad how she had held some. Steven then learned about a new library book they had read, Rebecca's bath where the water swooshed over her belly, the banana and peanut butter sandwich, which was still partly hiding under the couch, and their play in which Rebecca wore mom's jacket and hat and became "momma."

After supper, they checked the garden to see if the ants were still there. It wasn't very long until Rebecca was ready for sleep. After a little washing, finding her pajamas, two songs and a story, she was sleeping. By now, Jenny and Steven had also done the dishes and had time to talk. Jenny always had many details about Rebecca's day. She needed to tell Steven about each one, and he needed to hear them all.

Later, Steven told Jenny about his meeting with Dr. Kaplan. "She left me more mixed up then ever, yet somehow I think she's right. Katie just doesn't have a relationship with anyone. Not a real relationship. Not like Becca has with us. I never thought about it before. Probably Katie never had as much fun with her parents as we just did with Becca the last couple of hours. It's hard to imagine. It was always obvious to me what abuse would do to a kid. But, it seems now that it would be just as bad if she never got much hugging and laughing and singing and talking."

"From what Dr. Kaplan said, it might even be worse," said Jenny. "Rebecca so much needs for me to be engaged with her for hours each day. I can't imagine what it would do to her if I simply left her alone for long periods, ignored her movements toward me, and initiated nothing with her. I know it would hurt her a great deal."

"When you and Becca are together, it's like nothing else exists," said Steven. "You two are so in synch that I almost can't tell where one of you starts and the other ends. Like you're one being."

"I guess that's what attachment is all about," Jenny said. "It's such a unique experience. Different than you and me. I'm so aware of her feelings and thoughts and actions. Sometimes it feels like I experience them at the same time that she does. And I have a feeling of just wanting to help her to bring them out, to express whatever is going on within her, to let her know that whatever she feels, it's special to me and OK with me. To help her to discover the wonderful, incredible person she is—the person who has such a powerful impact on me!"

"Yeah, Jenny, I know what you mean. I feel that way with her, too, though not as often as you do. Right now in her life I think that she needs to be with you that way, differently or more intensely than she does with me."

They held hands and thought about their kid some more. Then Steven said, "I'm beginning to think I know what Dr. Kaplan was talking about. To deprive a kid like Katie of thousands of experiences like we've been talking about is nothing if it's not neglect. No wonder she can't live very well in a family. And she's almost seven. All those years! During the first five, no one wanted to hold and hug her, and during the last two, she hasn't wanted anyone to.

Jenny hugged Steven and suggested they not talk of it anymore that night. Her relationship with Rebecca made it very hard for her to think of this little unknown girl named Katie.

## COMMENTARY

Allison's evaluation of Katie consisted in obtaining her distant and recent history as well as in observing and gently addressing her interactions in the office. First she obtained from Steven a summary of her experiences of abuse and neglect as well as her placement history. She would want to know if Katie had any stable and positive relationships during her early years when her attachment history was unfolding. She would want specific details of her history in order to address them briefly with Katie and observe her response. Allison also would want to determine Katie's most recent functioning with Susan. She would want to know her symptoms as well as her strengths. She would ask about her response to intersubjective as well as shame and stressful experiences. She also would observe the interactions between Katie and Susan.

Allison related with Katie during the evaluation session in a manner similar to, although less intensely, than she would in a treatment session. She wanted to observe how Katie would respond to directives and to challenging themes for both diagnostic reasons but also for an estimate of how she would respond to therapeutic interventions. How easily would she respond to empathy and playfulness? Would she be receptive to Allison's curiosity about her thoughts, feelings, and behaviors—and would she be open to new explorations about the meaning of her experiences? How would she express her anger and would she resist being led from anger to the probable feelings of sadness, loneliness, and fear that were likely to underlie her rage? If there were a conflict between them, would Katie be able to accept aid to repair their relationship? Allison would observe and then attempt to develop a composite view of Katie that she could use for the purposes of her evaluation.

During the evaluation, Allison saw Katie alone for a while, something that she seldom did during her psychotherapy with children with significant attachment and trauma problems if they have an available attachment figure. If the children do not have an attachment figure, she would see them alone, while also advocating the search for such a person. She wanted to see if Katie responded differently than she did when she was in the presence of her foster mother. Had she used her foster mother's presence for any sense of security? Would she be more or less critical of her foster mother when she was not present? Would she be more able to express various emotions? Would she express any guilt or responsibility for the problems in her foster home or express only excuses and blame the rest of the family? Could she access any sense of sadness over being so alone in the world and any desire to learn how to develop an attachment with her parent? What psychological and physical boundaries would she have when speaking with Allison alone? How would she relate with her?

Steven and Jenny's relationship with their daughter, Rebecca, demonstrates the contrast between how a healthy attachment develops and how Katie was raised. The routine, but magical, intersubjective experiences between Rebecca and her parents serve as the foundation for the development of both her sense of self and the world and also her present and future attachment relationships. Without them, a child cannot experience herself as being special and worthwhile. Nor will she identify with her parents and make them unique and special to her.

# 7

## Choosing a New Approach

Two days later Steven went to meet Jackie Keller. She wanted to talk with him before deciding if she would bring Katie into her home. Jackie lived in the town of Vassalboro, about 10 miles north of Augusta. She lived in a gray cape-style house with a large dining area built around a huge stone fireplace. Steven would have to visit in the winter to feel the warmth it must create. Jackie's husband, Mark, was a science teacher at Gardiner High School. They had two birth children, Matthew and Diane, both in high school, and a foster son, John, who was 16 and had lived with them for two years. John apparently had suffered physical abuse at the hands of his father. He maintained a relationship with his parents but probably would not return to live with them. They also had a large, graying black Labrador, who licked and liked anything that moved. Except for flies in the spring. When they invaded the home on sunny spring days, he spent hours trying to spear them with his foot long tongue. When he managed to catch one, he seemed to be both surprised and pleased with himself. His name was Whimsy.

Two months before, Jackie's 11-year-old foster son, Gabe, moved to an adoptive home after living with the Kellers for two years. She missed Gabe and still had some contact with him. In fact, there were some initial plans for him to visit from his adoptive home in Pennsylvania sometime in August.

Steven immediately liked Jackie. She seemed warm and relaxed. Her home had a casual but organized and active quality. He imagined how it would sound when three teenagers returned from school. But in many ways Jackie reminded him of Susan. Would this be different? Would Jackie be able to give Katie the affection that she needed without being overwhelmed by her rage?

"Tell me about Katie, Steven," Jackie said as she brought him coffee. "You've mentioned that she's now in her third foster home. What's she like?"

"She's an angry and controlling kid. When things are going her way she seems just like any kid but if things don't go her way she immediately becomes outraged. Dr. Kaplan says that she has trauma and attachment problems similar to the boy who just left your home. That's probably why she suggested that I call you."

"So I might be getting myself in for quite a lot if I take her," Jackie said, "Though I like the idea of working with Allison again."

"Dr. Kaplan isn't treating her. She just evaluated her a few days ago," Steven said.

"I'm not sure I can take Katie unless Allison is her therapist, Steven," Jackie said.

"Why is it so important that she see Dr. Kaplan?" asked Steven. "She has a good therapist who could address Katie's attachment difficulties now that we know what they are."

"I don't know her therapist, Steven," Jackie said, "But I do know Allison and she knows how to connect with kids who don't want to connect with anyone. Just knowing that she has significant attachment problems does not guarantee that one is able and ready to treat them. Also, I completely trust Allison and believe that she trusts me. I need that kind of relationship with Katie's therapist and such trust develops slowly. This is very hard work, Steven, and if I can't work with Allison, I'm afraid I'm not ready to commit to start working with Katie. I don't want to become her fourth disrupted home."

"But she has worked with her therapist, Jan, for over a year and a half. It doesn't make sense to me to break her attachment with Jan if we're trying to help her to learn to attach to people," Steven said firmly.

"Steven, if Allison is right and she does have significant attachment problems, she is not likely to have a secure attachment with her therapist," Jackie said, "She may enjoy seeing her in order to get to play or to get snacks or to just get a chance to control someone. But she really would not miss her therapist if she has not formed a secure attachment. Just as she doesn't miss her previous foster parents and she won't miss her current foster mother. If a child is really unable to begin to form a meaningful attachment to a parent, she will definitely have much difficulty forming a secure attachment with anyone else."

"Well, I'll have to think about it and talk with Jan," Steven said.

"That's fine, Steven," said Jackie, "And while we're talking about Katie living with me, I should ask if Allison talked with you about how I would have to be raising her."

"No, she didn't," Steven said. "Is it that different?"

"Yes, it is. I didn't raise Gabe like I'm raising my own kids or even like I'm raising John. When I first started working with Allison, I had a hard time following her suggestions. I felt that I was being too hard on him, especially since he had been through so much already. But what Allison said to do did prove to be necessary. Without it, I know that Gabe would never have changed. So I'll need to know that I have your support in the ways that I'll be raising her before I can agree to become her mother and expect her to form an attachment with me."

"Could you give me an example of what you mean?" Steven asked.

"Well, if you stop by to visit you're likely to see that she's getting a lot of supervision. She'll be needing permission for just about everything in the early months. She'll be near me, following my schedule for her. Also, she has shown some desire to hurt others, Steven. Although I think the other kids can take care of themselves, I do have to be careful about Whimsy. That dog will love her silly and will need my protection or she is likely to be mean to him."

"Also, I'll have to ask you not to take her out and have a lot of fun with her. She does not really know how to have fun and if she's going to learn it's going to be with me first, and within my guidelines."

Steven didn't know what to say. No foster mother had ever been so direct with him about the kind of support that she wanted. Jackie seemed to be saying that she would be as tough as she wanted with Katie and Steven would have no say in whether or not she was being too strict. He didn't know if he could agree to this or even if he wanted to agree. He was Katie's guardian. "I don't know, Jackie. What am I supposed to do if I think that you're being too hard on her?"

"Steven, I will not do anything that violates your basic Department regulations and procedures. I've had to learn them well when I was caring for Gabe. If I do believe that she needs any form of parenting that steps outside your guidelines, I will get your permission first. But I have learned that within Department regulations social workers have a lot of flexibility about what is acceptable or not in raising a child. What I would want is for you to initially accept my decision regarding the care that I am giving her. You could then talk with me and Allison about it and we'll tell you why we're doing it. But unless I'm abusing her or breaking one of the basic regulations, I would need you to support me and I would need to have Katie know that you support me," Jackie said with certainty."

"You are her guardian," Jackie added. "I know that you have to do what you think is best for her. By telling you now how I'll probably have to be raising her, I want to avoid hurting Katie again by your removing her from my home because you disagree with what I'm doing. I want you to know as much as possible so that if you disagree, you can simply not consider me for Katie at this time and save putting her through another disruption. I know that some of the interventions I use are uncommon and you might have trouble with them. If you do, I want to see if we can resolve any differences now."

Steven was beginning to sense that Jackie would not allow Katie to overwhelm her. There was a strength about her and a confidence about what Katie really needed and what she would be getting from Jackie. Steven still wasn't sure if he could accept Jackie's having this degree of control over her care. It seemed that she was taking some of his responsibilities. She did say that she would follow the basic foster care regulations. But within those regulations, she wanted him to defer to her. He would have to discuss it with Kathy.

"I imagine that you think I'll be running an army boot camp for Katie, Steven," Jackie said. "And you can be sure that she'll think it's a boot camp. But it will not be. It will be a home that provides her with the structure and comfort, the enjoyment and care, the laughter and rules that good homes provide for their children. And when I'm with her I'll have an attitude toward her that you'll never find in boot camp. Allison calls it 'The Attitude.'"

"What kind of attitude are you talking about?" Steven asked.

"There are five qualities to The Attitude. They are *being accepting, curious, empathic, loving, and playful.* They will be a part of all of my interactions with a kid like Katie and they'll make all of the difference. Without this attitude, the firm behavioral structure and supervision that she needs to have would not really be therapeutic. They will help her to experience, hopefully, that the structure and supervision is a gift to her, not a punishment. A gift that will bring her success, not failure."

Steven thought about what Jackie said. "The Attitude" made the structure and supervision that Jackie thought that Katie would need a little more understandable.

Before Steven left, Jackie also told him that she would like to talk with Susan and meet with Katie before deciding. She also suggested that before he and she made a final decision, they should meet with Dr. Kaplan to discuss more details about their plans for Katie. Steven left feeling that he would be losing some of his authority if he worked with Jackie. It made him feel uncomfortable and somewhat vulnerable.

On May 19, 1994, Steven and Kathy met with Jackie and Dr. Kaplan at her office. Steven had anticipated that these two might request things that would require Kathy's OK, so he had asked her to be present.

"Jackie tells me that she's still interested in Katie becoming her foster child," Steven began. "She made it clear that she would want you to be Katie's therapist, Dr. Kaplan, so I discussed her request with Kathy and Jan Temple and we agreed that if we decide that Jackie will be her foster mom, and you were able to see her, we would transfer her to you."

"Jackie and I work well together and I am able to see Katie," Allison replied. "I'd be more comfortable if you would call me Allison, since we're going to be working closely and since that's what Katie will be calling me."

"That's fine, Allison," said Steven.

"Steven tells me that you and Jackie will probably be working with Katie in ways that he might disagree with," said Kathy. "It that why this meeting is necessary?"

"Yes," said Allison. "DHS has custody of Katie. It is your call as to what kind of treatment is in her best interest. I don't want to begin working with her if you have any fundamental differences about my approach with her or Jackie's way of raising her at home. It certainly won't be good for her if six months from now you say that you don't really believe in what Jackie and I will be trying to accomplish."

"That's fair," said Kathy. "Why don't you tell us the general outline of your approach?"

"Good," Allison began. "The first thing that I will stress is that if Katie is to ever change and begin to trust her mom and depend on her, she will need to reduce her pervasive need to control everything and become comfortable with Jackie being in control of the major realities of her life. As you have seen, waiting for Katie to voluntarily give up control will be a long wait and probably will make it too late for her to ever have the opportunity to be parented. She has lived for almost two years in three different homes and not shown any readiness to be parented. By her maintaining such a strong compulsion to be in control, she is avoiding experiences of healthy dependency on her mother and she is not able to learn that such experiences are pleasant and safe. *And* she is not able to develop in ways that require such experiences. Thus, Jackie will gently but firmly be in control at home just as I will in therapy. But we won't do this in a mean way. We'll give her a great deal of empathy and support for how hard it is for her not to have control. We will not become angry with her and we will accept her resistance to our making decisions for her. And when she's ready, we'll begin to slowly give her some control back. We don't want this control. We're taking it because she can't manage it at all. Her being in control prevents her from learning to develop a secure attachment which is crucial if she is to develop in healthy ways."

Allison turned to Jackie, "Why don't you tell Steven and Kathy some of the specific ways that you plan to structure Katie's life when she moves into your home."

"Sure," Jackie said. "Well, I'm going to begin the moment that she moves into my home. I'll be letting her know right away what I expect and what the structure and routines are in my home. I'll be telling her that it must be hard for her to have to learn how to live in so many different homes, but I'll be glad to teach her. I'll let her know that I'm aware of some of her past behaviors and I still want her to live with me. She'll be needing help to learn to change those behaviors in my home."

"And if she poops in your hamburger?" Steven asked.

"Good question," Allison said. "In fact I'll be discussing that with Katie in an early therapy session."

"My first goal will be to prevent her from pooping in the hamburger in my home. However, if she does," said Jackie, "there probably would be a variety of consequences. She might help to clean the kitchen and bathroom. She'd most likely have to do some chores to earn some money to buy new hamburger. She'd go to the store with me and order the meat and pay for it with her money. However, I want to prevent it from happening so that she has success, not failure. Therefore, she probably will be supervised more closely in the kitchen for quite some time. I may tell her that she will be supervised fairly closely around food for now because of my concern that she might decide to poop in our hamburger, or soup, too. But I will not threaten or shame her. I would just calmly make her aware that I know of her past behaviors and my knowledge has led to this plan, to help her to be successful with us."

"One reason we'd discuss it in therapy is to let her know that we know what she did and to help her to know some of the factors in why she did it," Allison said. "Her knowing why she does her outrageous behaviors is not to give her an excuse, but rather to help her to feel less profound shame for her behaviors so that she can gradually be able to face them."

"Do you really think that she feels shame?" asked Steven. "Her other foster parents say that she never shows any remorse for what she does."

"Shame is not guilt, Steven," said Allison. "Her sense of guilt may well be weak since it is a more complex and developmentally more mature emotion than shame. But she does have shame, probably just about all of the time, and she just will not let herself experience it. If she did access her inner life, she basically would feel and think that she is worthless and that conviction is experienced as shame. The rejection and humiliation that she must have experienced over and over with Sally and Mike must have left her convinced that she is 'just no good.' Her frequent rage is her effort to both control others and maintain her precarious sense of safety, but also to block out the painful experience of shame. Her constant lying and denial of her behavior also shows her intense effort to avoid experiencing shame."

After a pause, Allison continued, "In therapy I might be suggesting that family gatherings like the one at Susan's must be hard on her when everyone else is having fun and she doesn't feel that she fits in because she really doesn't know how to have fun. She decided to ruin everyone else's fun too. I'll give her empathy for those feelings and then tell her that it's probably best for now that at Jackie's she be supervised during the entire time of the family gathering. If that is still too hard for her, she will not be able to participate herself. But she will be told that she is missed at the gathering and that Jackie will work hard with her so that she will be able to successfully attend a gathering in the future."

"But wouldn't that make her feel that she's not a part of the family?" asked Kathy, "and slow down the development of the attachment that you want?"

"Great question, Kathy, because it goes to the heart of this approach," said Allison. "If we give her enjoyable experiences that she fails at, we will not be helping her to become securely attached. She will just be feeling more of a failure, her shame will increase, and she'll be less receptive to further enjoyable experiences. It's like taking a person who was lost in the desert for three days and giving him a gallon of water to drink. It feels right to give him a lot of water since he is dehydrated and seems to need that much water. But that much water won't help him, it will kill him. He needs it in small, carefully supplied amounts. He cannot receive it more quickly than he can absorb it or it won't help him. The same is true for Katie. If we give her a great amount of experiences that most children would find to be enjoyable, she will sabotage them all. She can't integrate them. They don't fit her self-perception or her view of parents. It's too great a stretch for her and it makes her anxious and uncomfortable and will elicit behaviors that will seek the rejection and anger that is more comfortable for her."

"I'm still lost, Allison," Steven said, "If her early years of deprivation are the source of her problems, how can depriving her of enjoyable experiences now cause the change that you want?"

"Our goals for Katie are the same as they would be for any kid having difficulties. We want her to experience a loving relationship with her parents, we want her to have many opportunities for enjoyment and satisfaction in her life, and we want her to have the freedom to choose, among numerous options, what is in her best interests. However, with Katie, and with other children who have difficulty forming secure attachments, she has extreme difficulty integrating experiences of fun, love, and freedom to choose. She sabotages fun, undermines efforts to love her, and her choices are invariably not in her best interests. Essentially, if she is to benefit from them, she needs training in receiving and accepting experiences of fun and love while learning to make better choices. Also, Katie's pervasive shame has to be reduced. We are not trying to eliminate it since limited experiences of shame, especially prior to the onset of guilt, is crucial for socialization. But we help her to remove experiences of rejection, humiliation, and contempt from socialization experiences. Most importantly, we will quickly reconnect with her emotionally after her experience of shame so that she will be able to sense her worth and feel the beginnings of security in her attachment with Jackie even when she must experience consequences for her poor behavioral choices."

"We want what you want for her. But from her activities over the past 21 months, it seems fairly certain that these goals must be long term. We must build up to them slowly, one step at a time, minimizing failure, and gradually showing her how to live well within a good family."

"But how are you going to motivate her if she has nothing to work for?" Steven asked, "If you are that restrictive, why should she want to change?"

"Jackie and I really won't be *that* restrictive, Steven," answered Allison. "And we definitely won't be angry and rejecting of her behaviors. More than anything else, we're going to be going back to the parent-child interactions that she should have received during the first two years of her life. We will be patiently and persistently providing her with the countless experiences of intersubjectivity that babies and toddlers should receive but which Katie did not."

"What do you mean by 'intersubjectivity?'" asked Kathy.

"Intersubjectivity refers to the early experiences of reciprocal interests and joy that the mother and her infant have over and over during the first couple of years of life and which actually will never stop in a good parent-child relationship. It refers to those moments when the mother and her infant are lost in their mutual eye contact, facial gestures, synchronized movements, and shared focus that eliminates every other reality when they are so engaged. The mother and her baby are sharing their affective lives. They are sharing their attention. And they are learning about each other's wishes and intentions. They are having an impact on the subjective experience of each other. Katie needs those experiences with Jackie and she needs to receive them throughout every day, regardless of her behaviors. In fact, if Jackie has some success in engaging her at that level, Katie's behavior is likely to become more oppositional and angry as she tries to get Jackie to stop. When she is providing these experiences for Katie, Jackie will be asking her to do something that brought pain and shame when she tried to do it in her early months and years. Hopefully, Katie will not ultimately reject these experiences and Jackie will be able to successfully give her what she needs—namely, the experience of mutual joy and interest with a person who loves her, and who will not reject her regardless of her behaviors."

Steven was now quite interested. Allison was talking about Jenny and Rebecca! But he still couldn't understand how Jackie could provide those experiences to a defiant child almost seven years of age. "How can Jackie give Katie all of that lovely attention and all the rest when Katie is constantly getting herself into trouble?"

Jackie laughed and said, "With difficulty. But also with practice and some rest, and some support from Allison, my husband, Mark, and from you and others. For me, my beliefs in God help, too. My discipline is not given in anger. I look on discipline as an opportunity to build the security of her attachment with me rather than as a hindrance to it."

"How is that?" asked Steven.

"I'll give her empathy rather than annoyance when I limit her and give her consequences for her actions. Experiences of mutual acceptance and enjoyment will hopefully precede and immediately follow the misbehaviors that trigger shame. I'll be letting her know that it's hard for her to make these changes and I'll be patient and thorough in teaching her how. Each time we resolve a conflict without abandonment or abuse will build her sense of safety in the context of her relationship with me. Each time I limit her behavior I also will give her empathy for her experience of the discipline given for her behavior."

"You're not going to get angry with her! Is that realistic?" asked Steven.

"I won't say that I'll never get angry, but I'm now confident, after having raised Gabe for two years, that during those times when I'm angry with Katie it will be in order to achieve a goal with her rather than because I lost control. When Katie is able to 'make' me angry, I'll know that she's winning, she's in control, so that both of us are losing. It was hard to develop this way of responding, but Allison showed me how important it is, and now it's fairly easy to attain most of the time. Also, if I'm going to help Katie, I don't think I have any choice."

"Are you saying, Allison, that if a parent gets angry at his kid that he is damaging him and hurting their attachment?" asked Steven.

"I'm not talking about healthy kids who have a secure attachment with their parents already," said Allison. "Those kids are able to deal with their parents' anger without undermining their own sense of worth or their trust in their parents' love for them. But with kids who have been abused and who do not have a secure attachment history, routine anger, or even mild annoyance when it is frequent, will damage our efforts to facilitate their ability to form a secure attachment, because it triggers a pervasive shame response with its related self-contempt and mistrust of the parents' intentions for the discipline. Habitual anger directed toward Katie would further solidify her core sense of worthlessness."

"I want to assure you," Jackie said, "that although I will be firm with Katie and my standards for her behavior will be high, I will not be rejecting her and I am not harsh. I was fairly 'easy' with my own kids; it's the way I prefer to raise kids. But Gabe, and I think Katie, too, could not handle 'easy,' so I was forced to change my style to meet his needs."

"But, Jackie," Kathy said, "how can you have high expectations if you're going to ask Katie to change 'one step at a time?'"

"If my expectations aren't high, she won't change at all. I will, however, be limiting her choices. I will not give her choices that will cause her to fail, even if other children her age are able to be successful with those choices. Within the choices that I give her, my expectations will be high. But when she does not meet my expectations early on, I will continue to accept her, not be punitive, and not be angry with her."

"I still don't get it," Kathy said.

"Kathy," Allison said, "although Katie is almost seven, Jackie will have expectations for her that are more similar to a two- or three-year-old child. But she'll be expecting her to do a good job at meeting those limited expectations. If Katie doesn't do a good job, then Jackie will be asking her to stay with it until she gets it right, or she might change her immediate goals and if Katie is only failing at what is being expected of her, lower the expectations but ask her to do a good job at those. But she will not accept Katie failing in her behaviors. Katie does need to be socialized successfully if she is to ever live within Jackie's home and our community. For example, Katie might not know how to share a family activity like playing a game together very well as is evidenced by her arguing over the rules, talking loudly, or cheating. Katie will be told clearly how to play the game with the family the acceptable way. If necessary, she'll receive practice doing it and close supervision sitting next to Jackie on the couch. The length of time she can play may be limited. She may only be able to watch others play the game for a while. But Jackie will not be correcting her a dozen times in endless conflict-ridden games. She will not be overlooking repetitive behaviors that are not appropriate. Katie will not be coaxed to do it right."

"What do you mean by 'coaxed?'" Steven asked.

"Too often, parents and other adults work harder to get a child to make the right choice than the child does himself," Allison replied. "The child might be given three chances which were preceded by two warnings. It must be confusing to the child. His appropriate behavior is of benefit to whom? If the parent is that responsible for the child acting well, then the child will become less responsible. Once Katie is told what is expected of her in a situation, she will not be given a second chance and she will not be reminded or coaxed to meet the expectation. The situation will be changed to make it more likely for Katie to succeed at it in the future. When we know that she is able to learn from a mistake, she will continue to have the opportunity to learn. We assume that she will choose what is best for her. If we disagree with her choice, the natural consequences to the choice will be evident, and she will have an opportunity to have a consequence more to her liking in the future. But when she fails repeatedly, that opportunity will be removed, she will be given opportunities in which she is more likely to succeed, and when we think that she is ready, she will be given assistance to manage the original failure better."

"Allison," Steven said, "Jackie told me the other day about an attitude that she'll have with Katie. How does that fit in with what you're talking about now?"

"'The Attitude' is another way of saying what we just described," Allison replied. "The five qualities of The Attitude provide the emotional context in which Katie will be able to accept intersubjective experiences. They will enable her to tolerate the stress of our behavioral expectations, supervision, and consequences, all of which might trigger shame. They will help her to reconnect with us after shame. In essence, they will help her to see what a secure attachment is all about."

"What Attitude?" Kathy asked.

"Kathy, over the past few years, some therapists, parents, and I have become increasingly aware of how we actually *are* when we relate successfully with children with attachment difficulties. We identified five features, which actually are very similar to the attitude that a parent has when she is in synchrony with her infant or toddler. The features are *playful, loving, accepting, curious, and empathic.* We think that all five are necessary and that this attitude needs to become the background atmosphere, both in the family and in therapy, if the child is to begin to respond to the interventions provided. When a parent like Jackie has developed this attitude to the extent that it's an easy and natural way of interacting with her child, then it's fairly easy to avoid angry, frustrated and tense interactions much of the time. Once the parent is good at maintaining this attitude, for both reciprocal enjoyment as well as relationship repair after shame experiences, parenting becomes a lot easier, regardless of how outrageous the child's behavior is."

"Easy for you to say!" Jackie laughed. "No, really, Allison is right. When I lose that attitude, every hour is difficult. When I can maintain it, I actually often feel that raising this very tough kid is challenging, but, at times, even fun. I can relax and enjoy her more. I don't try to predict and control her behaviors. I'm curious and accepting about them and I'm free to respond with empathy in ways that can best meet her needs. I can be playful and loving in my responses. She can't control my emotions so I can use them to remain emotionally engaged with her no matter what she does. This attitude does remind me of how I was with my birth kids, Matthew and Diane, when they were babies. It makes raising these tough kids so much easier. It's good for both parent and child."

"Could you summarize for us what happens in your treatment sessions?" Kathy asked.

"Certainly," Allison replied. "I'll meet with her at least weekly and the sessions will last around ninety minutes, possibly two hours initially. Jackie will always be present during the session. Her presence is needed because my goal is to facilitate a secure attachment with Jackie, not with me. Also, I do not want to meet with her alone because I will be sitting close to her and often touching her. Because of her history of abuse, both Katie and I will feel safer if Jackie is present."

"At the beginning of each session, I will speak with Jackie alone about what has been happening at home to develop some ideas for interventions that I might try in the session. I also might give her some suggestions for interventions that she might try at home. I don't want Katie to know what I am recommending until I know if Jackie agrees with me. Also if Jackie is exhausted, angry, and tense, I will need to attend to her first. I can help Katie more by helping Jackie at those times. I also do not want to address with Katie issues associated with terror or shame, if Jackie is not able to manifest 'The Attitude.'"

"Much of my routine in therapy is based on attachment sequences that occur in daily life in healthy mother-child attachments. I first want to establish a relationship with Katie in each session that has features of a shared affective state—attunement—and The Attitude that we discussed earlier. Then I'll most likely initiate a discussion about an experience associated with shame from her current life in her foster home or her early life with her birth parents. For that reason, I will want to know everything that you know about her early life of abuse and neglect. Finally, I will work to reestablish relationship repair with her, to help her to gradually begin to reduce and integrate her experience of pervasive shame and also become more receptive to comforting and to discovering that her experiences of shame will not hurt her relationship with Jackie or me."

"That sequence of establishing an intersubjective connection, experiencing a break in the relationship because of shame, and then reestablishing the relationship will probably occur one or more times during each session."

"I'm having trouble picturing how you'll be doing this," Kathy said. "Will you simply be sitting near her, playing with her, and then talk about her problems, before playing with her again?"

"The qualities of The Attitude will permeate all aspects of the sequences. Katie will be experiencing acceptance, curiosity, and empathy throughout every interaction. She will experience my intense curiosity about her inner life—about what she feels and thinks about everything—and she will often experience these interactions within a light and gentle, playful quality. While I will not be communicating that her problems are 'funny,' I will be showing confidence in her. I will be communicating that I see a healthy self within her that will not be destroyed, or even compromised, by whatever traumatic or stressful experiences that she has had. I will be "discovering" within her the wonderful qualities that every infant and young child possesses and which her parents seldom saw. As I discover those qualities, I will communicate my experience of her quite directly and Katie will then discover them, too. When she can smile with us over her difficulties in learning to live in Jackie's home, and manifest sadness when recalling her life with Sally and Mike while being comforted by Jackie, she will have taken a giant step in forming a secure attachment with Jackie while at the same time organizing a coherent sense of herself."

"Is your therapy called 'holding therapy,'" Steven asked, "and if so, what does that refer to?"

"My treatment is not 'holding therapy,' Steven. 'Holding therapy' was a form of therapy that was developed to work with children such as Katie. It ranged from having the therapist only hold the child to having the parent only hold the child. Some 'holding therapists' stress eliciting rage, and I believe, increasing shame, and are quite confrontational. Others emphasize the nurturing quality of holding a child."

"But your question about 'holding therapy' suggests that I should speak about whether or not Katie will be held. During much of the therapy session either Jackie or I will be interacting with Katie in ways that incorporate touch. Touch is a crucial way in which parents communicate love, enjoyment, comfort, support, nurturance, and guidance to their child," Allison replied. "Just as it is with infants and toddlers, touching her will be very helpful in efforts to help her to engage in intersubjective experiences including regulating her affect and discovering qualities about herself and others. She will feel closer to us, in spite of her well-established defenses, and she will actually feel safer when she feels herself being touched by Jackie or me. She will be more receptive to affective memories and current experiences that she habitually guards against. When Jackie or I am touching her hand, arm, or shoulder, or placing our arm around her or giving her a hug, I am confident that she will be more receptive to experiencing and more able to regulate both positive and negative affective states."

"In the past, either I or the parent routinely held the child through significant parts of the session. I had thought that this was more crucial to the treatment than I now know it to be. I am able to achieve the same results through nurturing facial expression and voice tone, more gradual pacing of the sessions and touch. Now, during particularly stressful discussions or during times characterized by relaxation or reciprocal enjoyment I encourage the child to be held by the parent or ask them to sit closely and snuggle. If the child does not feel comfortable with that I suggest that they both find another way for the adult and child to co-regulate the affect that is present."

"I seldom hold the child myself now, believing that since the parent is the primary attachment figure, the child should become comfortable with the parent's safe and comforting arms. At times I thought that the parent and child's relationship was not strong enough yet for the parent to give the child the sense of safety and comfort that she might need, so I would do it. Now, I believe that if that is the case, then I should work harder to make their relationship stronger, and go slower in therapy until it is stronger. If the child periodically sits in my lap it most likely represents a spontaneous initiative of the child, expressing fun and joy or possibly gratitude."

"Will you or Jackie hold her against her will?" Kathy asked.

"Not, Kathy, as part of therapy or for the purpose of doing therapy. If she is ever held against her will it is because she is out of control, aggressive and destructive, and the only way to keep her and us safe is to hold her until she can control her behavior. This would be no different than if she were engaged in such dangerous behaviors at home or in public. If she needs to be held—or restrained—at home regularly because of explosive behaviors following routine frustrations, then my guess is that at times in therapy she may need to be restrained, too. However I will never provoke her into having to be restrained. If she does not need to be restrained at home, she will not need to be restrained in therapy."

After a pause, Kathy said, "I think that we can and should give approval for you to work with Katie, Allison, and for her to move into Jackie's house. I like what you're saying, although I still will want to see how it works from day to day. Would you have any objections to Steven regularly talking with you about how the therapy is going as well as stopping by Jackie's house on a more frequent basis than he otherwise would?"

"None at all," Both Allison and Jackie responded. Allison added, "Actually, if Steven would like to sit in on some sessions with Katie, Jackie, and me that would be fine, too."

"I'd like that," Steven replied.

"Let's try it, then," Kathy said. "You can be confident that we won't interfere with what you are doing even if we're not sure about it being helpful. We'll let you call the shots. We will expect you to be following Department Foster Care regulations. If you think any regulations may need to be modified, check with us, and if we agree, we will see if we can obtain an exception from the central office. We will be committing to six months until the first treatment and placement review with Katie. Is that sufficient?"

"While it may not be sufficient for Katie to make substantial progress," Allison said, "it should give us enough time to show you what we're doing and for us to see some initial changes that we'll hopefully be building upon."

"What are the rates of success in using this approach with kids who have such difficulty being able to make progress in good foster homes?" Kathy asked.

"I wish that I could provide you with well-established research findings," Allison replied. "But there is little research on complex trauma and attachment difficulties in childhood and even less on therapeutic and parenting approaches to take for children with these severe difficulties. I can tell you about my own experiences over the last 20 years."

"That would be helpful," Kathy said.

"Well, a rough estimate would be that about 40 percent of the children like Katie that I have worked with have made very significant progress, another 40 percent made some progress that proved to be quite helpful, and a final 20 percent made little if any progress. About all I have been able to accomplish in the 20 percent group has been to assist their families in learning to live with them in ways that help to preserve the family, keep the child safe, and hope that in the future the child—or young adult—may be able to attain a better life. My goal then is to keep the consequences of the child's problems within the child rather than having him or her hurt the other members of the family. And I help the parents explore the painful possibilities involving having the child placed in a group facility if that seems to be necessary."

"I have to say that your results leave me somewhat discouraged," Steven said.

"I understand that," Allison said. "But they are much better than the results that I saw before when I used the traditional approaches of play therapy and cognitive-behavioral child-rearing interventions in which I had been trained. Back then, I would have had to say that for children like Katie, my interventions had little or no effect 90 percent of the time. Now I see positive effects four-fifths of the time and in many of those cases the effects have been very significant. For that reason, I'm elated with the results that I now see, although I grieve for the children and families that I cannot reach. We need good research on creative and comprehensive approaches to these children. They have very significant psychological problems which do not respond to treatment easily."

"Are there any other approaches for these very traumatized, untrusting children?" asked Kathy.

"None based on research, I'm sorry to say," Allison replied.

The four of them sat quietly for a few moments. They all experienced sadness for every child who had been hurt or abandoned by their parents, and who lacked the ability to have a secure attachment with capable and committed parents when finally given the chance. A nightmare life.

"OK," said Kathy. "Why don't we set a date for Katie to move to Jackie's home?"

## COMMENTARY

Allison and Jackie needed to present a detailed account of the way that they would be intervening in Katie's life because it was crucial that their strategies be understood and accepted before she were placed in Jackie's home, with Allison as her therapist. Some of the interventions at home and in therapy vary from the traditional views of what constitutes appropriate child-rearing.

Allison and Jackie repeatedly stress the need to maintain a therapeutic attitude if they are to be able to have an impact on Katie's development. It is that attitude that makes the strategies employed therapeutic. If Katie requires restriction from a family party or if she has to take an hour to clean up the milk spill because she is choosing to do her task slowly, Jackie must present these consequences in the manner conveyed by The Attitude described above if they are to be therapeutic. Jackie will say to Katie, "I'm sad that you're not ready to join the party with us. I can't wait until you can handle having fun with us better so that you can be with the rest of us at times like this." Such a statement is therapeutic. It is never said with sarcasm and it is only said when it reflects the true intentions of the parent.

Contrast that statement with, "You're not allowed to be in the living room while we're having the party. Until you learn how to act right, we don't want you with us!" Another comment to avoid would be, "You never do what you're told! It's your fault that you can't be with us!" Each of the three interventions involved restricting her from the party. The nature of the attitude conveyed to her determined whether or not the intervention was therapeutic. An equally destructive way of managing the situation would be to allow Katie to attend the party, with five warnings about how she had to behave properly, even though, in the last three similar parties, her behavior was very disruptive and aggressive, and there was no reason to think that this party would be any different. Then when she failed and had to be removed, she would be yelled at with, "You had your chance! I told you what would happen!" Such interventions would not help Katie.

Too often, caregivers present children like Katie with dozens of chances to make the appropriate choice, even when they have failed on every occasion. The caregivers respond to each failure with annoyance, a lecture, and a "fresh start," which would be more accurately described as a "stale repetition" of failure. This would be an excellent way to increase Katie's sense of shame and worthlessness. If a child in the seventh grade can read only at the third grade level, should that child endure a "fresh start" everyday to read a seventh grade book? Is it not much better to recognize that he reads at the third grade level, give him a third grade book, expect him to work at his level of ability and encourage his small steps toward further development of his reading skills? Children restricted by unresolved trauma and disorganized attachment behavioral skills do not function, emotionally, cognitively, or behaviorally, in appropriate ways. They need an environment that recognizes that fact, is sensitive to levels of success, and builds an environment with parental care, supervision, and expectations, appropriate to that level. If Katie is functioning with a level of skills that is more like a toddler's level—*and she is*—then she needs the same degree of intersubjective experiences, supervision, and parental expectations that we might give a toddler. The Attitude of acceptance, empathy, love, curiosity, and playfulness will insure that by treating her in that manner, the interventions will be successful and therapeutic and not be punitive or humiliating.

# 8

## Jackie Keller (Foster Home #4)

On Thursday, June 9, 1994, Katie moved into the home of Jackie Keller in Vassalboro, Me. Still six years old, she had been in foster care for 21 months, and, counting her life with Sally and Mike, she was moving into her fifth home. As he had done in the previous moves, Steven drove her with most of her clothes to Jackie's. Susan had told Katie about a week before that she would be moving to a new home that would be more able to meet her needs. Katie did not show much of a response. She certainly made no efforts to change Susan's mind. Rather, she was interested in what Jackie's home was like. She had met Jackie a few weeks earlier but didn't really remember her.

Jackie and Mark lived on a winding road a mile off Route 201 about 10 miles north of Augusta. Mark had built a two-bedroom addition on the home five years earlier when they had decided to care for foster children. Katie would sleep in one of the two downstairs bedrooms. Jackie and Mark slept in the other one and the three adolescents slept upstairs.

When Steven arrived at 2:00 p.m., Jackie and Whimsy were waiting for them in their large dining room. No one else was around. Jackie greeted Katie with enthusiasm. Whimsy licked her and immediately wanted to be her best friend. Katie patted Whimsy's neck as she looked around the kitchen. Jackie then helped her with her suitcases and boxes and brought them to her bedroom. Steven and Whimsy waited in the kitchen until they returned for some milk and crackers.

"Well, Katie, I'm pleased that you're here. I'm glad that you're becoming a member of our family. You'll be meeting your new dad, Mark, and your older brothers and sister before dinner. Now we'll have some time for you to get to know me and what it's like living here. You can have some crackers and milk."

"I want some cookies. That's what I eat in the afternoon for snack," said Katie.

"I'm glad that you let me know what you want, Katie. I like cookies, too. Here we have crackers and milk or fruit for afternoon snack. You might be sad about that but you'll get used to it after a while. Would you rather have the fruit?"

"I don't like those crackers!" said Katie.

"Well, you certainly don't have to eat them, Katie. You can just drink your milk if you want, or you don't even have to drink it, if you don't want. Or you can have the orange," said Jackie.

Katie stared at her milk and crackers in front of her. She seemed to be pouting. She didn't seem to know what to do.

"I can see you don't like only being able to have crackers rather than cookies. You might be thinking that I'm kind of mean. And you just met me! You might even be wondering if this is going to be a rotten home that you won't like at all. Looks like a hard start for you."

"You are mean!" Katie exclaimed and she suddenly moved her arm and sent the glass of milk flying. Most of the milk hit the table and the rest went right to the floor. A fair amount of what hit the table seemed to actually bounce before falling into Steven's lap.

Steven jumped back and up from his chair, grabbing his pants and yelling, "Katie, why did you do that?"

Jackie quickly moved between Steven and Katie, focused all of her attention on Katie, and said, "Wow, you really are mad! You don't waste any time showing me how mad you get when I won't let you do something. My guess is you wanted to say, 'I don't want any of your milk!' I'll bet that you wish that you had gotten the milk on me rather than Steven!"

Jackie turned to Steven and suggested that he might use a towel in the bathroom if he wanted to try to dry his pants. She then turned to Katie again and bent down, placing her arm on the back of her chair. She quietly said, "Katie, I can see that this is hard for you. You've had to move so much. So many families! Cookies, crackers, fruit! Always something new to get used to. Wow, it must be hard."

Katie only continued to stare at the table, where her glass of milk had been a moment earlier.

"I'd like to make it as easy as I can for you, sweetie. It's so important for me to show you right from the start how we live here. It wouldn't be fair to trick you into thinking that you can have cookies for snack, when it's crackers or fruit. You probably think that's dumb. 'No cookies for snack.' But that's the way we all live here. Even I don't get cookies for snack."

She stood near Katie for a few moments while this six-year-old survivor seemed to weigh her options. Jackie was relaxed and accepting. Katie's behavior might be very understandable if one could watch a videotape of the millions of moments of parental anger and indifference to her wishes that she may have experienced during those early years of her life. Any refusal to grant her wish might now be felt as another sign of contempt for her and complete apathy about what she felt and wanted.

Katie might have sensed Jackie's acceptance. She might have thought that she would take another approach or she might simply have decided to wait for another day. Katie reached for a cracker, and as she raised it to her mouth, she quietly asked for some more milk.

"Oh, Katie, I wish you could have milk but you threw it all over the table, the floor, and Steven's pants. I'll tell you what. While you're cleaning up the milk, I'll get you a glass of water to drink with your crackers."

"I want more milk!" Katie screamed and threw her cracker across the room. It hit a cabinet, broke into a hundred pieces, and joined the milk on the floor.

Jackie reached down and removed the two remaining crackers. "I'll save these, Katie. You are so mad at me! No cookies, no new milk, and no more crackers to throw! You probably feel like throwing me, but I'm too heavy."

Katie stood up and tried to grab the crackers in Jackie's hand. Jackie held her hand away as she placed the crackers on the counter. "Now, Katie, I'll show you the bucket and sponge that you'll need for wiping up the milk from the floor."

"No I'm not!" Katie screamed and tried to kick Jackie.

Jackie took Katie's wrist, and, escorting her to a chair, said, "Oh, this is a hard start for you Katie. No fun at all. I have to teach you, sweetie, that here, if one of us throws stuff on the floor, that person has to clean it up. You'll probably hear me tell Daddy Mark that a lot." Katie began to struggle to get away.

"You're really mad at me now and I can see you're not ready to clean up the milk.

You can sit in the chair for a minute before cleaning it up. But I can't let you kick me. You're so mad you might throw more things and break them or hurt yourself or hurt me."

Katie sat with obvious rage. She looked away and slammed her arms on the table. Just then, Steven came back into the room.

Katie looked up and screamed, "I don't want to live here! I hate her! Take me back to Susan's!"

Steven was speechless. Jackie quickly filled the silence. "Katie is really mad at me, Steven. First, no cookies. Then I wouldn't let her have more milk. Then I told her that she had to clean up the milk. And finally, after she threw her cracker, I took the other ones from her, then she tried to kick me, and I had her sit there since she's too mad now to clean up the milk and cracker from the floor and she probably still wants to kick me. And I still haven't even told her yet that she has to tell you that she's sorry for spilling milk on you and then ask you what she can do to make up for it! Katie doesn't like me at all."

"I hate you!" Katie screamed.

"I guess right now she even hates me! No wonder she doesn't want to live here with me," Jackie said. Then she spoke more quietly, directing her words to Katie. "She probably was hoping that she'd finally get a mom that she'd really like. And now she's afraid that I might be the worst mom that she ever had. This must be so hard for her."

Steven sat down and spoke to Katie. "I'm sorry that you're mad at Jackie now, Katie. I'm not taking you back to Susan's, though. I know Jackie, and I think that once you get to know her too, you'll like her."

"I don't want to stay here!" Katie screamed again.

"I'm afraid you have to, Katie. This is your new home and I hope that someday you'll like it and Jackie," Steven said, without much confidence in his own words.

"I never will!" Katie screamed.

"Steven, right now Katie is really, really, mad. I don't think that you'll be able to change her mind. Maybe it would be best if you left now and Katie could start to get used to being here."

"No!" Katie screamed and jumped up from her seat.

Jackie went to her quickly and took her wrists again as she reached for Steven. Katie spun and tried to kick Jackie again. After two years of caring for Gabe, Jackie anticipated the move and in one easy motion spun Katie in her arms and sat back down in the chair with Katie securely held in her lap.

"Why don't you call tomorrow, Steven, and I'll let you know how Katie is doing. Maybe the next time you come she'll be ready to say that she's sorry for spilling the milk on your pants," Jackie said.

Steven did not know what he could do besides leaving as gracefully as possible. He could not think of anything to say to Katie that would help the situation so he settled for "Goodbye, Katie" as he reached for the door.

As Steven drove down the driveway, Katie continued to scream at Jackie while she tried to scratch, bite, hit, and kick her. Jackie held her securely, with the back of her head against Jackie's chest. If Katie were bigger she'd have to hold her another way. Jackie would be able to keep them both safe this way while Katie expressed her rage.

"Oh, Katie, how hard this must be for you! You don't even know me and now you're all alone in the house with me. Steven left you here with someone you hate and don't know. I know you might not believe me but I can promise you that you'll be safe no matter how mad you get at me. I'll keep you and me safe while you're being so mad at me."

"You're hurting me!" Katie exclaimed.

"You might think I'm going to hurt you, Katie, and it must be scary that you can't move your arms and get away from me but I'm not hurting you. As soon as you're calm I'll let you go," said Jackie matter-of-factly.

"Yes, you are!" Katie screamed again.

"Oh, Katie," Jackie said quietly, "how much you've been hurt in your life. I'm sorry that you've been hurt so much."

"Shut up! You are hurting me!" Katie screamed.

"Oh, Katie," Jackie said quietly.

Over the next 15 minutes, Katie's struggles and screams gradually decreased. Then a car pulled into the driveway. A minute later, Diane, John, and Matt could be heard on the porch and they bounced in through the door. They stopped and stared at their mother, a sweaty, wrinkled little girl, and the milk.

"Kids, I'd like you to meet Katie. She's your new sister and she's living with us now." Jackie said in a casual and relaxed manner.

"Hi, Katie!" Diane said. Her brothers followed with less enthusiasm.

"Katie is having a hard time now, but things are OK," Jackie said. "If you want some milk and crackers you'll have to get your own now. And don't step in the milk."

Diane came over to Katie. "Well, so you're my new sister. I'm glad that I'll no longer be the only girl. Looks like you and Mom are having a disagreement. What does she want you to do?"

"She says I have to clean up the milk!" Katie said with both interest in Diane and annoyance at her situation.

"Too bad, Sis. Well, if you get it done soon, I'll show you around the place." Diane left for her room and Katie followed her with her eyes.

"You can let me go now," Katie said firmly. "I'll clean up the milk."

Jackie felt surprise at the suddenness of her mood change and her willingness to do what she expected of her. The arrival of three teenagers might have simply broken the atmosphere. Maybe she wanted to impress Diane and did not want to start on the wrong foot with her. Diane and her brothers might be allies against this evil mother.

"It sounds like your anger is gone, Katie. But I don't know you very well. Are you able to handle it if I let you go?" asked Jackie.

"Yes, I won't hit you," Katie said evenly.

"Fine, Katie." She stood up and released her arms. She took a small bucket and sponge from under the sink, filled it partly with water, and gave it to Katie. Katie took it and proceeded to wipe up the milk. Just then, Diane came in and got an apple.

"You're doing a good job, Katie," said Diane. "Maybe now Mom won't ask me to help her all the time."

Katie smiled and continued her cleaning. She actually did a good job and gave the bucket to Jackie when she finished.

"Diane, Katie is probably still kinda mad at me. Would you show her the rest of the house and the garage and swing set?"

"Sure, Mom." Diane smiled at Katie, "Come on, Sis. We'll start with your bedroom and then I'll show you mine."

Katie walked off with Diane as if she had never been happier. Whimsy followed them. Jackie was a little worn out, but Katie seemed to be full of energy. Jackie would never get used to how kids like Katie could move so abruptly from one mood and activity to another, with no signs of anything remaining from the last event. Jackie wondered if that would make life easier—just move on and have no regrets. It was more likely, however, that one's life would be more fragmented, with less continuity and integration of the various experiences that life brings.

On the way back to his office, Steven had his doubts about Jackie and Allison and everything that they had said. It may have sounded good but the real thing seemed to be different from the theory. Didn't Katie need to feel welcomed and relaxed the first day? Why couldn't Jackie have given her a damn cookie? What was the big deal? And then she had to make an issue of the spilled milk! And telling me that she was sorry! Couldn't she see that the kid was off to a bad start? Why did she have to push it? She seemed to want Katie to fight with her! She should have known that Katie wouldn't smile and clean up the milk!


Three days later Steven arrived at Allison's office for Katie's first treatment session. He met with Allison and Jackie first while Katie remained in the waiting room.

"How are things going?" Allison asked Jackie.

"Things are pretty much going as I expected. Steven saw her first tantrum, which happened about five minutes after she arrived. She's had a few more since then but I mostly think that she's mainly biding her time until she has the lay of the land. She's putting much more energy into trying to be nice to the other kids than she is trying to get closer to me. I suspect that she's looking for weaknesses that she could attack at some future opportunity."

"I was wondering why you seemed to want Katie to have a tantrum when she first arrived," Steven said. "You probably could have avoided her tantrum if you had tried."

"Maybe I could have, but I don't think that would have helped her any. She wanted her way and she was checking to see if having a tantrum would help her to take control in our relationship. I had no wish for her to have a tantrum. However, if I had actively avoided it, I would have to avoid countless more in the days and months ahead."

"With kids like Katie, Steven, it's generally not a good strategy to try to avoid her tantrums. *She* needs to be working to avoid tantrums," Allison suggested. "If she sees us doing the work she's likely to think that either we are afraid of her getting angry or that she is not able to manage routine frustrations. Either message is not what she needs."

"But the first minute she was there? Why not let her choose between cookies or crackers?" Steven asked.

"Then she would have searched for something else to justify a tantrum," Allison responded. "She wanted to find out how easy it would be for her to take charge of this new family. She needed to see that if she wanted to have a tantrum, that was OK. Jackie would not reject her for the tantrum, nor acquiesce to it. If she had chosen to accept what Jackie offered her, that would have been OK, too. Actually, Katie probably benefited more from having her tantrum and seeing Jackie's response to it than if she had chosen to be 'good.'"

Steven was still skeptical, but he decided not to push the issue further.

Jackie continued to describe the first few days. "Katie seems to be sleeping OK so far. Her appetite is OK, too. She fussed over her daily chores the first two days, but then she did them. I'm staying pretty close to her. She was annoyed that she couldn't go out with the older kids a few times."

After some additional discussion about Katie's recent behaviors and strategies for the next week, Allison went for Katie in the waiting room. Jackie and Steven heard Katie chat excitedly on the way back.

"What are they doing here?" Katie asked Allison upon entering the treatment room.

"Good question, Katie. You're used to having therapy with Jan and she saw you by herself, didn't she? Well, in therapy with me your mom, Jackie will always be with us and sometimes Steven will be here, too," Allison said calmly.

"I don't want them here!" Katie yelled.

"I didn't think you did, Katie," Allison replied. "You sound kinda angry about their being here with us."

"Make them leave!" Katie yelled at Allison.

"You *really* don't like them here! And I can tell that you want to decide what happens here," Allison said. "Well, I'm glad to hear what you want, but I need to decide what's the best way to use therapy to help you with the troubles that you've been having in your life for such a long time. And your mom really needs to be here."

"She's not my mom!" Katie yelled again. She was looking for something else to be in control of since her command that Jackie and Steven leave did not work.

"But she is, Katie. She's not your birth mom, but she is your foster mom, the mom who is taking care of you now."

"She's not my mom!" Katie was not ready to concede to Allison.

"Wow, Katie, you really sound mad at me and at your mom. Things just aren't going the way you want them now, are they?"

Katie did not respond. She was sitting on the corner of the couch looking away from Jackie and Allison. She was not a happy girl! She did not like the idea of therapy, unless she could control what were to happen there. She certainly didn't want Jackie to be present. Allison wasn't going to make Jackie leave but she certainly couldn't make Katie talk to her. Katie would ignore her!

Allison sat on the couch near Katie and said quietly, "It's too bad that this has gotten off to a hard start for you, Katie. Your mom says that you haven't wanted to talk much with her at home, either. It must be rough having to get used to so many moms in six years! No wonder you don't want another mom. No wonder you want to say to moms, 'Leave me alone!'" Allison added emphasis on the last phrase to try to let Katie know that she understood her anger at having to have a relationship with Jackie. She went on, quietly, and more slowly, "You're so tired of moms. They have hurt you so much. Especially Sally. No wonder at times you'd rather be all alone than to get close to a mom. No wonder you probably often want to say, 'No more moms.'"

Katie was sitting motionless, withdrawn into a reality that she seldom attended to. She normally didn't let any feelings or thoughts stray into those experiences that had caused her to give up on people. She wasn't aware of where her thoughts were taking her or she would have been yelling about something else by now. Anger was always her favorite distraction.

Allison could tell by her lack of movement and her distant and sad gaze that she was responding somewhere within herself to Allison's words and to her empathy. She continued with her comments, even more slowly and deliberately than before, watching Katie for any clue of her emotional response. "You probably wish that you didn't need any mom. You might wonder why someone else can't give you food, and clothes, and a place to stay. Someone who isn't a mom! Someone who doesn't try to get you to like her and be close to her." Allison gently rested her hand on Katie's hand, and then removed it before Katie could protest. She allowed a moment of silence before she continued.

"Let's talk about something else for now, Katie," Allison said, changing her tone of voice and posture. "I hear that Diane is taking you swimming after therapy today!"

"Yeah! We're going to a big lake. And we're going to bring some food!" Katie replied with enthusiasm.

"She sounds like she's going to be a neat big sister!" said Allison.

"Yeah!" Katie smiled.

"So I guess that you'd like it if we got this therapy over with for today so you can get to the lake with Diane," Allison suggested. Katie looked at her, waiting for what was next.

"Well, Katie, I know that you've had some hard times and probably not been real happy with Sally and Mike and then in the three other homes that you lived in before coming to live with your mom, Jackie. Is that right?"

"Yeah," Katie replied.

"Do you think that you probably did some things that made it harder for you in those foster homes? Do you think that it might be a good idea for me to be able to help you to be happier in this home than you were in your other homes?" Allison asked.

"Yeah."

"Well, OK, Katie, but it probably means that you'll have to work pretty hard because you've had a lot of troubles for a long time. Is that OK with you?"

"Yeah."

"Is that all you can say, 'Yeah?'" Allison smiled and took Katie's arms in her hands. With a big smile, she went on, "Well, cut it out! No more 'Yeah.' Give me a few of those 'No, I won't!' that I know you can say."

Katie paused, smiled and hesitated further, not sure what to say.

"I said to say, 'No, I won't!' and say it now!" Allison held her closer and smiled even more.

"Yeah!" said Katie with her biggest grin yet.

"No!" screamed Allison. She lightly touched her side for a moment and Katie laughed loudly.

"I said to say, 'No, I won't!'" Allison yelled again.

"Yeah!" yelled Katie in reply.

Allison lightly touched her again, and this time added a quick hair rub. "No, I won't!"

"Yeah!"

"No, I won't!"

"Yeah!"

"Katie, if you don't say, 'No, I won't' you'll be in big trouble!" Allison said with a forced frown on her face.

"Yeah!"

Allison wrapped her arms around her and gave her a quick hug. "You say that one more time and I'll give you two more hugs!"

"Yeah!"

Allison again hugged her as she said "one" forcefully. She released her, smiled into her eyes, and said "two" as she hugged her again. "I thought you said that you wanted my help." Allison said in the same tone of voice.

"Yeah!"

"Well, Katie, if I'm to help you you'll have to agree to cooperate. OK?" asked Allison.

"Yeah!"

"Great, Katie! I know that I'll be able to help you when you work hard with me. You get a big hug for that!" Allison squeezed her again.

"No!" Katie yelled while she laughed.

Allison then leaned over and whispered. "I can be a tricky therapist. You better watch what you say or you'll be getting a million hugs."

Katie looked at Allison, smiled, and said, "No, I won't!"

Allison smiled and again leaned over and whispered, "You can be tricky, too. That's neat, we must be twins!" She hugged her again.

"No, we're not!" Katie continued to laugh and yell. Her smile was genuine, spontaneous, and unexpected.

Allison sat back, breathing deeply. "Wow, this kid is smart. She knows what's going on. It's going to be fun getting to know her."

Katie watched Allison without knowing what to say or do next. She was much more receptive to Allison than she had been initially. She had some fun in spite of herself. She had fun in spite of Jackie sitting near her and smiling at her working. Did she do any work? If she did, she hadn't intended to. Maybe she would have to watch that tricky Allison more carefully.

Allison alternated between small talk and playful interactions involving gentle pushing, touching, a brief, light tickle, and one screaming hug. She seemed to establish an interaction with Katie and then leave it, over and over again. Katie followed her lead each time and Allison did not want to maintain the connection beyond what Katie would accept. She broke it before Katie did, making it easier for her to direct the interactions and the overall affective tone to the session. She was pacing Katie's ability to tolerate reciprocal communication and enjoyment. Such interactions—so basic for healthy children—were a stretch for Katie. Allison recognized this and paced the session accordingly.

Allison decided that Katie must now begin to benefit from being led into an area of her self that had not yet received attention. She knew that central features of Katie's personhood were buried under shame. As long as these areas were untouched and unexplored, they would effectively maintain the barrier that separated her from others, especially from Jackie.

Shame! Shame would descend over Katie whenever she did anything that met with the slightest question, limit, or criticism. Shame would equate her with Bad, Worthless, and Unimportant. Shame would prevent her from accepting the reality of discipline as central for socialization into the human community. Shame would make her unable to understand how her behaviors connected to the consequences that followed. And if Shame were to remain entangled throughout her sense of self, she would never . . . could never . . . believe that she was special to someone. Such Shame would not leave room for meaningful attachments; it would not allow a self whose features and sense of worth emerged from a secure attachment.

As she would throughout therapy, Allison approached the realm of shame in a calm, caring, and matter-of-fact manner. She wanted Katie to know that this area of her self and her life would be explored like every other. Her attitude and her emotional tone would not change. She accepted and did not judge this area of Katie just as she accepted and did not judge any other area.

"Well, Katie, our meeting will be over soon. I do want to talk briefly about one more thing. But this will probably be hard for you." Allison leaned forward and said very quietly near Katie's ear, "When I talk about this you might get mad at me and want me to shut up. You might think that I'm being very mean to talk about it. If you think or feel that, it's OK. Just let me know if you want to." Then she gently patted her hand a few times.

"Katie, I hear that you had a hard time when you first got to your new home. You really didn't like those crackers. You wanted cookies. And you thought that your mom was being mean to you for not giving you any! So you knocked over your glass of milk! Wow, were you mad! And it went all over Steven's pants! And he got upset! And you thought that it was all your mom's fault."

Katie did not respond nor look at Allison. Neither were expected or encouraged now. Allison thought that they would be too difficult for Katie to do and still maintain some active emotional connection to Allison. She hoped that her empathy for what Katie had probably been thinking and feeling would enable her to remain passively responsive.

"There are two things that I'd like you to do, Katie. I know that this might be hard." Allison paused, and again gently touched Katie's hand. "First, I'd like you to look at Steven and tell him that you're sorry for getting the milk on him."

Allison left her hand on Katie's and calmly waited. If Katie would not apologize, she would accept the decision and "help" her by doing it for her, by pretending to be Katie. Since she didn't need to have Katie respond, she was able to remain accepting and nonjudgmental. This attitude would make it easier for Katie to choose to do it.

After some delay, Katie looked up, looked out the window, and said that she was sorry for spilling milk on Steven.

"Your words came out fine, Katie, but your eyes missed. Steven is not standing in the window. Try again." Allison smiled and gently encouraged her.

"I'm sorry that I spilled the milk on you," Katie said quietly, while looking at Steven.

"Thanks for telling me, Katie," Steven replied. "That was the coldest milk in Maine!"

"Way to go, kiddo," Allison said casually. "Now I'd like you to tell Steven that the next time he comes to your home to visit, you'll serve him milk and crackers without spilling one drop."

Katie smiled and looked at Steven again. "The next time you come to my house I'll get you milk and crackers and I won't spill any."

"That would be great, Katie," Steven responded affectionately.

Allison smiled and gently pulled Katie toward her. She held her close and said, "Guess what happens if you spill one drop on Steven?"

"I don't know," Katie responded with some confusion and interest.

"Steven will tell me and the next time I see you, you'll get seven hugs, four tickles, two nose squeezes, and three hair mess-ups. So you better be careful!"

Katie laughed and Allison sat back. She turned to Jackie and said, "I think that Katie really was with us today."

Jackie agreed. "It seemed that it didn't bother her that I was here and know what she did with you. That should help me to help her better at home."

"Yeah," Allison said. "And she sure needs mom-help, although right now she doesn't like it very much."

After the first session, Steven was again uncertain about Allison and Jackie. What they did made sense. But didn't they ever give her a break? He knew that Allison hadn't pushed her too hard. But at the same time it seemed that she did. Was it really necessary to bring up the milk again after they had a pretty good session? Was it worth the risk? Why rub it in? She's had such a hard life. Why make a fuss about something so small, that only happened once in Jackie's home? Also, didn't Katie have the right to ask that Steven and Jackie leave her session? If she's more comfortable seeing Allison alone at first, shouldn't her wishes be granted? Steven didn't know what to think. In such situations, he talked to Betty Norton back at the office. Betty always had a gut reaction to things and, more often than not, her response made the most sense. He told her about the milk and crackers episode as well as the first treatment session.

"Let me get this right," Betty said with interest although she seemed to enjoy Steven's struggles. "This kid threw a glass of milk on you and you wanted to wring her neck. Then you got mad at her foster mother, argued with her therapist, and felt sorry for her. Then the kid had a lot of fun with the therapist, did what she was told and told you that she was sorry. Am I right so far?"

Steven was both uncomfortable with where Betty was going with this story, while at the same time, enjoying her pleasure over his doubts.

"And finally you get a promise from this kid to serve you crackers and milk, *without spilling any*, and you think that maybe things should be different. Right?"

Steven smiled and replied with difficulty, "Right."

"Well, Steven," Betty said seriously, "you have a good point. You should have held out for milk and *cookies* served by Jackie and Allison. How dare they get her to face behaviors that have gotten her moved from three foster homes?"

Steven laughed.

"I think that they're doing great so far. I don't know if it's going to help Katie but I think that they're on target so far. This kid has major problems. We can't simply have business as usual."

The next few days were fairly uneventful at Jackie's. Katie wanted to spend her time with Diane and whenever Diane was around, Katie was helpful and charming. However, when Diane was gone with friends or wanted to be alone in her room, Katie's mood was more variable. When Jackie spoke to her, she might or might not respond. When Jackie showed her how to do something, she might or might not do it as she was told. Sometimes she seemed cheerful and friendly, sometimes indifferent and irritable. When Katie wanted something from Jackie, she was more friendly and "giving," but not nearly to the degree that she turned on her charm for Diane. Katie might be looking for an edge, for a way to establish some control over Jackie. When she found it, Jackie would know who was actually in charge!

On June 20, Katie was eating her breakfast slowly. Jackie already knew her well enough to guess that this might be one of her "might not" days. Katie finished her cereal and juice, got up, and headed for her room, probably to see if Diane were up yet.

"Not feeling like doing your job today, I see. Well, sweetie, I can help you if you need some help," Jackie said with a smile.

"What?" Katie asked angrily.

"*What?* You want to pretend that you don't know what to do after you finish your breakfast. You *really* don't feel like doing your job." Jackie continued to smile.

"What am I supposed to do?" Katie demanded.

"Sweetie, if I thought that you forgot, I'd certainly tell you if you asked in a nice and friendly way. But I know that you know. And you would have to ask me differently than you just did." Jackie paused as Katie stared toward the table. "Why not ask in a friendly way and I'll pretend that you don't know and I'll tell you."

"What do I have to do?" Katie demanded again, with almost as much rage as her last statement.

"That's not what I'd call 'friendly,' sweetie. Do you want to try it again?" Jackie asked, continuing with her caring and accepting tone.

Katie decided that being friendly to Jackie now was the last thing in the world she wanted to do. She rushed to the table, grabbed the bowl and glass, brought them to the counter, and roughly placed them down. She turned to leave.

"Slow down, Katie. Good job of remembering what your job was. Now I want you to tell me something before you leave the room."

"What!" Katie yelled.

"Ask me more quietly," Jackie said in a relaxed manner.

"What?" Katie asked quietly, though her facial expression could have scared a cat.

Jackie walked over to her, smiled again, and said quietly, "I want you to say—"

Then she suddenly raised her voice, "I HATE YOU TELLING ME WHAT TO DO!"

Katie was startled for a second but then quickly screamed, "I HATE YOU TELLING ME WHAT TO DO!"

Jackie maintained her relaxed and accepting attitude. She gave Katie one last look and said, "You have a great grouchy yell!" She then turned back to the counter. Katie seemed to be confused and she wasted no time leaving the kitchen.

Later that morning, after Diane had left to baby-sit for a neighbor down the road, Katie turned on the TV in the family room. Jackie had told her twice during the first couple of days that she needed to ask before turning on the TV. Jackie needed to know what she intended to watch. Jackie told her that she'd usually only be able to watch one hour a day. Jackie told her that TV was not something that the family watched much. Jackie explained that kids were better off doing active things rather than just staring at the TV.

Jackie made a point to know where Katie was all the time so she was immediately aware that the TV was on. She walked calmly into the room. "Katie, are you pretending that you forgot another rule?"

"I didn't turn it on!" Katie yelled.

"It is hard for you to tell the truth, isn't it? Well, turn it off, please."

"Why? Diane turned it on before she left." Katie was almost convincing.

"Then Diane will be grateful that you turned it off for her," Jackie replied.

"I didn't do it!" Katie screamed.

"It sure is hard today to do what I tell you, sweetie."

"I didn't do it!"

"I'm willing to turn it off for you, honey, but then you won't get to watch it at all today." Jackie remained calm. Her attitude indicated that she really didn't care if Katie turned it off or not. Jackie didn't mind doing it for her.

Katie stared at the TV, as angry as ever. Jackie waited a moment and then reached for the TV.

"I'll do it!" Katie yelled.

"Too late, sweetie." Jackie pressed the knob, turned, and left.

On the way back to the living room, Jackie heard the TV again. She stopped, chuckled to herself, and returned to the family room. "Well, I guess it REALLY, REALLY, is hard to do what I tell you. And you're SO MAD AT ME!" Jackie turned off the TV and walked over to Katie. She sat down on the couch next to her.

"Katie, I want you to tell me how mad you are at me," Jackie said.

"Shut up and leave me alone!" Katie yelled.

"That's the idea. Say it again, 'SHUT UP AND LEAVE ME ALONE!'" Jackie said.

"Shut up!" Katie replied.

"AND LEAVE ME ALONE!" Jackie added.

"SHUT UP!" Katie said more loudly.

"That's it, kiddo. Now I know how mad you are at my telling you what to do. You're so mad now that I think you might get yourself into some trouble and not do things that are good for you unless you stay close to me for a while. I'm doing some work in the living room; you can play on the floor there. Let's go and get the Legos."

"No, I want to go to my room!" Katie yelled.

"I know that you probably don't want to be near me very much, but you need to be for a while. I'll let you know when you can go to your room."

"No!" Katie screamed and stomped her foot.

"Yes, sweetie. I'll take your hand or you can walk in front of me," Jackie said.

"No!" Katie yelled again.

"I'll hold your hand, then, Katie," Jackie calmly said.

As Jackie reached for her hand, Katie kicked her arm and yelled, "Leave me alone!"

In one easy motion, Jackie pushed down her leg, wrapped her arm around her shoulder, took her other wrist, and pulled Katie to her on the couch.

Katie screamed and tried frantically to release herself.

"I'll just hold you here and keep us both safe until I know that you won't be trying to hurt me. Then I'll let you go and you can come into the living room with me." Jackie was clear and firm but her matter-of-fact, accepting attitude had not varied in spite of Katie's physical outburst.

"I know it's hard for you to do what I say. So hard. That's OK. I don't mind helping you and I certainly don't mind holding you when you need me to," Jackie added.

"Let me go! You're hurting me!" Katie screamed.

"I imagine that you're afraid that I might hurt you, Katie. But I won't. You're safe," Jackie said.

"You *are* hurting me!" Katie screamed again.

"I've held a lot of kids, Katie, and I know I'm not hurting you. But it must still be scary for you."

"You're hurting me! You're hurting me! You're hurting me!" she continued.

"Oh, Katie, this must be so hard for you. You probably were hurt when you were little. Well, you're safe now." Jackie was sure that Katie was not being hurt, but she also knew that Katie might almost believe that she was. Arguing would not do any good. She'd just keep affirming that she was safe.

After about 10 minutes, Katie's intense rage and efforts to hit and kick began to lessen. After another 10 minutes, she was quiet and still. She seemed worn out and resigned—not resentful.

"Well, Katie, are we safe if I let you go?"

"Yeah," Katie replied with a touch of annoyance.

"It's sure been a hard day for you so far. I'll bet it's not your idea of a fun summer day," Jackie said.

Jackie stood up and took her hand. Katie quietly walked with her into the living room. "You sit there and I'll get the Legos." Katie complied, again with a subdued manner. Jackie found the Legos. She gave them to Katie and then turned to her paperwork at the desk near the dining room. She spent the next 30 minutes at her work, commenting on Katie's construction, chatting about lunch possibilities, and singing quietly to herself. She wanted Katie to be aware of her calm and accepting presence. Their conflict would not damage their relationship. Jackie would be communicating that to her more times than she would care to count.

At the second therapy session, Jackie informed Allison that Katie was relating with her in an unpredictable, moment-to-moment manner. She might be friendly, helpful, and seemingly content. Or she might be tense, withdrawn, and irritable. There seemed to be little connection with what was happening at the time. Katie appeared resigned about Jackie's behavioral expectations. She had unleashed a number of verbal outbursts each day and since her arrival she had incurred restraint five times for aggressive behaviors. Generally she would complain, then comply when Jackie told her to express her anger more directly, and finally follow the directive.

Steven asked if there was anything that she could do differently to avoid holding her.

"I don't mind restraining her if that's what she needs," Jackie said.

"But for Katie's sake, isn't it better to find an alternative?" Steven asked.

"She always has alternatives, Steven. If she wants or needs to be held, that's OK with me." Jackie remained firm, not being willing to follow Steven's way of approaching Katie. Steven saw restraints as a failure that must be damaging Katie; Jackie didn't.

"Steven, I know that it takes some getting used to that we believe Katie's being restrained is acceptable and even beneficial for her," Allison commented. "But when it is done with a loving attitude, she is learning some very important things. First, she will not be rejected or hurt when she is enraged and aggressive. Second, she will be kept safe. And finally, that Jackie is so committed to her that she will get sweaty, tired, and possibly bruised, to give her what she needs. If Katie were held three times every day I wouldn't be concerned about it as long as Jackie can remain loving and accepting. I might worry about Jackie's health and stamina, but I won't be worrying about Katie! She may really need to be held when she is aggressive now. We can't avoid holding her if she needs to be held. I truly believe that at some point Katie will become angry and not aggressive and the restraints will no longer be necessary. Now, Jackie is co-regulating her rage through the restraints. At some point, Jackie will be able to co-regulate her rage with a look or tone of voice. Finally, Katie will be able to regulate her rage by herself."

"Of course, we will not 'set her up' to be held by giving her expectations that are just too difficult for her. We will try to structure her day and give her supervision that will enable her to stay regulated better in both her affect and behavior. But we will not avoid important situations for learning in order to avoid restraints."

Allison paused and then added, "Actually, Jackie is probably helping Katie to avoid being held, if that's what she wants, by her own calm and accepting attitude. Unnecessary restraints occur most often when the caregiver is tense and angry herself and her annoyed attitude is felt by the child. That's not happening with Jackie."

"You're right. It does take some getting used to. I've spent a lot of time talking with parents and foster parents about avoiding conflicts, especially those that get physical," Steven said.

"And in many families that's probably the safest course. Jackie is good at dealing with these conflicts in a way that facilitates the relationship and does not hurt it. With Katie, I really don't think that she'll learn to truly rely on Jackie if she doesn't lose control of her affect and behavior at times and then experience Jackie as accepting the rage and keeping her safe. These are shame experiences for her and she needs to be able to experience them without being rejected or humiliated and she needs to sense that Jackie's emotional support and empathy remain available to her. If Jackie couldn't deal well with Katie in these situations we'd have to try to avoid them. But that would not help Katie as much as what Jackie is doing now," Allison said.

"Anything else we should discuss before I get Katie?" Allison asked.

"I've noticed that she doesn't sleep well at night. It takes her awhile to get to sleep and she's restless. I never had that trouble with Gabe."

"You might try tucking her sheet in on three sides." Allison said. "That will keep some gentle pressure on her body and may help her to feel more contained and secure. Let me know if that doesn't help and we'll explore some other ideas. Possibly she's having some dreams that we might help her with."

When Katie entered the therapy room, she was friendly and expressive. She told Allison that she was going swimming with Diane that afternoon. Then she began talking about how much she liked her new home. Then she asked if she could play with the stuffed bears in the corner of the room. Allison could see that Katie had decided to try to control the session through her chatter and questions. If Katie could direct them toward playing with the toys, so much the better. Her angry orders at the onset of the first session had not led to controlling the situation; maybe her charm would be more effective.

"Well, Katie, you sure seem to feel like talking today. That's what I'd like to continue doing now rather than playing with the bears," Allison said cheerfully. "I'm interested in knowing more about why you like your new home."

"Diane is my new sister. I like her," Katie quickly replied.

"I'm glad that you have such a nice big sister, Katie," Allison replied. "What do you think about your new dad, Mark?"

"He's nice. He pushed me on the swings."

"Great, Katie. Your dad does seem nice. How about your mom?"

"She's OK," Katie replied evenly.

"Is she a good cook?" Allison asked.

"Yeah, we had pizza!"

"Pizza!" Allison exclaimed. "No wonder you like your new home and your mom. Did you bring any with you? I'm hungry," Allison asked with a smile.

"No!" Katie grinned and replied.

"No!" Allison looked shocked. She reached over and put her finger in Katie's shirt pocket, "Maybe you're hiding some. I have to find it."

Katie laughed and pulled back, "It's all gone!"

"All gone, and you didn't save me any! Katie, how could you do that?" Allison laughed too.

"She ate some, too!" Katie pointed toward Jackie.

"Who did?" Allison asked.

"She did!" Katie pointed again.

"Who did?" Allison moved closer to Katie and took her hand.

"Jackie!" Katie replied.

"Who?" Allison asked.

"Jackie!"

"Who is Jackie?" Allison persisted.

"My foster mom," Katie finally answered.

"Oh, your mom! Well, that's OK. Since she made it," Allison said.

"She didn't make it. We got it at Pizza Hut," Katie replied and smiled.

"I thought that you said that she was a good cook? And she bought it? Are you sure she's a good cook?" Allison smiled.

"Yeah, she made a chocolate cake!" Katie said.

"Well, Katie, I guess she is, then. For a second I thought that she really wasn't a good cook. I thought that you just made it up so your mom wouldn't get into trouble for being a bad cook. Sometimes daughters are that way in defending their moms," Allison said reasonably. Then she moved closer and lowered her voice, "Now I have a big question for you. I heard that Steven stopped in to see you yesterday. What about the crackers and milk?"

"I gave them to him and I didn't spill any," Katie said with a smile.

"You didn't spill any!" Allison seemed surprised.

"Not any!" Katie was definite.

Allison turned to Steven, "Is she telling the truth, Steven?"

"She sure is. And they tasted good, too."

"More proof that Jackie is a good cook!" Allison replied. Then she looked at Katie with a look of utter annoyance, "And you didn't spill any! So I can't pick on you like I said I would if you spilled some. Darn it. I wanted to pick on you and I can't!"

"No, you can't!" Katie seemed pleased and excited.

"Well, then I'll just have to show you how happy I am for you that you didn't spill any." Allison reached down and removed Katie's shoes. She took one foot in her hand and said with a large smile, "This little piggy went to the market . . . ."

Katie was taken by surprise. She seemed to be trying to remember something from her past, but she wasn't sure what Allison was doing. Allison was going to do something unexpected and Katie became alert.

When Allison began, "Wee, wee, wee, all the way home!" Katie screeched with laughter. Then Allison took the other foot and repeated the game. Katie screeched even louder.

"Well, Katie, you must wonder why this lady is teasing you and tickling you and playing silly games," Allison said.

"Yeah," Katie replied.

"Well, I guess it's time to tell you," Allison said as she smiled and squeezed Katie's big toe, "You see, I want to be able to find ways to help you live a regular life as a kid in your new family. I know that you've been in THREE other foster homes and I've been thinking that FOUR is TOO many for a girl. Moving is TOO hard—new parents, new bedroom, new rules, new school, new friends. It's just TOO much. NO MORE MOVING!"

Katie nodded yes.

"So I thought that I might be able to find ways to help you to learn to live in a good family." Allison then leaned forward and said slowly and quietly, "I know that when you were very little you didn't live in a good family. Sally and Mike did not take good care of you. They didn't know that babies and little kids need to laugh . . . and be held . . . and be warm and fed . . . and be smiled at . . . and tickled. . . ." Allison smiled, lightly touched Katie's toe until she smiled in return, and then went on, "So you never learned what living with a good mom and dad was like. Well . . . Katie . . . Jackie is a good mom . . . and Mark is a good dad . . . but it's hard . . . so hard . . . for you to know that they are. How would you know that? It's hard to tell a good mom from a not-good mom when your mom made big mistakes when you were a baby."

Allison leaned back again, smiled in a gentle way, and then squeezed Katie's toe again. Katie was very quiet and attentive. She lay motionless on the couch with her legs folded and Allison at her feet. Her eyes locked on Allison's eyes. Allison took a deep breath and quietly said, "It's hard . . . so hard."

Then Allison leaned forward and with a twinkle in her eye whispered loudly, "Look at Jackie, Katie. Can tell you that she's a good mom by her black ponytail? No? How about that little dot on her cheek? How about those white sneakers with the red line on the side? No? There must be something about her that will show you that she's a good mom. Let's stare at her for a while."

Katie began to giggle and Allison joined in. Soon Jackie and Steven began laughing, too. Finally Jackie groaned, "Oh, cut it out, you two. You're making me feel embarrassed!"

"Well, Katie, I guess there's no way of telling that Jackie's a good mom by looking at her. So I'm going to have to teach you how to know for yourself that she's a good mom. Once you know that, it will be so much easier to live with her. You'll begin to . . . feel happier . . . and not mind it when she teaches you stuff . . . and want to make cookies with her . . . hand pick corn in the garden with her . . . and even hug her when she helps you to find your special doll that you lost. OK with you?"

Katie nodded yes.

"So, kiddo. Katie kiddo. What a neat name! I'll be asking you to say and do stuff here. And I'll be suggesting that you and your new mom do stuff at home. I'd like you and your mom to agree to do the stuff that I tell you. If you both do, then you'll be able to learn if Jackie is a good mom. If she is, your life should be a lot better than it has been for so long. Does that make sense, Katie kiddo?" Allison asked.

"Yeah," Katie replied.

"Great, kiddo. In therapy I'll have many suggestions for you and Jackie. If you both do what I suggest, things will get better faster. When you two don't, they go slower. Sometimes you won't want to do what I suggest. No big deal. No kid wants to do what she is told all the time. It's OK for therapy to go slower, too. Fast, slow. Slow, fast. Jackie probably won't want to do some things, too. Either way you get some hugs." Allison smiled. "And Jackie does, too! So, kiddo, ready to begin?"

"Yeah," Katie said.

"There's that 'yeah' again. Is that all you ever say?" Allison asked as she squeezed her toe.

"No!" Katie yelled and laughed.

Allison turned to Jackie, "Will you help Katie to learn whether or not you're a good mom, Jackie?"

"I *will* help Katie to learn that," Jackie replied. "And I'll work hard, too."

"Great. With both of you trying so hard, my job will be easy," Allison said. "Now we need to do something to find out what Katie is going to learn." Allison sat quietly, put her hand to her face, said, "Hmmm, hmmm," looked around the room, suddenly yelled, "Yes!" and looked at Katie and smiled mischievously.

Katie's eyes got wide, she smiled broadly, and she said, "What?"

"Jackie, I want you to take Katie's left big toe. I'm going to take her right big toe. If my little piggy gets home first then that means that you're a good mom. If your little piggy gets home first, that means that you're a great mom!" Allison said cheerfully.

Katie screeched and yelled, "Noooo!"

Jackie leaned over, grabbed Katie's left foot, and shortly thereafter the piggy race began.

"She's a great mom!" Allison yelled at the end of the race. She could barely make herself heard over Katie's laughter, wiggling, and yelling. Allison continued, "What a great start, Katie kiddo! There's going to be so much that you'll be learning about your new home and new parents. I'm happy that after all those years you now have a chance to really know . . . what a great mom . . . is really like."

Allison paused, took a deep breath again, and then continued, "Now I'd like you to practice doing some things that I tell you. Get up."

Katie smiled and quickly got up.

"Now jump up and down three times." Katie did so.

"Good job. Now walk around your mom's chair two times." Katie did, with a big smile.

"Way to go. Now go over and shake Steven's hand." Again, Katie did as she was told.

"Three in a row. Now, Katie, stand in front of your mom and look at her. That's it. Now say to her, 'My name is Katie.'"

"My name is Katie," Katie said while controlling her laughter.

"I'm now living with you." Katie repeated what Allison said.

"Sometimes, I don't like what you tell me." Katie again complied.

"Sometimes, I get mad at you." Katie repeated it, more seriously now.

"Your eyes are missing your mom's," Allison said.

"Sometimes I don't think that you're a good mom." Katie said what Allison directed, more quietly than before. She made eye contact for only a second.

Then Allison said, with her head behind Katie's ear, almost in a whisper, "And sometimes I think that you don't like me." Katie quietly said what she was told, without looking at Jackie. She said it again, with fleeting eye contact.

"Now, Katie, look at your mom as she tells you what she thinks about what you just said," Allison said.

Katie stood quite still as Jackie said slowly and calmly, "I'm glad that you're now living with me and the rest of the family, Katie. I know that sometimes you don't like what I tell you to do. And that you get mad at me. I know that sometimes you think that I'm a bad mom. It's OK being mad at me and thinking that I'm a bad mom. I know that it's hard at times getting used to living with me and following my rules. That's OK. I'm happy to keep teaching you. And finally, Katie, I do like you. I like you a lot. Even when you get mad at me and think that I'm a bad mom. I still like you then."

Katie seemed to become anxious as Jackie spoke to her. Allison noticed this and said, "Tell your mom, Katie, 'It's hard hearing you say that, Mom.'" Katie quietly complied.

"Now tell her, 'I'm not sure if I want you to like me, Mom.'" Again, Katie complied. She stood motionless, seemingly confused and not knowing what to feel, or think, or do. Allison asked Katie to sit down on the couch next to Jackie. She did so and Jackie briefly squeezed her hand while Katie sat passively.

"Now," Allison continued, "Katie, we're going to be having a number of talks like we just did. I know that talking is hard for you. Often, I think you just don't know what you think and feel. Or maybe you're just not sure if you want to say it. We'll be talking about all kinds of stuff—hard stuff, easy stuff, fun stuff, scary stuff, silly stuff, sad stuff. When it gets hard I might suggest that you get a little hug from Jackie or sit in her lap, or let her hold and rock you a little bit. I'd like you to be able to learn how to let Jackie help you during hard times. And how nice it might feel when she does. Or if you want her to hold you during a hard time—or a fun time—just let her know and see what she says. My guess is that she will feel fine about it. Does this make sense so far?"

"Yeah," Katie replied.

"Great, Katie. I'm going to talk now about all kinds of stuff. Are you ready?"

"Yeah." Katie remained fairly passive, but not uncooperative.

"Tell me how many elbows you have."

"Two!" Katie hollered and laughed.

"Now tell me how many fingers you have."

"Ten!" She yelled.

"Now, tell me how many freckles you have." Allison said.

Katie paused, surprised. "I don't know!" she exclaimed.

"You don't know!" Allison seemed shocked. "Well, we just have to find out. Jackie, count them!"

Jackie proceeded to touch the freckles on Katie's face and count quietly as she did. Katie initially laughed, but then became quiet and eventually peaceful.

"72! Wow, Katie, that's a great number of freckles to have." Jackie said with a smile. "That means that you are going to learn how to be a special kid in a good family! If you forget that, just look in the mirror and see your 72 freckles. They'll remind you what you're going to learn. Isn't that great?"

Katie did not reply.

"Isn't that great?" Jackie persisted.

Katie laughed and said, "NO!"

"No!" Jackie screamed. "Say yes, kiddo!"

"No!" Katie continued.

Jackie seemed horrified and tickled her side. "Say 'Yes!' Katie."

"No!" Katie laughed and yelled. She continued to yell "No!" as Jackie touched her cheek, messed her hair, and gave her a hug. When she tickled her neck briefly, Katie yelled "Yeah!" Jackie yelled "Yeah!" along with her and gave her a quick hug.

"Well, Katie, you already learned how to do this therapy! Way to go." Allison leaned back and took a deep breath. Often when she changed the tone from one of active excitement to one of quiet and relaxation, she made it obvious. Katie so far followed the change in tone quite readily without being aware of it.

"Now, Katie, I want to talk with you about something that is going to be harder for you." Katie immediately appeared tense. The muscles in her face and body tightened up. Jackie gently stroked her hair and rubbed her shoulder and arm until Katie began to relax again.

"Your mom told me how you got mad at her at home the other day because she turned off the TV. I wonder what made you so mad! I wonder what was so hard for you about that! What do you think?"

"I don't know!"

"That was my guess, Katie, my guess was that you really didn't know why you got THAT mad when your mom told you to turn off the TV. Wait, Katie, why do you think your mom said that?"

"She's just mean to me!" Katie was now raising her voice.

"Wow, Katie, now that makes some sense to me. You got so mad because you thought that your mom was being mean to you. Wow, Katie, that would be hard. If the mom who is supposed to keep you safe and help you to be happy wants to be mean! Very hard!"

Katie sat quietly, staring into Allison's eyes, seeming to be stretching to make sense of what Allison was saying. Katie rarely thought about her rage outbursts. She never asked why she might do something in anger. Most likely, she assumed that it was simply another example of how bad she was.

Allison continued, "I'm thinking, Katie, how hard that would be if you think that your mom wants to be mean to you. Why would she want to be mean to you? Why?" Allison's voice grew more animated, suggesting her deep desire to understand something important, very important.

"She doesn't like me!" Katie shouted out quickly.

Allison matched the intensity of her expression. "Oh, my goodness, Katie! That's why you got so mad. You thought that Jackie did not like you when she turned off the TV! You thought that she didn't like you! What a mother if she didn't like you! No wonder you got mad, Katie! No wonder!"

Katie stared at Allison and her face became soft and vulnerable. She looked so tired!

"Look at your mom, Katie, look at your mom," Allison said quietly.

"Now say to her, 'Mom, when you say 'no' to me I think you're mean.'"

Katie quietly said, "When you say 'no' to me I think you're mean."

"Now say, 'Mom, when you say 'no' I think that you don't like me.'"

"I don't think that you like me."

"Now say, 'That's why I get so mad at you, Mom.'"

"That's why I get so mad."

"Good job, Katie." Allison looked at Jackie.

Jackie squeezed Katie's hand again and said quietly, "Oh, Katie, that must be so hard for you. When I say no, you think that I'm mean. And you think that I don't like you! Now I know why you get mad at me. Now I know. Thanks so much for telling me, Katie. Thanks so much."

Allison responded, "Jackie, I think Katie was so brave to tell you what she thinks and feels when you say 'no' to her. So brave."

"Yes, Allison, I agree. Very brave."

Jackie took Katie's hand and she did not resist.

Allison leaned over and calmly said, "That's it, Katie, good job of telling your mom what you were thinking and feeling. I know that was hard for you. When your mom holds you when you're really mad, you probably really don't like it. You might think that she's going to hurt you. No wonder you don't like it."

Katie became calmer fairly quickly. She was listening intently to Allison.

"Look at your mom, Katie, look at your mom."

Jackie squeezed Katie's hand. Katie looked at her.

"Now look at your mom, Katie, and say, 'I don't like your holding me when I'm mad.'" Katie said what Allison said to her, while looking into Jackie's eyes.

"Now say, 'It's scary when you hold me when I'm mad, Mom.'" Katie complied.

"Say, 'I'm afraid you might get mad at me and hurt me.'" Katie repeated it.

"Say, 'Will you get mad and hurt me, Mom?'" Katie did.

"No, sweetie, no matter how mad you get at me, I won't get mad and hurt you," Jackie replied gently.

"Say, 'Thanks, Mom. But it's hard to believe you.'" Katie did.

"I know it's hard, sweetie. I hope that it will get easier for you," Jackie said.

"Say, 'I hope so too, Mom,'" Allison said and Katie repeated it.

"Now ask your mom for a quick hug, Katie," Allison directed her.

"Can I have a hug, mom?" Katie asked quickly. Jackie immediately gave her a big hug.

"Good work you two!" Allison said cheerfully. "What a mom and daughter you two are going to be! You two are really something together!" She smiled at them both.

For the remaining minutes of the session, Allison directed the discussion toward Jackie's thoughts about Katie's swimming abilities. She ended the discussion by saying to them both. "I'd like it if you would both do something before the next session. Katie, I want you to draw a picture of a time when you think that your new mom is being mean to you and another picture of a time when you think that she's being nice to you. Jackie, I'd like you to draw two pictures, too. I want you to guess what pictures you think Katie drew and draw those. Then during the next session we'll look at all four pictures. OK with you both?"

Jackie and Katie both agreed. "Finally, Katie, I'd like you to tell Mark what we did in today's meeting and see what he thinks about it. If you don't remember it all, that's OK. Your Mom will help you."

Katie agreed and the session ended. Allison heard Katie talking excitedly to Jackie as they left the building. Steven waited for a chance to talk with Allison for a few minutes.

"That seemed great, Allison," said Steven. "But did Katie really mean what you told her to say?"

"What does 'really mean' mean, Steven? Would Katie have said that on her own? No. Does she feel what I had her say? To some degree. Did those words resonate with a small, deeply hidden aspect of herself that needs to develop if she's going to make it? Yes. Did those words hopefully raise a doubt and a possibility within her awareness that there might be something special in a child's relationship with her mother? I truly hope so," Allison said calmly.

"You mean that if you tell her often enough about healthy parent-child relationships, she'll begin to believe it?" Steven asked.

"Not simply 'telling' her. As you noticed, the words were always embedded in an interaction that was emotionally meaningful to her. She was alert, receptive, and curious. Just giving her a 'lecture' will have no effect. The words that she receives must naturally arise from an empathic, nurturing attitude from me and Jackie. What is being communicated is done so mostly nonverbally. That's the way language develops in healthy infants and toddlers and that's the way it has to be if it's going to stay with her and affect her. Also, Jackie's behavior toward her at home, hour after hour, day after day, will have to make those words real to her if she's to begin to 'feel' what they mean and truly believe them. Jackie's goal will be to maintain that playful and/or empathic and nurturing attitude throughout as many interactions with Katie as possible. Again, that's how babies form an attachment with their mothers. Have you seen the special way that a mother interacts with her six-month-old infant?"

"Now that you mention it," Steven smiled, "my wife, Jenny, and I have an 18-month-old daughter, Rebecca. And yes, I know what you mean, although I think you should include fathers in your description of the way parents interact with their babies."

"Wonderful, Steven, and yes, I'm sorry for not including fathers," Allison said. "So when you are with Rebecca, imagine that that's the way Jackie will be trying to relate to Katie. And that's the way I'm trying to relate to her here, too."

"Sounds easy, Allison," Steven said.

"I wish it were. The problem is that Katie now does not want that way of being with her parents the way Rebecca does. She has so much that she needs to unlearn. Also, her behaviors are tough and they make it a lot harder for Jackie to maintain that attitude toward her. I promise you, this will not be easy."

"I know that you're right," Steven said quietly, "I just worry a lot about that kid and I want her to make it."

"We'll just have to keep working at it, then," Allison said calmly.

When she and Katie arrived home after the session, Jackie anticipated that Katie might not do well. Katie had relaxed her efforts to control the session and Jackie expected that she might quickly do something to establish her idea of how their relationship should be. Katie would try to negate anything that she may have said or done during the session.

When they got out of the car, Jackie stood on the walk toward the kitchen door, waiting for Katie. She looked back and saw Katie on the other side of the car. Katie bent over, seemingly to pick up something. She didn't get back up.

"Katie, come on in the house," Jackie said. There was no reply or movement.

"Katie!" Jackie said more loudly.

"What?" Katie yelled back, with an edge of anger in her voice.

"Come here, Katie," Jackie said. She saw Katie stand up straight and walk quickly around the car. Something wasn't right.

"What were you doing?" Jackie asked.

"Nothing!" Katie was now more annoyed.

"What were you doing behind the car?" Allison asked.

"I said nothing!" Katie yelled.

Jackie took her arm and said, "I need to check, sweetie. The way you're talking makes me think that you did something that you shouldn't. Maybe I'm wrong. We'll see." Jackie was matter-of-fact.

"Leave me alone, I didn't do anything!" Katie was becoming upset but she came along with Jackie.

Jackie went around the car and looked at the ground. Nothing was there. Nothing was wrong. "Well, Katie, I guess you were right and I was wrong. Oh, well. Someday I'll be able to know that you're telling me the truth and I won't have to check. But now I have to check."

As Jackie turned toward the house, again she glanced at the car. She immediately noticed a scratch, about six inches long, on the passenger door. She knew that it was new, and she knew now why Katie knelt down after getting out of the car.

"Katie, I am angry at what you just did! You scratched the car. In our home we don't damage each other's stuff just because we are angry at each other. I don't like that you did! If you are angry with me you can yell and moan and groan . . . or tell me, but I don't want you to damage something!"

Katie looked down and did not move. Then Jackie took a deep breath and spoke again, this time with her usual empathic and nurturing tone, "I know it is hard, Katie, learning to live with good people in a family. And learning that you fit. We'll get through things like this. I'll help you. You're part of the family and we'll all help you learn these things." Jackie gave her a quick hug, took her hand, and walked her into the house.

"Well, it looks like I was right after all. It's sad that after you and I had a good time together at Allison's you needed to do something wrong. I guess you really wanted to get me mad at you. Well, sweetie, I was mad at what you did for a minute and now it's over. Let's go into the kitchen," Jackie said.

"I didn't do anything!" Katie screamed. She struggled to get her arm loose but Jackie held her tight. "Let me go!"

"I need to have you near me now. I can see that you're getting all worked up. I'm afraid you'll get into even more trouble if you don't stay near me." Jackie was clear. Katie was going with her.

They came up the walk, Katie was resigned, still yelling that she didn't do "it," but without much confidence that she was going to get her way. Jackie opened the door and brought her to the table.

"Sit here for now, Katie," Jackie said calmly. Katie sat. Jackie went to the counter to begin preparing lunch. "I'll be checking with Dad to see how much it's going to cost to get that door fixed. I'm afraid that you're going to have some work to do to pay for it."

"I didn't do it!" Katie screamed.

"I'm fixing some tomato soup. We'll have cheese sandwiches, too."

"I don't want cheese!"

"No problems, sweetie, soup is a good lunch." Jackie didn't mind.

"I want baloney!"

"Only have tomato soup and cheese sandwiches today. But you don't have to eat it," Jackie said. She continued to prepare their meal when Diane and John came running in. They were dressed for swimming.

"Better hurry with your lunch, Katie," Diane said. "My friend, Susan, will be here in 15 minutes to take us to the lake."

"I'm afraid that Katie won't be going with you, Diane. She scratched the car door with a stone and she's going to have to do some jobs this afternoon to begin to pay for it," Jackie said with disappointment.

"I'm going swimming!" Katie screamed. It never had occurred to her that her scratching the door would prevent her from going swimming. This made no sense to her. She had been told at breakfast by Diane that she would take her! How could Jackie stop her from going? "I'm going swimming!"

"I wish that you could go. It would have been fun, it's such a nice warm day. But when you ruin something like the car door, you have to work to pay for it to be fixed. You'll have more chances to go swimming." Jackie showed empathy for her rage and confusion.

"I'm sorry that you can't go, Katie," Diane said. "I'll take you again when Mom says that you're ready."

"No!" Katie screamed and she lifted the soup spoon to throw it. Jackie was standing near and she knew to expect something like this. She reached over quickly and grabbed the spoon from Katie's hand.

"I hate you!" Katie screamed at Jackie and she jumped up to try to run from the room.

Jackie stopped her. "You need to sit at the table during lunch, sweetie. I know you're mad at me! That's OK. But you're too mad to be alone now. You have to sit here."

"No, let me go! I hate you!" Katie screamed again. When she tried to hit Jackie, her mom took her arm, pulled her to her, and sat down on the chair with Katie on her lap.

"Would you check the soup, Diane, please? And would you put the cheese away. Katie needs me to hold her now and help her with her anger."

"Let me go! Let me go!" Katie struggled to get loose. But she needed to re-main in Jackie's lap for a while after Diane and John left for the lake. Finally, when she calmed down, Jackie sat her in another chair. She then got her soup and sandwich and sat near her. "Do you want your soup or cheese sandwich now, Katie?" Katie ignored her. "This sure has been a difficult day for you so far and it's only 1:00."

That afternoon Katie spent her time with her new mom. Jackie had beans to pick in the garden and Katie helped, reluctantly. Jackie estimated that she worked for about 30 minutes of the time that they were in the garden. Then they did the laundry together with Katie sorting the clothes. Jackie chatted away as if they were on the best of terms. Katie said little, and that with effort. Jackie was pleased with herself. She was quite calm and engaged. Her patience was there, as was her empathy. But she thought to herself that it might be a re-ally long summer. This kid was not going to give up her way of living easily!

## COMMENTARY

From the moment that Katie entered her home, Jackie related with her as if she had lived with her for months. Jackie did not want to be "nice" to Katie during the first day and ignore her misbehaviors. She needed to demonstrate quickly what life would be like in her home. She did not do that in an au-thoritarian, harsh, manner. She simply commented on what was expected and she presented various consequences to Katie's choices depending on whether or not she met Jackie's behavioral expectations. She also was quick to express empathy for Katie's anger and distress, to remain accepting of her and in charge of her own emotional response to the "milk and crackers" incident. Jackie wanted Katie to know what she might expect in the months to come. If she "gave in" to Katie because it was her first day, Katie would expect her to "give in" forever. When Jackie finally began to assert the regular routines and expectations, Katie would think that Jackie was getting stricter. She would conclude that as Jackie got to know her more, she liked her less, and therefore that Jackie was becoming more mean to her.

Often when children with a history of trauma and attachment disorganization are restrained, they complain that they are being hurt. Assuming that Katie was not being hurt, there were various reasons for her to make that statement. First, she might have been trying to trick Jackie into letting her go. Second, she might have feared Jackie's control of her and she might have experienced vulnerability to being hurt. Third, she might have experienced a reenactment of a time when someone hurt her. When Katie said that she was being hurt, Jackie needed to first check to be certain that she was not accidentally hurting her. When she was certain that Katie was physically OK, she needed to express empathy for how frightening it must be to be held and not to be able to go. She then might imagine some of Katie's fears and reassure her that she was going to keep her safe and not hurt her. Jackie might also recall for Katie possible acts of abuse from her past that she was aware of in order to help her to recognize that the present situation is different and not abusive. However, it was too soon for Jackie to speak with Katie about her specific abusive history unless Katie initiated it.

Various brief courses instruct parents and childcare workers in techniques for safely holding children who need restraint. Many therapeutic foster care programs, residential facilities, and group homes for children and adolescents train their parents and staff in utilizing those techniques.

During the first therapy session, Allison established the general framework of the treatment. During the second session, she verbalized what Katie could expect to occur in therapy and what Katie would be asked to do. Allison made it clear from the outset that Jackie would be present during the sessions. The reasons for Jackie's presence are numerous. Jackie would be providing Katie with emotional support and she would be having opportunities for mutual enjoyment with her. Her presence would also help Katie to differentiate her from her birth parents and to carry over therapeutic experiences into the home. Jackie would also be available to address Katie's lies and excuses and to share her own thoughts and feelings about her. Allison would also use Jackie's presence to reinforce her parental authority to Katie and to communicate her confidence in her parenting abilities and in her commitment to her. Finally, her presence serves to provide safety to both Allison and Katie, while they are engaged in these intimate and stressful interactions.

During the first two sessions, Allison demonstrated that therapy would provide the setting for facilitating intersubjective experiences and for decreasing shame. She would initially establish a supportive atmosphere characterized by playful, empathic, and accepting interactions. Later she would explore shame-related themes in a way that would reduce Katie's sense of shame and make her more able to address and integrate these experiences. Allison initially spoke for Katie a great deal since it was most unlikely that Katie had the ability or motivation to speak for herself. In the first session, Allison focused most of the interactions on Katie's response to her. In the second session, she was beginning to direct Katie's attention and responses to Jackie more often.

As she would do throughout the course of therapy, Allison accepted Katie's resistance whenever it arose. When she asked for a specific response and Katie refused to give it, Allison gave it for her or she accepted and developed Katie's resistance. She wanted to communicate to Katie that she would remain engaged with her, doing this very difficult work, regardless of what Katie did to avoid engagement, elicit anger and frustration, or resist a therapeutic theme. Allison would not become angry with Katie nor allow her to avoid exploring these important themes. She understood the reasons for the resistance and she was patient. Throughout the sessions, she would be maintaining the same attitude in therapy that Jackie was maintaining at home.

Toward the end of the second session, Allison mentioned calmly to Katie and Jackie that the session might have been stressful for Katie and that she might find herself becoming angry and wanting to do something to get Jackie angry when they got back home. This happens frequently. As the child steps into an anxious way of relating and viewing self and other, she often seems to do something to suggest that she really does not want to change and that she is still the "bad kid" that she always was. By acknowledging that such a response may occur, it becomes less likely to occur or it may not last as long. Then the parent and therapist can calmly show empathy for the anxiety associated with change and make it clear that the progress that occurred during therapy or a home event was real.

After Katie scratched the car door Jackie became angry briefly, focused on the behavior, and then repaired the relationship. Certain behaviors do require a brief angry response. Caregivers should express such anger with "I-messages," focusing on the behavior and an alternative. For such a response to be effective, the parent needs to repair the relationship quickly as the child is moving just as quickly toward shame. With shame, the angry response to the behavior will have just the opposite effect. The behavior will be likely to increase.

Jackie made a mistake by allowing Diane to tell Katie in the morning that she would be taking her swimming in the afternoon. Such long waiting periods before something is to occur often create anxiety and the child frequently does something to make it less likely to occur. Also, if bad behavior or an outside circumstance cancels the scheduled activity, the child often experiences something close to betrayal. At this stage in Katie's placement, it would have been better to tell Katie that she could go swimming just before they were leaving.

# 9

## Life with Jackie

By July 12, Katie had managed to pay off her responsibility for the car door. She even was swimming with Diane some days. Of course she was supervised a great deal of the time. When Jackie or Mark was not actually watching her, they knew exactly where she was and what she was doing. They remained alert for any strange sounds or movements from Katie's direction. Katie's mood was unpredictable. If she wanted something, she was cheerful and helpful. Most of the time she was simply planning what to do next, while complaining about what she was doing now. She wanted to know everything that was going on. If Mark and Jackie were talking, she would be nearby until directed to wait in a specific chair. When the teenagers were around, she would constantly interrupt them or ask to be involved in their plans. She did not want to be alone. But she could not relax and enjoy herself when she was with any family member. Rather, her energy seemed entirely taken with finding ways to get something. When redirected, she would sulk and complain.

By now the teenagers were losing patience with her. Diane had given her some of her old dolls and Katie quickly destroyed them. She also had taken some money from Matthew's wallet and she had broken John's watch. They had begun avoiding her which meant that they spent less time with Jackie and more time in their rooms or out with their friends. Jackie had seen this happen before—just after Gabe had come to their home. His negative attitude soon affected the whole family. The atmosphere at home had become tense and angry and even she and Mark had begun to quarrel over numerous small things. They also had disagreed a lot over Gabe. Mark had thought that she was too strict with him because his misbehavior had led to days of high structure and supervision. Jackie wanted to be sure that Katie was not able to ruin their family atmosphere, too. If she could maintain her empathy, acceptance, and playfulness, while being loving and curious, then Katie's effect on the other family members would be less. Katie needed to become like their family at its best: friendly and helpful, relaxed and supportive. Each one in the family had their own space and interests. They also cared a lot for each other and everything else occurred in that context. They did not need to become like Katie. There was too much rage, terror, despair, and shame in the world already.

On August 4, 1994, Katie became seven years old. Allison and Jackie had discussed her birthday in the last therapy session. They knew that Katie would find a way to ruin it. There had not been one happy and fun activity since she had been in Jackie's home that had not left her tense, irritable, and in need of sabotaging. She would find something destructive or defiant to do either during the activity or immediately afterwards. Should Jackie give her the opportunity to do the same to her birthday? Would the brief "pleasure" of having a big party with nice presents be more beneficial than the shame that was sure to follow when she did something to ruin the day for herself and the family? Would the message conveyed by receiving the nice presents outweigh the shame that she would feel after she destroyed them? Should Jackie give her the chance to learn from the "natural consequences" of ruining her special day?

Jackie and Allison decided that she probably had experienced the "natural consequences" of destroying happy experiences and nice gifts and possessions dozens of times in her short life without showing any signs of learning from those compulsive acts. The odds that she would respond differently this time were extremely poor. Why set her up for failure at what should be a happy celebration of her life. It was hard to imagine that she could "celebrate" her life, given her self-contempt and her mistrust of everyone around her. Thus, Jackie and Allison decided to have only a small acknowledgment of Katie's birthday. Possibly that would not be too great a stretch for her and she would be able to successfully integrate it. Steven was not convinced of the wisdom of their plan. But as usual, he deferred to their judgment. It was left to Jackie to tell Katie.

At breakfast on the morning of August 4, Jackie had some time alone with Katie. Katie had not mentioned her birthday to her. Diane said that she had told her about it a few days before.

"Well, Katie, today is your birthday. You are seven years old! I hope that you have a happy day!" Jackie said cheerfully.

"Am I going to have a party?" Katie said with her innocent, lovely, facial expression that could even melt the heart of someone who hates kids.

"Not a very big one, honey. You get to pick the dessert tonight and your dad and I bought you a small gift. I thought that we'd sing "Happy Birthday" to you after dessert."

"Why can't I have a big party?" Katie asked. She seemed to be confused. Not really angry and certainly not sad. Just confused.

"Well, honey, your dad and I decided that you're not ready for a big party yet. I wish you were. We'd love to give you one and we're sad that we can't. It's just that when you have too much fun you do get all mixed up inside and then you do things to mess it up. We decided that it wasn't fair to you now to give you too much fun and we decided that what we're going to do would be just right for you now." Jackie was clear and calm and very receptive to Katie's mood.

"But it's not fair! Every kid gets a party! I did last year!" Katie was becoming upset.

"I know you did, honey. And Ruth said that you screamed and threw things after the party and had to be held. And the next day you broke all of the presents! You must have been so sad when you did that. We think that it would happen again if we gave you too many presents and you had too much fun." She believed what she was saying, but desperately wished that she could be saying something else.

"You don't like me at all!" Katie screamed.

"Oh, Katie, it must be hard now if you think that I don't like you. Wow! I'm your mom and if I don't like you, you would probably think that I won't keep you safe and no one will like you. I do like you, sweetie. And now that I've gotten to know you, I'm beginning to love you. I want to give you a big party and I'm really sad that I can't. I sure understand why you're mad at me and think that I don't like you. It must be hard for you to know that you're not ready for a big party and a lot of presents."

"I am ready!" Katie screamed.

"I wish you were, honey. It's sad that you're not ready yet," Jackie said quietly.

"I am ready," Katie said. Her anger seemed less. She seemed to withdraw into her thoughts. She did not seem to be planning to try to change her mind or to strike out at her. As Jackie watched her, she wondered if this were the closest thing to sadness that Katie could feel or show. She thought that if Katie were to begin to cry now, her resolve not to give her a party might evaporate. She'd be tempted to rush out and fill the car with presents and the biggest cake in Augusta. But it didn't happen. Katie didn't cry. She never did. And the car stayed in the driveway—which was for the best.

After their discussion, Katie acted as if nothing had been said and it were a regular day. As she usually did, she complained about restrictions and also about her chores, but she wasn't unusually upset. She had picked chocolate cake for dessert and she ate her piece as rapidly as ever. Katie could devour sweets faster than they could be served to her. She smiled at everyone when the family "quietly" sang "Happy Birthday" to her. After she opened her gift to find a jump rope and a bright blue swimming suit, she thanked everyone and seemed content. That night at bedtime, Jackie sat on the edge of her bed as she always did and talked quietly about the day.

"I enjoyed spending your birthday with you, Katie. I'm glad that you picked chocolate cake. That's one of my favorites, too."

"Can I have some more tomorrow?" Katie asked.

"Well, Katie, I know that there's some left, so I'll make sure some is saved for you so that you'll have some if you eat your dinner," Jackie replied. Then she added quietly, "You might feel mixed up about that jump rope and swimming suit, Katie. I know that it's hard for you to accept presents, even if they are small. I'll be happy for you if you don't have to destroy them. That would probably make you sad. But they are yours and it's up to you if you keep them safe or wreck them. If you want me to keep them for you so that you don't wreck them when you get angry, I'd be glad to do it for you."

"Can I wear my swimming suit at the lake?" Katie asked.

"Sure, sweetie, if you want. The next time you go swimming," Jackie replied.

Katie did not have anything else to say. She again seemed more distant and thoughtful than usual, but Jackie had no idea what she might be thinking or feeling. She did wear the swimming suit the rest of the summer. The jump rope disappeared. It would be a long time before Jackie would know whether it survived as a present that Katie could accept.

Jackie saw no signs of progress in Katie's functioning during the rest of the summer. She knew that she had to be careful not to expect continuous progress, but it was hard not to hope for signs of change each day. She had already made that mistake with Gabe early in the placement. When he did not show signs of improvement, she became discouraged and she began doubting her ability as a foster mother. Every day she found herself judging her own success as a parent on whether or not he "behaved." Allison had been able to help her to focus more on her own attitude and behavior, not Gabe's. She began to review how she had related with him and responded to crises and conflict. When she judged that she had cared for him in the way that he most needed for her to care for him, she was content regardless of his behaviors. By maintaining this outlook, she was able to be more accepting of him, and this was central to the progress that he eventually made. It also enabled Jackie to avoid following the mood and behavioral extremes that Gabe manifested. By remaining more stable herself, she was able to help him to reduce his extremes. This also prevented him from gaining control of her emotional life. She hoped to maintain this attitude with Katie and she generally was able to do so more often than she had with Gabe.

Early in the third treatment session, Allison focused easily with Katie on her daily routines as well as her moment-to-moment comments, facial expressions, gestures, sighs, and even the color of her socks. Without making demands on Katie, while at the same time relating with her in a light, gently teasing and relaxed manner, Katie became fully engaged in the immediate interaction.

Allison led Katie and Jackie to her desk and indicated that she wanted them to show their drawing abilities. She placed a large white paper on the desk and asked Jackie to sit down and then place her cheek on the paper. Allison asked Katie to trace Jackie's facial profile with a long pencil. On a second sheet of paper, Katie traced a second profile. She then cut out the two silhouettes and pasted one of them on a blue paper and the other on a red one. On the first silhouette, she filled in Jackie's face, with a large smile. On the second, she gave Jackie an angry look. Then it was Jackie's turn to trace Katie's profile twice, cut them out, and fill them in with happy and angry expressions. Allison then taped the four profiles on the back of the rocking chair and she asked Jackie to sit with Katie on the couch.

"There you both are—and there are TWO of each of you," Allison said. "Since BOTH of you can be BOTH happy and upset, I thought that we should be able to see what you look like both ways."

Jackie briefly "complained" that her nose was not as large as Katie had drawn it.

"Now I'd like to look at the homework that I gave you both last week. Katie was to draw a time when her mom seemed to be mean to her and another of a time that she seemed to be nice. Jackie was to guess what Katie drew and then draw her guesses."

When they were comfortably resting on the couch, Allison showed them the picture that Katie drew of a time when Jackie was being "nice" to her. The picture was of Jackie giving Katie some paper and crayons. Both figures were smiling, but there was little detail. They discussed the picture and Katie acknowledged that she liked Jackie when she gave her something. They turned to the second picture in which Katie saw Jackie as being "mean" to her. In this picture, Jackie was taking a game away from her. Katie drew Jackie as a very large and menacing figure, with large eyes and hands. Katie was small and sitting on the floor. In spite of Jackie's frightening posture, Katie appeared to be very angry, rather than scared. Katie told Allison that she does not like Jackie when she will not let her have something.

Allison handed Jackie some markers to give to Katie. They both smiled as Jackie placed them in Katie's hand. Allison directed Katie to thank her mother for the markers.

"Here, Katie, these are for you," Jackie said.

"Thanks, Mom."

"Do it again," Allison said. They repeated it three times, laughing at this activity that seemed quite silly to Katie.

"Now, Jackie. Tell Katie to give you the markers." Jackie did and Katie relinquished them to her, with less humor than was present during the first script. They repeated it again.

"Katie, tell your mom to give you the markers."

"Give them to me."

"Look her in the eyes and yell at her to give you the markers."

"Give them to me!"

"Again!"

"GIVE THEM TO ME!"

"Say, 'You never let me have anything!'"

"You never let me have anything!"

"You're mean to me!"

"You're mean to me!"

"You never give me anything!"

Katie repeated what Allison said, growing more animated with each phrase.

"Why are you always mean to me?"

"You think I'm bad!"

"You think I'm the baddest girl in the world!"

"I am bad!"

"WHY AM I SO BAD?"

Allison repeated the phrase again, this time with less intensity.

She noticed a few tears in Katie's eyes and she whispered it again. Katie responded. After a short pause, Allison quietly said, "Say 'I think I'm bad, Mom.'"

Jackie softly embraced her and whispered, "I thought that you thought that about yourself, Katie. I thought so. I'm sad for you. It must be so hard for you thinking that you're bad so often."

Katie immediately became uncomfortable and her body became rigid and she yelled, "Let me go!"

Jackie pulled back somewhat and said, "I guess you've had enough of this for today."

"I guess she has," Allison said. Then she turned to Katie and added, "I think you were kind of surprised at what you ended up saying. I can understand why you want to stop now. What you just did must have been hard."

"Stop talking!" Katie exclaimed again.

"Soon, Katie," Allison replied. "First, I'd like you to do one more thing with Jackie that's a little different and not so hard." Katie stared at her, waiting to hear what Allison was going to say.

Allison did not comment on Katie's few tears. The experience of intense affect was stressful for Katie and Allison did not want to push her into having an experience beyond what she thought that she could integrate. Attempting to go too far in the early sessions would prevent her from integrating important, though incomplete, glimpses into her inner life and they would not remain available to her as something to build on. Pushing her too hard would elicit a more global denial of the experience, which would make it harder for it to remain accessible to her in later sessions.

Allison took a marker and asked each of them to hold one of its ends. She suggested that they take a deep breath and smile before they began. Katie waited for a moment but smiled when Jackie did. Allison knew that she was ready to become engaged in a new activity.

"Now you two, I want you to pull the marker back and forth without letting it go," Allison said, "When the marker is close to you, Katie, you and I will yell, 'Thanks, Mom!' and when it is close to you, Jackie, Katie and I will yell, 'No!'"

Allison sat behind Katie, put her hand on her hand, and they pulled the marker toward them.

"Thanks, Mom!" they both yelled.

When Jackie pulled the marker back toward her, they screamed, "No!"

They pulled the marker back and forth, faster and faster. The first five or six times their yells were in time with the movement of the marker. After that, synchronization gradually eroded and their cries seemed to emerge randomly. Trying to get back the rhythm, Katie yelled "No!" three times in a row, while Allison was continuing to alternate her cry. With that, they finally all exploded in laughter.

As Allison sat back, they continued to laugh, with the three of them truly feeling merry all at the same time. This did not happen often with Katie.

Casually, Allison said as they came to rest, "You know, Katie, having a mom can get a kid—ALL MIXED UP. First she gives her something, then she takes something away. Then she gives, then takes away. Yes, No. Yes, No. What's a kid to think! It's almost like she has two moms, but there's only ONE! One, two, two, one, how confusing! You must have a Yes-and-No-Mom!"

"A Yes-and-No-Mom!" Katie chuckled.

"That's me!" Jackie exclaimed. "Your Yes-No-Yes-No-Yes-No-Mom!"

"Makes it hard for a kid to figure out, doesn't it, Katie kiddo?" Allison asked.

"Yeah."

"Well, kiddo, that's why we drew those two pictures of you both." Allison said. "You see, you are both Yes-and-No-People. When your mom says 'yes' she probably looks happy to you and 'good.' When she says 'no' she looks mean to you and 'bad.' And you, kiddo, when you feel happy, you have that smile and think you're 'good.' When you feel angry, you have that look, and you think that you're 'bad.'"

Allison allowed Katie to look at the pictures for a while. She then added, "You both did a great job with those pictures. We're going to be looking at them a lot so that some day, Katie, you won't be so MIXED UP about who you and your mom are."

## COMMENTARY

During sessions four through nine in therapy, Allison continued to engage Katie in a playful, accepting, and curious way. She explored current experiences and wondered what Katie thought and felt about them. She frequently raised other possibilities about what she might have thought or felt, while showing empathy that a girl with her early experiences would most likely think and feel as she did. Rage emerged toward her and toward Jackie when she discussed some shameful experiences that Katie wanted to deny. She returned a number of times to how mixed up she must feel, having a "Yes-and-No-Mom." She suggested that Katie might also have feelings of sadness and fear, but Katie usually rejected those ideas. Throughout the sessions, Jackie touched Katie a lot. She hugged her, played with her hair, tickled her, and made circles on her face. On a number of occasions, Allison gave Katie a hug. Katie was clearly tenser with Jackie hugging her than when Allison did. It was a beginning. At the end of a few of the sessions, Jackie read her a story. On some occasions, Allison played quiet music that helped to set a relaxed, mutually enjoyable mood. In general, Katie followed the directives set by Allison and tolerated a bit more easily the exploration of shame-inducing experiences.

Allison also spoke more about Katie's birth parents, Sally and Mike, in the therapeutic sessions. She spent some time covering what the DHS records said about Katie's first five years of life. Katie listened closely to the records and she even asked Allison to read over again some of the reported incidents. But, apart from the incident that actually brought her into custody, Katie seemed to remember very little about these crucial formative years. Allison, however, would be covering this period of her life again and again in treatment, usually in small amounts unless Katie initiated a longer discussion.

Katie would most likely gradually remember more about her years with Sally and Mike.

When Jackie informed Katie that she would not be having a party but only a small acknowledgement of her birthday, Katie's response took her by surprise. Katie showed more sadness than rage over this restriction. Since Katie's habitual response was to be outraged at the source of her frustration rather than to allow herself to feel sadness, Jackie rightly saw this as a step toward Katie learning to become aware of more of her inner life than her anger. If Katie could begin to notice her sadness or fear, she might gradually come to accept those feelings as well as her profound vulnerabilities. She might also begin to allow herself to feel the shame that permeated much of her waking life. What a goal—to help a child to access her inner life of sadness, fear, and shame. But what an important step if Katie was to ever reduce her denial, avoidance and rage. If she could confront such painful work, she would be likely to turn to Jackie for aid and comfort. Jackie would not be solely her antagonist; she also would be her guardian. But, one incident does not make a pattern. One pattern does not create a self. Jackie would have to be patient, and continue to with her therapeutic attitude, as Katie continued being whoever she was.

During the third treatment session, Allison wanted Katie to begin to be aware of the inherent nature of ambivalence in healthy parent-child relationships. Jackie was a Yes-and-No Mom because she gave Katie both nurturance and discipline, acceptance, and socialization expectations. Given that, it was not surprising that Katie would like her sometimes and dislike her at other times. It was almost as if Katie had two moms, a good-mom and a bad-mom. This psychological reality is present often in the world of the toddler who has not yet integrated these opposing experiences and internalized a coherent relationship with her one mom. It is also present in the world of abused and abandoned children, often for a much longer period of time.

Throughout most days, Katie engages in "manipulative" behaviors. Parents often respond to these behaviors poorly. They experience themselves as "being used" by the child. They experience the child as being deceitful and they experience the overall behavior as being "bad." It is helpful for parents if they are able to remind themselves that such "manipulative" behaviors were very adaptive when the child was living in circumstances of abuse and neglect. The child could not assume that the parent would naturally anticipate and meet the child's needs. She could not assume that if she made a direct request for something that she wanted and needed that the parent would respond positively. As a result, the child had to devise strategies for "tricking" the parent into meeting the child's needs. If the child did not become proficient in "manipulating" or "intimidating" the parent, she might have suffered unmet needs. Keeping this in mind is likely to help the parent not to respond to "manipulation" with rejection and anger or even consequences. "Manipulation" is likely to decrease if the parent is able to respond to it with a playful, accepting, curious, and empathic attitude. As the parent is able to increase the child's sense of safety and confidence in the good motives of the parent, the child will be more direct and open in her requests. In the meantime, the parent might simply acknowledge the apparent motive for the behavior and then grant or deny the hidden request.

# 10

## The Quilt

In mid-September, about two weeks after school had begun, an incident occurred that made it clear to Jackie how far Katie still had to go. It was Saturday morning, which meant that everyone was doing a few chores. Since Katie's readiness to do her work independently was still not evident to anyone, including Jackie, she, therefore, did her work wherever Jackie happened to be able to do it with her. Movable jobs, such as sorting laundry, dusting, and tidying up were ideal now. Jackie also might have her practice some school work or organize her bureau drawers. Katie's complaints about the need for her to stay near Jackie were less. Jackie was starting to imagine that she might be accepting it.

About 10:00 a.m., Whimsy started to bark and Jackie heard a car coming up the driveway. Judy Morris was stopping by. Judy was active on the Vassalboro School committee and one of her kids was a classmate of Matthew's. She had spent much of her spare time that summer working on a quilt that the school committee planned to raffle off at the Fall Festival that would start early in October. She was now bringing it to Jackie who would be responsible for displaying it at various community gatherings over the next month before the actual raffle.

Jackie brought Judy into the living room where she and Katie were working. She admired the quilt and showed it to Katie. They discussed the raffle and Jackie's plans to show it. Judy could not stay long and Jackie walked her to her car. They stood outside for a few moments to discuss a new after-school program and they planned to see each other the next week.

When Jackie returned to the living room, she wanted to admire the quilt again. Fear struck her immediately when she saw that it was not on the table.

Isn't that where she left it? Of course it was. Katie! She looked over at Katie, who was sorting socks on the living room floor. "Katie, where is the quilt?"

"I don't know," Katie replied, her standard response to most any question.

As she was about to address her again she saw the quilt on the couch, folded neatly as it had been on the table. Katie must have just wanted to look at it! She went to the couch and picked it up. Something was wrong! It was wet! Fear returned. Jackie was horrified. She knew what she had to do, but she was afraid. She raised it to her face and smelled it. Urine! It was urine! Katie had peed on it!

Jackie was in shock. She couldn't move. Tears came to her eyes. She wanted to scream and cry and erase the last 10 minutes from her life. How could she have done it? How could she have left Katie alone with this quilt? What could she say to Judy? What could she do?

First, she needed to clean the quilt before the pee really sank in. She knew that Judy had made it for "rough wear." She ran to the kitchen sink and she soaked it in warm water. She held it with the water running through the fabric. She squeezed the water out and did it over again and again. Her own tears mixed with the water running through the quilt. Finally, not knowing what else to do, she laid it out on towels spread out on the kitchen table. She would wait to tell Judy until after it had dried and they would know if there was any permanent damage.

She finally returned to the living room. Katie was still sorting socks although she could have been done long ago. She looked up at Jackie as if nothing had happened. "Can I have lunch now?" Katie said, without any hint of something being wrong.

Jackie got down on the floor, kneeling in front of Katie. She took her arms in her hands and leaned closer to her.

"Katie!" Jackie yelled. She was angry and Katie would know it. "I am very, very angry with you for peeing on that lovely quilt. That was a very mean thing to do to Mrs. Morris after all the work she did to make it. That was not fair to all the kids at your school who will not be able to do some special things if the quilt is ruined. And it was not right to do that to me since I'm responsible for it. I am angry with you. Members of this family do not treat other people that way! You are a member of our family. I am angry that you have done this to Mrs. Morris and to our family."

Jackie was watching Katie's response. She saw her usual guarded, resentful look that she often had when being confronted with her behaviors. But she also saw another look. Katie seemed to be both somewhat afraid of Jackie's anger but also pleased that Jackie was mad at her. Katie got Jackie mad! She was in control! And Jackie was finally telling her that she *was* a bad girl.

Jackie kept staring into Katie's eyes. She took a deep breath. This would be hard for Jackie to do but she needed to continue talking to her.

"Katie," Jackie said in a much quieter voice tone, "I love you, sweetie. I love you a lot and it's very important that I continue to teach you how important it is *not* to do things like this to people. I know that it's hard for you to learn this stuff, but since I love you, I'm going to keep teaching you until you get it." Jackie continued to stare into Katie's eyes. Katie now seemed to be more frightened than she was when Jackie was yelling at her. Katie seemed lost and afraid. Jackie reached over and gave her a hug. She continued to embrace her while her own tears came. She pulled back, staring into Katie's startled eyes. Katie was bewildered. She could not begin to understand or express the affect that now enveloped her. Jackie was crying just like her other foster mothers had done. But this felt different and she did not know why. Katie sensed that she was not in control and she was frightened. Jackie gave her one last hug. Then she got up and went into the kitchen.

Telling her that she loved her then was the hardest thing that Jackie had done since Katie came into her home three months before. It would have been so easy to keep yelling at her—and threatening her with having to move to another foster home if she ever did anything like that again. It would have been easy to look at her with disgust and either not touch her or else grab her arms tightly and squeeze them. If she did that to Katie, she would become like her birth mother, Sally. She would be telling her that Sally was right—she's not special, she's just a bad kid and nobody should bother with her. If she did that, she would be telling her that Katie's self-hatred was right, too. She *was* no good and there was *no* reason for her to try to learn how to live like the Keller family. She *never* would belong in their family or any other good family. Jackie would not do that. She knew that Katie had enormous amounts of shame for her behavior—for the self who did it—and very little guilt for the behavior itself. She had to reestablish a connection with her, not reject her. Katie would learn—feeling some empathy for hurting someone and then feeling some guilt and remorse. It was a question of when. Jackie would keep working. And crying.

That evening Jackie sat close to Mark on the couch. "I was so close to shaking her and screaming how bad she was for what she did. Gabe had never gotten me to feel so much anger. I kept thinking, 'What am I going to tell Judy?' I kept picturing the quilt having a big brown stain, and a smell that would make it unfit to put over a horse in the winter."

Mark never did talk much about his feelings but he was interested in Jackie's thoughts and feelings, listened well, and thought a lot about his family and his life. He was strong for Jackie when she needed him to be. He also was able to recognize that Jackie was strong for him when he needed her to be. At times, Jackie was not sure what he felt about things since he tended to understate what was on his mind. But she had learned to read him much better over the years. She knew that he chose his words with care; they represented what was most important, and thus, most private, to him. And Mark had learned to express his inner life more openly with words since it was important to Jackie. In doing so, he had discovered that he was more aware of himself.

"I'm sorry that this happened, honey. But you seemed to have handled it about as well as anyone could. I don't think that I could have been so understanding with her."

"If only I hadn't left her alone with it. What was I thinking?"

"You were thinking about Judy for a second. Is the quilt OK?" asked Mark.

"So far I think so," Jackie replied. "I'll be able to tell better when it's dry."

"You sure did a good job dealing with your anger with her," Mark said.

"Maybe, but I sure felt like rolling her up in that quilt and shipping her back to Steven."

"Would the post office take her?" Mark asked with a smile. After a moment he added, "If we're really keeping the kid, I want to be able to help more in any way I can."

"Thanks, honey," Jackie replied. "I know you do and believe me, you'll be the first to know if there's something else that you can do. Just promise never to take her side if she's complaining about me. Do that, and you get wrapped in a quilt, and the post office *will* take you, believe me."

"What else?"

"Mainly being here for me like you are now. How about if we also work out some times when you are 'in charge' and I can go out more with a friend. That would be nice."

In therapy that week, Jackie told Allison about the quilt and her response. Steven was present, although he now attended only one out of every three or four sessions. Allison felt sad for Jackie. She knew how difficult it must have been for Jackie to tell Judy about Katie's urinating on the quilt that she had worked on for weeks. And it had happened within 10 minutes after Judy had given it to Jackie! Allison focused on Jackie's feelings now, to see if she were able to maintain her therapeutic attitude toward Katie at this time. Allison knew that without that attitude, Jackie would be in no position to continue to raise Katie well and certainly in no position to be able to facilitate Katie's attachment security. Allison's first task each session was to focus on Jackie and her needs. Nothing that she could do with Katie would have any beneficial effect if Katie went home to a mom who wanted little to do with her.

"Jackie, I'm so sorry that happened. I know how hard it must have been for you."

"I was not a happy camper!" Jackie replied.

"No, I imagine that you were not a happy foster mother," Allison said quietly.

"Sure, I was mad at Katie," Jackie said. "But I was even more angry with myself. How could I have left the quilt alone with her? What was I thinking?"

"For a minute, Jackie, you were just being a regular mom in a regular home," Allison suggested. "It's so hard to be a therapeutic mom with a kid with Katie's troubles every second of the day."

Jackie seemed discouraged. Allison had not seen her this worn out since Gabe was in one of his very difficult periods.

"You're right, but it doesn't feel any better. With Katie I can't afford to 'forget' or she could really hurt someone or herself. If it were just more predictable! If I knew that she was upset about something, I would have known not to let her out of my sight. But she seemed OK. I can't think of anything that she might have been upset about!" Jackie was so frustrated.

"And there probably wasn't one specific thing upsetting her then. With kids like Katie, simply living makes them angry. Being who they are makes them ashamed. Being with people like you and not having a secure attachment with them makes them feel lonely and scared. She's sitting with nothing particular in her mind. Something special, like the quilt, is left near her. No adults around. Feelings burst from within her! Impulses follow that make them concrete. There's no healthy *self* to be aware of, monitor, and integrate those feelings and impulses. They have a life of their own. The excitement of getting even with you and everyone else in her life! The satisfaction of expressing her deep sense of being evil and worthless! The anticipated thrill of seeing you scream, or cry, or possibly even hit her. Those feelings exploded from within her when she saw that quilt, left alone with her."

"Why can't I remember that?" Jackie asked.

"Jackie, why aren't you a saint? Or a robot we could program to be 'correct' 100 percent of the time? You're a real person! You've probably given more to this kid in the past three months than anyone else has in the past seven years. She doesn't need a saint or a robot. She needs a mom who loves her. Who sweats for her? Who cries for her? And, at times, who gets angry with her. She doesn't need you to be perfect, Jackie. She simply needs for you to remain committed to her, find ways to enjoy her and teach her. And that's probably often harder than being perfect. I couldn't do what you're doing for her," Allison said, with compassion and admiration for this woman.

Jackie took a deep breath. There were tears in her eyes. "Thanks. I need to hear that once in a while." She blew her nose and laughed. "That little kid sure knows how to get to me. I could hug her one minute and strangle her the next. I know that you're right about what is going on under that angry mood and mean behavior of hers. If I didn't know that, I could never live with her for more than one day."

The three of them sat quietly for a moment. Then Allison suggested that she get "the kid" from the waiting room.

With Katie sitting next to Jackie on the couch, Allison began exploring with her some recent events in her life in the Keller home. It was immediately obvious to everyone present that Katie was not thinking about the quilt at all. It could have happened a year ago. It was as if someone else had been involved in peeing on it, not her.

Allison fairly easily got into her usual relaxed and playful manner of relating with her. At first, Steven had some trouble getting used to her approach with Katie. No matter what Katie had done, Allison always spent the first part of her interactions with Katie laughing with her, touching her, teasing her about something she said or did, challenging her to do something and then enjoying Katie's resistance, or doing something unpredictable and surprising that would leave Steven as confused as Katie as to what Allison was up to. Today was no exception. The quilt would obviously wait.

Steven noted Katie's response to Allison. As usual, she quickly fell in with Allison's playful, friendly, and interested manner. Katie was alert to Allison's every move and statement. She clearly enjoyed teasing Allison about her graying hair and she roared with laughter while screaming, "I will!" when Allison warned her not to tell anyone how many gray hairs she has. She would shriek when Allison would start searching for fuzz between her toes. She would squirm and moan at first when Allison would tell her that it was time for the "friend circle." With her finger, Allison would trace a large circle around Katie's face five times. Then she would gently tap her nose five times and finally kiss her forehead five times. Although she usually would express annoyance about that practice, Katie often found a way to "remind" Allison about it near the end of the session if she had not given her one. She would say, "I'm glad that you're not doing the 'friend circle' today." She then expressed great annoyance when Allison thanked her for reminding her of the need to demonstrate their friendship. Initially, Katie would wipe the circle and kisses off her face. Then Allison told her that "everyone" could see the "friend circle" and that it would remain on her face for one week if she did not wipe it off within three seconds after the last kiss was planted on her forehead. Allison then held her hands while she counted to three and she asked Jackie and Steven if they liked the circle. Both agreed that it was lovely and Katie expressed her usual annoyance. Jackie reported that later that day she noticed Katie staring at herself in the mirror, searching for the circle.

As she sometimes did, Allison began discussing one of Katie's "behaviors" without a pause. She simply moved from the playful and light content into the difficult area without any change in voice tone or general expression of enjoyment of Katie.

"Oh, Katie, your mom mentioned about your peeing on the quilt. I was a little mixed up. What made you decide to do that?"

Katie immediately tensed up and became annoyed. "Don't talk about it!"

"But, sweetie, it's something we need to talk about because I know that you and your mom have had a lot of feelings about it this week and that makes it important to both of you."

"It's not important to me!" Katie declared.

"Oh, I think it is. But I know it's hard for you to talk about. No problem. I can help," Allison said in a matter of fact tone.

"I don't want your help!" Katie screamed.

"Great, Katie, say that again!" Allison raised her voice.

"I don't want your help!"

"Great job, Katie!" Allison's words matched Katie's in intensity and cadence. Allison then leaned closer to her and spoke quietly and slowly near her ear. "I know that taking our help is hard for you, sweetie. But you need it so much. And your mom loves you and I like you a lot, so we're going to keep helping you to have a happier life."

Katie screamed, "No!" Allison had pulled her chair close to the couch in front of Katie and Jackie. Katie tried to kick Allison and Jackie reached over and pulled her to her. She put her arms around her and held her hands. Katie tried to kick as she screamed at Jackie for holding her.

"Oh, you're mad at me!" Allison yelled, again matching the intensity of Katie's "No!" "You want to kick me and hit me. You want to never see me again! You really are mad at me now!"

"Shut up! Shut up! Shut up!" Katie screamed as she continued to try to find some way to escape Jackie's hold.

"You want me to shut up!" Allison continued to speak loudly to Katie. "You want me to stop talking to you about how mad you are at me, and at your mom, Jackie." Allison waited for a pause in Katie's thrashing and she continued, now much more quietly, "But I need to keep talking, sweetie, because I know that you're a sad and scared little girl, and you don't like yourself very much."

Allison's quiet tone and her moving the focus toward her vulnerabilities, mobilized Katie's rage again, but now with her voice, rather than efforts to kick or hit. "I do like myself!" she screamed.

"Say it again!" Allison said loudly.

"I DO LIKE MYSELF!" Katie now had tears running down her cheeks.

"One more time." Allison said more quietly again.

"I do like myself."

Katie was barely moving. She was not looking at Allison. She was lost somewhere in the despair of her past.

Allison leaned forward and whispered into Katie's ear, "I wish you did, sweetie. I want to help you to really like yourself." Katie began to shake as the tears continued to flow down her cheeks and onto Jackie. Jackie hugged her tighter and Katie squeezed her in return. Jackie began to rock slowly, while holding her closely.

Allison and Steven sat motionless, watching Katie and Jackie, not wanting to disturb the mood. They had never seen Katie cry before this moment. Jackie now knew that what had happened around the quilt was important to Katie after all. Her empathy for Katie became strong again.

"Katie, Katie, Katie," Jackie said quietly as she rocked slowly in her arms.

Allison waited until she became quiet and then she told Katie to open her eyes and look at her mom. When Katie did, she immediately noticed that Jackie had been crying, too. She stared at her for a moment, and then Allison said, "Now, Katie, say to your mom, 'Mom, I'm sorry for peeing on the quilt.'"

Immediately Katie said to Jackie, "Mom, I'm sorry for peeing on the quilt." She began crying again, and Jackie embraced her again. "I'm glad for you that you're sorry, Katie. I'm glad for you. And I'm glad for us now. Our hearts are together now," Jackie said quietly.

Moments of silence supported their continuing embrace and affirmed what had just occurred.

Allison spoke quietly, "This kid is a hard worker, Jackie. I can see why you love her a lot."

"Yes, she is," Jackie replied. She then took some tissue and began wiping the tears from Katie's face and from her own. Katie watched her without moving.

"I need a tissue, too, I guess all three of us had a lot of tears that needed to come out," Allison said.

Katie looked over at Steven. "He did, too. Steven cried, too."

"Yes, he did, Katie. We all know how hard this is for you. We all get sad when we see how hard you have to work to have a happier life," Allison said.

All of them, including Katie, were enjoying the quiet of the moment.

Allison gently asked Katie, "What is your consequence, sweetie, for peeing on the quilt?"

"Mom said that I have to help clean the house. I even have to wash the kitchen floor." She then turned to Jackie, seeming to have a new thought. "Do I still have to do it, Mom?"

Jackie smiled, "Yes, you do, honey. But don't worry. I'll make sure to show you how to do it right."

Allison smiled and said to Katie, "Say, 'Thanks, Mom!'"

Katie smiled and thanked Jackie and they all laughed. They then spent some time checking to see who had the stickiest tears. They agreed that Steven's were the stickiest, which meant that he had to get glasses of water for the other three.

At the end of the session, Steven waited a few minutes to talk with Allison, a habit that he found to be very helpful in understanding Katie. "I think you really got somewhere with her today, Allison."

"Important experiences did occur for her. But they will not stick unless we are able to create for her hundreds of similar experiences, in therapy and at home, in the months ahead. She needs to share many, many such intense affective experiences with Jackie before she will begin to believe that she is a good kid, and that her mother's love is a wonderfully important, pleasurable, and healing reality for her."

"Before we started with Katie, you spoke with Jackie a lot about her feelings toward Katie after the quilt incident. Did you think that she was going to ask her to leave?" Steven asked.

"No, but I wanted to be sure she was able to get back the therapeutic attitude that she needs if she is going to be able to help Katie's attachment with her. It takes two to develop a secure attachment."

"I see what you mean. I know what you're talking about," Steven said. "You were able to show The Attitude in therapy today."

"I try to, Steven, or I don't think that I would be able to help her. She needs to have adults relate to her in that way, as much, or even more than, your daughter Rebecca does. Without those intersubjective experiences, she never will attach to Jackie and she never will begin to have a healthy 'self' that she likes. With these experiences—her experience of our experience of her experience— enable her to discover parts of herself that have never seen the light of day. It's easier to keep this attitude in therapy than it is at home, hour after hour," Allison said.

"Well, I better get going. I'm glad you spent the time supporting Jackie. She seemed to need it."

"She did. And because she did, Katie needed to have me help Jackie before trying to help her," Allison replied.

"Makes sense to me," Steven replied.

As Steven headed toward the door Allison said, "I saw some ancient wisdom on a T-shirt once."

"What's that?" Steven asked.

"It said, 'If Mom ain't happy, ain't nobody happy.'" Allison replied.

Steven smiled. He might just stop on the way home and get Jenny some flowers.

On the way home from therapy, Katie asked Jackie if they could stop at McDonald's for a snack. Since they never had gone there after therapy and because Katie had long since stopped asking, Jackie assumed that Katie wanted a reward for her work in therapy. Katie knew that the adults liked what happened in therapy so she might use it to her advantage.

"No, sweetie," Jackie said. "I'd like to get on home like we usually do."

"I want some french fries," Katie yelled.

"I'll bet you do, Katie, you worked hard in therapy and I imagine you might be hungry."

"Then get me some."

"I'll find you an apple or orange when we get home."

"No, I want french fries."

"It sure is hard for you sometimes when I won't give you what you want."

"Get me some french fries!" For emphasis, Katie slammed her foot against the dashboard. Jackie immediately pulled the car over to the side of the road.

"Katie, I sure understand why you're mad at me for not stopping at McDonald's. You can tell me about your anger, but you can't kick the car."

"I don't care. I hate you."

"That's the idea."

"I'm glad that I peed on that quilt!"

"I'm sure that part of you is glad, sweetie."

"You're not my mom! I hate you!"

Jackie was silent. The kid certainly was using words to express her rage over being deprived of her french fries. She probably was also telling her that everything that she felt and said in Allison's office was a lie. Katie didn't want hugs, she wasn't sorry, and she didn't want anyone to help her, especially Jackie. Katie was frightened, she had revealed a lot in therapy, to Jackie and to herself. She now was trying to minimize or deny her earlier expressions. Jackie thought about conveying empathy for how confused and scared that Katie must be now, but she decided that this was not the place to do it. She did not want to have to search for Katie in the woods. Nor did she want to spend the next few hours sitting in the car with a snotty kid. She decided that silence would be in her own best interest.

After about five minutes of quiet, Jackie decided to continue on her journey home. She guessed right. Katie did not have the energy to fight further. She pouted the rest of the way home.

The next day Steven called Jackie to see how Katie was doing. He expected that the therapy session would have brought about some changes for the better. He was surprised to hear about the car ride home. He was further disappointed to hear that when he called, Katie was kneeling on the stairs, washing off the pee. Early that morning, she had stood at the top of the steps and peed down them.

"It must have been quite a waterfall," Jackie said with her dry sense of humor.

Steven was frustrated. Would Katie ever change? Why would she do that?

"Steven, she has a long way to go," Jackie said calmly. "I knew what I was in for. She can't take giant steps. Yesterday's session was important, but I imagine only a small part of it will stick. She needs many experiences like that, with me and with Allison, before we can hope to see real change. I am hoping that washing down the stairs after peeing on them will be another experience that will also help the process."

"How will that help?" Steven asked, wondering how Jackie could consider it similar to yesterday's therapy session.

"Katie is saying that the therapy session was all a lie and that she's no different. I'm going to accept her action and accept this part of her, too. If I get angry and discouraged now, she will be able to minimize the session. She'll convince herself that even I don't believe that what she showed yesterday is real! It's as if she is searching for shaming experiences to convince herself that she's still bad. By responding with soap and water, along with The Attitude, I'm showing her that I do think therapy was real, just as the part of her that peed down the stairs is real. I am still connected to her. I'm going to be the same, in responding to both parts. Hopefully, someday the part of her that we saw in therapy will be a lot stronger and she'll be able to bring both parts together."

"I'm glad that she didn't pee on my stairs, Jackie, I don't think that I'd be so understanding," Steven said with admiration for her.

"Once you got used to trying to raise a kid like Katie, you would. Or else you couldn't keep doing it. And I'm not a martyr. I do get a lot of satisfaction when I see that frightened and sad little girl inside of her take a few steps into the sunlight."

Steven told Barbara and Al about Katie's behaviors in therapy and afterwards. He needed to sort out his thoughts about her. He concluded that he really did not know Katie. That "part" of her that was so angry and destructive, and . . . *mean*, seemed to have a life of its own. Would they get through to her? A larger question was who was the *her* that they were trying to find? When they found *her,* would they be pleased or frightened? Did this *her* even exist?

Steven decided that if he thought about Katie anymore right now he would only worry more. He turned to his paperwork. That would calm him down. He could lose himself in the words and rules. He could avoid experiencing the profound terror, rage, and despair that many of his foster kids faced every moment of their lives. For him, paperwork did the trick. For Katie, it was kicking dashboards, peeing down stairs and on quilts, and eating french fries.

That weekend Steven and Jenny decided to work outside. They had been busy canning the tomatoes and beets the previous few weeks and it was time to put the garden to bed. It was a clear and cool autumn day. By far, this was their favorite season of the year.

Rebecca was now 20 months old! What a free spirit! She walked fast and she ran faster. Which means that she fell as often as she saw something new to explore. Certainly, the task of cleaning the garden held endless opportunities for adventure. Dirt and stones, plants and weeds. Things to grab and break open, taste, and throw. She found the cherry tomatoes, which were a favorite of hers when she spotted them in her salad. And now there seemed to be millions of them! Just hanging from the branches waiting for her fingers and lips. Her face was soon red, her parents were busy deciding how many she could safely consume without creating havoc in her sensitive stomach, and Jenny decided to get the camera to record one of the many moments of Rebecca's life that Alice had insisted should not be lost to future generations.

Steven hauled more plants to the wheelbarrow and turned to see if Rebecca had reached her limit. His red-faced child was careening through the garden toward him with a giant smile on her face and the trowel in her hand. Without thought his heart stopped and his voice shouted, "Rebecca, stop!" while he visualized her falling and striking her face with the trowel. A heartbeat later he leaped toward her, her smile disappeared, her legs stopped and a startled expression covered her face. By now, Steven was next to her and he reached down and quickly removed the trowel from her hand. Her eyes met the tension and fear in his face. Her mouth quivered, she sat heavily on the ground, and her face turned away from him and down toward the ground. A cry erupted from her lips.

Steven tried to console her as he picked her up but she arched her back and looked and turned her shoulders and face away from him. Just then, Jenny came running up with her camera and Rebecca heard her and turned in her direction. She reached up her arms and almost flung herself out of Steven's arms. She wanted Jenny with as much force and need as she had ever shown. With the same degree of intensity, she did not want Steven!

Jenny took Rebecca and held her tightly. She spoke in her calming and reassuring voice as her daughter shook and sobbed in her arms. She walked around the garden slowly, holding their clinging child.

Steven watched them. He was relieved that Rebecca had not gotten hurt. He could understand that he had frightened her and that she now needed her mother. He needed to have her understand that he had not been mad at her. He had yelled and scared her because he was frightened for her. Maybe he could have managed it differently but his motive was to keep her safe.

Jenny quietly told Rebecca how Steven had been frightened because she was running with the trowel. She explained that he had not been angry with her, just frightened for her. Rebecca seemed to peek out from over Jenny's shoulder at her dad. Jenny walked slowly toward Steven. He reached out toward his daughter and, after a moment's hesitation, she came into his arms. He hugged her, reassured her, and found her eyes. She smiled and pointed toward the cherry tomatoes. He carried her to the nearest plant and they sat on the ground. She pulled one ripe tomato off the plant and fed Steven. He fed her. Now Jenny had another photo opportunity.

Rebecca lost interest in the tomatoes and Steven and wandered off toward the cucumber vines. Steven sat there watching her. Just a routine event in a routine day with the two most important beings in his life. She often got upset with him or Jenny. She wanted to touch and hold so many things wherever she found herself. She did not take "No" lightly. She seemed surprised whenever her parents thwarted her desires. Especially when they got upset over something that she had done.

He sat for a few minutes more. Rebecca had felt shame! Of course, that was an example of what Allison and Jackie had been discussing. Certainly, Rebecca had experienced shame on numerous occasions but this was the first time that Steven actually connected her distress to what Allison had so often talked about. And Rebecca's shame was brief and left suddenly as her parents comforted her. That is what Katie experienced every moment of her life. Shame defined Katie's existence. Rebecca had simply integrated shame, and later guilt, into her developing sense of self and her relationships with her parents. They were vehicles for learning limits to self-expression, the need to integrate one's own wishes with the desires of others, and the necessity of considering the consequences of one's acts. For Katie, her pervasive shame was not such a vehicle. Shame proved her worthlessness. She could not learn from it; she wanted to destroy it through her rage. She needed to conceal what it said, for it said that she was unwanted on this earth.

## COMMENTARY

Katie's urination on the quilt created the first crisis in her placement. Such incidents are certain to happen in any placement with a child who is manifesting the effects of trauma and attachment disorganization because such children are experts at sensing what will infuriate their parents. With that awareness, they do not avoid those behaviors, rather, they embrace them. They have a compulsion to recreate their early experiences of rejection, abuse, and disgust directed at them from their parents. They actively seek that sense of being worthless that such shaming experiences create within them. Feeling worthless affirms the reality of the "hated self" and destroys any reason for trying to form a relationship with Jackie. There could be no way that Jackie could love her. Or, if she had loved her, there could be no way that she would continue to do so once she really saw how bad she was. Katie would put a stop to the placement herself, on her terms, rather than wait for Jackie to do it. That it would end, either through rejecting Jackie or being rejected by her, was inevitable.

Therapy began, as it always did, with Allison talking with Jackie about how Katie was functioning at home. This enabled Allison to know how both Katie and Jackie were doing. After the incident with the quilt, it was crucial for Allison to focus on Jackie and her immediate emotional response to what had occurred as well as her current thoughts and feelings about it. If Jackie was not able to maintain her therapeutic attitude toward Katie, progress would stop and the placement would be in jeopardy. Allison needed to attend to Jackie's needs if they both were to be able to address Katie's needs. Allison also valued Jackie for herself, not simply as Katie's foster parent. She needed to communicate that Jackie's well-being was important to her and her distress would receive her full attention, before turning to Katie. In working to facilitate the attachment between Jackie and Katie, Allison needed to communicate that they were both important to her. Allison must not forget Jackie.

The therapy session at least temporarily derailed Katie's quest to terminate the placement. Allison had led her, through pacing her affective experiences, from her rage and her resistance to help, to her self-rejection and despair. She cried, with deep sadness, something that she had not done in years, and she became receptive to the healing and caressing words and touch from Jackie and Allison. In spite of her self-loathing and her distrust of feeling close to others, she felt their comfort and warmth and she could not deny or refuse the experience. But, of course, it had to end and her habitual mode of experiencing herself and others returned quickly and forcefully. She now felt a compulsion to invalidate what had occurred in therapy and she did so in the car after therapy, and by peeing on the stairs the next morning at home. Jackie's acceptance of Katie's attempts to sabotage the therapeutic experience was crucial in preventing Katie from minimizing its validity. Jackie was maintaining her affective connection with Katie in therapy, but also in the car and while she supervised her washing the stairs. The soap and water, applied with Jackie's therapeutic attitude, maintained the validity of Katie's tears.

Jackie's response to Katie for peeing on the quilt raises the important question of what a therapeutic parent needs to do with her anger at her child. For good reasons, the *attitude* that these children need if they are to learn to trust their new parent does not include anger. Katie's early life with Sally and Mike was permeated with rage directed toward her. Such rage contained rejection, contempt, and disgust and served as the cement for the foundation of her self-contempt. That rage had nothing to do with her behavior or with healthy socialization experiences. How can a therapeutic parent express anger without triggering a cognitive and affective response that lies within that old template for defining self and other?

Jackie expressed anger without calling Katie names, threatening her, or expressing contempt for her. Jackie used "I-messages," connected her anger toward the specific behavior, and stated why the behavior was not acceptable to her. She immediately followed her anger with a gentle expression of her love for her and her commitment to teach her how to live well in her family. This expression served to repair the relationship that her anger had threatened. Jackie's tears conveyed both her anger at the behavior, but also her fear for Katie's future, a fear interwoven with her love for her. Jackie was communicating her continuing commitment to Katie. Through Jackie's complete response, Katie was not able to simply interpret the experience as proof that she was bad and that Jackie was disgusted with her. Katie engaged more in their relationship and in what her action and Jackie's response said—both about her worth and the meaning of Jackie's love for her. The experience was unsettling to her and it made her more receptive to her underlying terror and self-contempt when Allison explored the incident in therapy.

Jackie expressed her anger very quickly and immediately followed it with efforts to repair the effects of her anger on their relationship. Without repair, Katie would be likely to enter her pervasive shame states, which would only make her more likely to engage in similar behavior in the future. With repair, there is some possibility of eliciting guilt over her behavior, which would reduce that likelihood.

At times, every parent, including therapeutic parents will be having an especially hard day. They will be irritable and impatient and will have difficulty maintaining The Attitude consistently throughout the day. Even their usual methods of self-motivation that get them through such days and enable them to still respond quite well to the attachment needs of their child are ineffective. On those days, the parent needs to face the truth, accept the reality that she has little empathy for others, especially her child who is persistently misbehaving, and take care of herself. If possible, she might ask another adult to assume the primary role of caring for her child. If not possible, she might structure the day so that less interaction is required and the routines in place are likely to reduce the probable conflicts.

Parents also need to "own" their affect, and not project it on their child. Rather than saying, or even thinking, "You're making me mad!" they need to be able to say to themselves and their child, "I don't have much patience today. I'm in a grouchy mood. It has nothing to do with you, but I thought that you should know it so that if I get angry, you'll know where it's coming from." Or the parent might say, "I'm kinda angry and grumpy today, so I need to spend some time alone. It has nothing to do with you, and don't worry, I'll get over it. But you might give some thought as to whether or not it would be smart for you to make a lot of bad choices today."

Steven's experience in the garden with Rebecca contrasts the normal and brief experiences of shame that occur repeatedly within a healthy parent-child relationship, with the pervasive shame that Katie had constantly experienced. When Rebecca ran to Steven with the trowel, she experienced much excitement and she anticipated a response from Steven closely attuned with her own affective state. His clearly misattuned response to her affective state caused her shame. Her sense of self found no validation. It felt smaller and less special. She immediately withdrew into herself, physically and psychologically. Jenny and Steven immediately provided her with reassurance that she is special to them. They attuned to her distress and they enabled her to experience the security of the attachment from which she could again know that her self had value. Through interactive repair, her parents were able to convey to her the meaning of the experience. Its intention was to socialize, to show the danger of running with a sharp object. Her parents' motives did not indicate that they hated her or that she was bad. Rather, their motives indicated how truly special she was to them through their commitment to keep her safe.

# 11

---

# Fighting with Jackie

At the start of the next therapy session Jackie told Allison about how intense Katie's resistance had become. "She is looking for every chance that she can to have a fight with me. Her arguing is more intense. She's doing a lot of staying close to me since she does not want to follow the most basic expectations. Yesterday I asked her to hand me the paper that was next to her and she refused. She even yelled at Diane, something that she rarely does."

"My guess is that the incident with the quilt as well as our last session really bothered her," Allison said. "She cried and she let you support her. She also felt her self-hatred. Now she might be looking for a way to make the statement that she is bad and that she doesn't want your support. Besides, she believes that you don't really want to give it to her anyway. She wants to wear you down."

"Her comment that she was glad that she peed on the quilt did not endear her to me," Jackie said.

"No, I imagine it didn't," Allison smiled. "Well, if she's making a statement to us, I guess that we have to make a statement to her."

"What's that?" Steven asked.

"She's got to hear that we are going to help her because she *is* the kid whom we care for. She's going to hear that we understand and accept her decision to fight our help. She's also going to hear that we're not agreeing with her sense of worthlessness. She is going to hear that the parts of her that we see and respond to are real," Allison replied.

"How can you accept her decision to fight and still disagree with her?" Steven asked.

"We have empathy for her fear and resistance that motivates her fighting. We'll actively communicate our empathy—we'll share her distress—by letting her know that we understand how hard this is for her, given her past. In fact, we'll be trying to show her that her actively fighting us now is a measure of how hard she is actually working to make some sense of her life. She's fighting to maintain the view of the world that she learned from Sally and Mike. We'll understand her need to do this, but we'll keep making it harder for her by continuing to show her another world. This world is based on maternal love for her, enjoyment of her, commitment to continue to reach out to her when she is covered with shame, and confidence in her ability to eventually agree with us as to what is in her best interests." Allison stopped, knowing that it was easier to talk about this than actually do it. "Well, why don't I get the kid."

"Well, Katie kiddo, you look kinda perky today," Allison said as Katie sat between her and Jackie on the couch. "Your hair looks extra curly, your nose looks kinda bouncy, and your freckles look kinda bossy. Is that right?"

Katie smiled in response to Allison's smile and friendly tone of voice. "My nose isn't bouncy!" She laughed.

"Oh, no! Let's see." Allison took her forefinger and lightly bopped her nose twice. "Yes, it is! I knew you were extra perky today."

"No, it isn't!" Katie yelled, now smiling even wider.

"Oh, Katie, I can tell by how much you want to disagree with me that you're extra perky," Allison said, running her hand over Katie's hair.

"No, I don't!" Katie said.

"You are so great at arguing, Katie. You do it without thinking," Allison replied.

"No, I don't!" Katie laughed.

"You're so good at it I'm going to give you a hug." As Allison did so, Katie shrieked. They were both laughing now. Katie smiled and looked into Allison's eyes. Allison was often surprised how easy it was to initially engage most of the children with trauma/attachment problems that she saw. She would set a playful, accepting, and curious tone and most kids most of the time would spontaneously follow wherever she led. She knew that it was much more difficult for Katie to do it at home, hour after hour, with mom, the woman she most resisted. She also knew that therapy with these kids needed to begin with those playful attuned experiences, but it needed to go far beyond those. It needed to address her negativity and shame if she were to be able to integrate these aspects of herself with the parts that were easy to elicit in therapy. Without such integration, whatever experiences that she had in therapy, no matter how enjoyable, would not continue beyond the moment that Jackie limited her or told her to do something that she did not want to do.

As she often did, Allison related with Katie in a quieter, less joking manner that also was mutually enjoyable. She told Katie of a recent adventure that her cat had with a raccoon. It was usually easy to maintain her interest in stories. Jackie joined in with a tale of how Diane and Katie raked the leaves around the house and eventually had a pile of leaves so high that they buried themselves in them and Jackie and Mark had the hardest time finding them.

"Sounds like you had some fun this week, Katie. Jackie told me that you had a lot of hard times, too. She said that you were unhappy much of the time." Allison maintained her accepting and curious tone while noting Katie's sudden tension and withdrawal. "I felt sad when I heard what a hard week you were having. It seems like just about everything at home has been bothering you. Anything we could do to help?"

"Nothing's bothering me," Katie said firmly.

"I wish that were so, honey. But when you need to be near your mom a lot, I think that you must feel kinda grumpy."

"I do not!" Katie replied. Just as her playful and friendly manner of engagement had been total, now she was completely annoyed, without any sign that she had been laughing one minute earlier.

"Say it loudly then, Katie," Allison said. "Say, 'I do not feel grumpy!'"

"I do not feel grumpy!"

"Good job, Katie, now say to your mom, 'Leave me alone!'"

Katie looked at Jackie and said, "Leave me alone!"

"Now say, 'I don't want your help!'" Allison said, matching Katie's speech tone and intensity.

"I don't want your help!"

"You don't love me anyway!"

"You don't love me anyway!"

"Katie, say, 'You're just like Sally!'" Allison said rapidly.

"You're just like Sally!" Katie followed Allison's lead, but now braced tensely.

"I don't want any mom!" Allison said, again matching Katie's intensity.

Katie did not say anything. Allison quietly said, "That's OK. I'll say it for you." Allison again said, "I don't want any mom!" This time she spoke with a more child-like voice. She continued to talk for Katie, watching her facial expression as she did so.

"I'm too scared to love a mom," Allison said, quickly, but much more quietly.

"I'm afraid that you'll hurt me," Allison was almost whispering.

Allison rested her hand on Katie's shoulder and said quietly, "Good job listening, Katie. I know that those are some of your feelings and they are hard to talk about. Or even think about."

Katie was quiet. Allison continued, "It must be hard to think that every mom won't care for you. . . . No wonder that you have a hard time . . . letting yourself get close to this mom." Allison spoke slowly and quietly. Her hand moved on Katie's back in rhythm with her words.

"Tell Jackie, Katie, that it's hard to get close to her," Allison said, still quietly.

"No!" Katie screamed.

"Then say, 'I don't want to tell her that!'" Allison said quickly, matching Katie's intensity.

"I don't want to tell her that!" Katie responded.

"I don't want to get close to her!"

"I don't want to get close to her!"

"Good job, Katie. I know that . . . most of the time . . . you don't want to be close to Jackie. It's so hard . . . after the way Sally treated you . . . for . . . so . . . long." Allison spoke slowly and quietly again. Katie barely moved. Allison could generally tell when a child was being receptive to what she was saying. She knew from Katie's relaxed muscle tone and good eye contact that she was listening.

"I don't know why Sally did not love you in ways that you needed, Katie. Maybe she has lots of problems that make it hard for her to be a mom. But I know that . . . it . . . hurt you . . . a lot. Sally hardly ever showed you . . . that you were special to her . . . that you were lovely to her. She hardly ever . . . played with you . . . and touched . . . your face . . . and ran her fingers over your arms . . . and fingers. . . . No wonder that you don't want a mom. When you were a baby . . . you needed a mom . . . so much! . . . You needed your mom and she didn't often enough act like a mom should act. You must have been . . . so sad!" Allison continued to run her hand over Katie's back and shoulders. Katie continued to listen.

Without changing her voice tone and pace, she continued to soothe Katie with her hand while talking with Jackie, "I know . . . that you know, Jackie . . . how hard it was for Katie when she was a baby. Sally did not hold her enough . . . and play with her enough . . . and rock her enough the way she needed. No wonder she gets mad at you a lot, Jackie. She's still mad at Sally for not being the mom that she needed often enough."

"I agree. I know that it's hard for Katie to let herself like me and trust me. I know that she often really does not want me to be her mom."

"Are you mad at her for her anger at you?"

"No. I know why she gets mad at me a lot. I can handle it OK"

"Are you going to stop loving her?"

"No, I do love Katie and I don't plan to stop."

Katie remained motionless. She was listening to Allison and Jackie.

Allison looked again at Katie. She said quietly, "Katie, while you sit there, I'm going to draw a picture."

Allison began drawing a series of pictures of Katie beginning with when she was a baby with Sally and Mike and ending with her at seven years of age and living with Jackie.

"In this first picture, you were a happy and loving baby. See, there's your heart. It was working well and hearts are for loving. Then in this picture you can see that your heart was starting to get cracks in it. It was loving but not getting much love back so it was being hurt every day. In this third picture, you can see that you're older and bigger. Here you can see how you built a wall around your heart to protect it from being hurt more. See, none of the hurt can get through the wall. It was a really great way to protect your heart and try to keep yourself safe." Allison paused and watched Katie study the pictures.

Then she continued, "The problem with your plan to use the wall to keep your heart safe is that the wall also keeps out love. See, when you went into your foster homes, you weren't being hurt anymore so you really didn't need your wall. But it is hard to take it down now. So when your foster parents tried to love you, you didn't feel it! The wall caused the love to bounce away from your heart. No wonder that you often don't feel that Jackie really loves you. No wonder you don't trust her!"

"Now, Katie," Allison could see that Katie was very attentive, "we have to figure out ways to help you to take the wall down. You don't need it anymore, but it's very hard to take down."

After a considerable pause, with Katie remaining responsive and quiet, Allison said, "Do you want our help to take down the wall, Katie?"

"Yes," Katie replied quietly.

"Great, sweetie, with you wanting our help it will be a lot easier for us to really be helpful." Allison placed her hand on her shoulder again.

"Now, Katie, there's some more hard work to do. Are you ready?"

Katie replied that she was.

"Good, then look at that mark on the wall by the lamp. Pretend that you're looking at Sally. Good. Now say to her really loudly, 'I'm mad at you, Sally!'"

"I'm mad at you, Sally!"

"You didn't take care of me very well!"

"You didn't take care of me very well!"

"You hit me and called me names!"

"You hit me and called me names!"

"You let Mike hurt me!"

"You let Mike hurt me!"

"I'm mad at you, Sally!"

"I'm mad at you, Sally!"

**"I'M MAD AT YOU, SALLY!"**

**"I'M MAD AT YOU, SALLY!"**

"Good job, Katie, I could feel how mad you are." Allison was silent as she watched Katie. The fight seemed to be leaving her. She seemed worn out.

"I can see, Katie, how hard this is for you. You wanted Sally to be a good mom for you. You wanted her to hold you . . . and rock you . . . and play with your toes. . . . When you were a baby . . . you must have been so sad that she didn't show you enough that she loved you." Allison spoke almost in a whisper, "Say, 'Sally, I wanted you to love me better.'"

"Sally, I wanted you to love me better."

"Why didn't you love me very well?"

"Why didn't you love me very well?"

"I was a good baby."

"I was a good baby." Tears were now in Katie's eyes.

"Why wasn't I very special to you?" Allison whispered.

"Why wasn't I very special to you?"

"Say it again, Katie."

"Why wasn't I very special to you?"

Allison removed her hand from her shoulder and Jackie replaced it with hers as tears rolled down Katie's cheeks. Allison leaned closer to her and whispered, "I don't know why Sally didn't treat you in ways to make you feel very special to her, Katie. You were a baby and babies need so much to feel special to their mom. . . . Jackie and I are going to be looking for ways . . . to help you . . . to feel special to Jackie." Jackie then pulled her closer to her and Katie did not object. Jackie began to rock with her and she hummed softly. Katie did not resist her. She continued to cry. Jackie began to cry.

After a time, Allison began quietly talking with Jackie about how hard Katie had worked again. She added that she had worked a lot at home that week, too. Allison said that she thought that Katie was trying to figure out if she wanted Jackie's help and if she was an OK kid. They then chatted about the recent boat ride that Allison had taken searching for finback whales. The boat, which was doing research for The College of the Atlantic, had found a number of whales, many of which they had seen often that season. Katie was interested and asked Jackie if they could go looking for whales too. Allison indicated that the season was now over and Jackie said that she might take her the next summer.

"Jackie, I have just the book for you to read to Katie," Allison said as she walked to the bookcase and Jackie gave Katie another hug. Allison gave them a book of drawings of various animals and their babies and Katie sat in Jackie's lap. The next to the last page had a whale and her baby. The final page had a mom like Jackie in bed with her baby. They both smiled and chatted while Jackie read the book and they hugged again after the last drawing.

"We're going to be stopping now, Katie. I know that this was another hard meeting for you. And it probably has you more mixed up than ever. I wish that it was easier for you. But you're getting it. One of these days it won't be so hard as it is now." Allison indicated in her matter-of-fact, accepting tone, "After today's meeting you might decide to fight with your mom again, like last week. If you do, that's OK. Your mom will be able to handle things and she'll still love you."

Of course Katie fought with Jackie that week. And the weeks after that week. Katie knew no other way to live and her strength and persistence in trying to take control of the Keller home were incredible. She seemed to live from event to event, each time looking for what she wanted from it. She would decide how best to get what she wanted—whether by charming and trying to conceal her motives or by lying and stealing—and then try to get it. Generally, Jackie would notice her strategies and interfere with her plans. Inevitably, Katie would rage at Jackie for being so "mean" and "cruel." Just as inevitably, Katie would receive some sort of consequence either for her original act—such as stealing—or for her response to Jackie's intervention—such as throwing a cup.

As night follows day, a consequence from Jackie followed Katie's behaviors. Jackie was often amazed that Katie seemed to fail to see the connection. Each time Jackie would give Katie a chore in restitution for taking or breaking something from someone in the family, Katie seemed shocked at how unfair it was. It was as if Katie were thinking, "I wanted it, what's wrong with my taking it? You're mean for not letting me have what I want. And you're even meaner for giving me a chore for simply trying to get what I want!" Sensitivity to the rights and wishes of the others in the family was not Katie's strength. The others were there to serve her! Empathy for others! What a strange concept! Considering what others wanted before deciding whether to do something made no sense to Katie. Everyone was out for herself. Why should she worry about what others thought or felt? She could not imagine that anyone would really care about what was best for her. She had to conclude that Jackie only wanted to control her, just as Katie wanted to control Jackie.

What wasn't fair was that Jackie was bigger and had the power to make the rules. Someday Katie would be bigger and then she'd be happy! Being a kid was awful! First Mike and Sally hit her and said mean things to her. Now Jackie tries to trick her and say she loves her, but she never lets her do what she wants! Some love! She really just wants to boss her around and make her unhappy! Katie couldn't wait to grow up and live by herself!

When kids who lack basic trust in their primary caregivers enter one of their incredible spells of negative thought, affect, and behavior, it tests the strength and commitment of therapeutic moms like Jackie to continue to maintain "The Attitude." It is hard to avoid having a negative family atmosphere as well as a "vicious circle" of behaviors and punishments. Specific consequences given repeatedly in response to negative behaviors create a sense of punishment, no matter what attitude the parent tries to maintain. As a result, many parents have found that they need to change the overall structure of the home environment for the child as well as increase the amount of supervision. The added structure does not assume that the child will act in a friendly and cooperative manner. The child does not have the opportunity to ruin the tone of each day. Rather, the parent assumes that the child is now not able to tolerate fun, having choices, and many expressions of affection. The parent now meets the needs of the child by removing most choices, greatly reducing free time, restricting opportunities for fun that the child will sabotage, and limiting obvious demonstrations of love. Jackie informed Katie that her recent behaviors indicated that she needed to spend more time with Jackie and she needed to be asking Jackie for permission to do just about everything. She also told her that they would both be fairly busy, but that it wouldn't be too hard because Jackie would be at her side.

Along with the added structure and supervision, Jackie made sure to keep her sense of humor in her interactions with Katie. When Katie screamed at Jackie for five minutes one afternoon, Jackie assembled the three teenagers and asked them to participate in the Katie-scream-alike contest. The one whose scream was the most similar to Katie's would win a pack of lifesavers. Katie was asked to be the judge but she refused. John won, although Matthew insisted that Whimsy, who was now howling, should have been the winner. Once, Katie was especially angry and instead of slamming her door once as she usually did, she slammed it three times. Jackie went to her room and insisted that if she was going to slam the door more than once she had to do it five times. She indicated that Katie owed her two more "slams." Another time Katie put water in Jackie's rubber boot. At dinner that night, Katie's glass was empty. She immediately asked for milk. Jackie quietly poured the water from her boot into Katie's glass. She set the boot on the corner of the table and indicated that there was some left if Katie wanted some more. After a few moments, she quietly replaced the water with a new glass of milk. When Jackie responded to Katie's behaviors in this way, she was careful to do it with a twinkle in her eye, and not with ridicule or sarcasm.

For the remainder of September, October, and into November, Katie was receiving a high level of supervision, practice on her personal and social skills and choice selection, and chores that benefited her and, at times, the rest of the family. Jackie often worked with her in performing the chores since Katie had extremely little ability to work independently. Jackie anticipated that it would most likely be at least six months before Katie was likely to do the most basic chore alone. Jackie alternated work and play, active and quiet, interactive and solitary activities within the structure of each day.

When Katie awoke in the morning, she found the clothes that Jackie had selected for her to wear that day. At breakfast, she found the food that Jackie had chosen for her to eat. After breakfast, Jackie went with her and chatted about the day as Katie washed her face and brushed her teeth. Jackie continued to talk with her as they waited for the school bus. When Katie returned from school, Jackie was waiting at the door with a greeting and with milk and crackers. Then, Katie changed from her school clothes to her work clothes and then she and Jackie had a few chores to do together. Playtime followed with some time on the swing or the bike with Jackie admiring her abilities. When Jackie began to prepare dinner, Katie sat at the kitchen table and listened to some music while drawing and coloring. At times, Jackie would tell her to do something to help with dinner. Katie always set the table.

After dinner, Mark would supervise Katie for an hour or so while Jackie took a break and the teenagers managed the dishes. "Mom time" then followed, with Jackie and Katie spending some special time together prior to bedtime. Jackie might give Katie a back rub, shampoo her hair, play with baby dolls with her, tell stories, read books with her, sing and show her how to play the recorder. When Katie was in a pouting and complaining mood, Jackie would still remain with her and refuse to be rejected or to reject Katie. Jackie then might read out loud, listen to music, or quietly sit and rock while watching Katie. At those times, her message for Katie was that she was there for her. If Katie did not want to engage her with pleasure, Jackie would accept her wishes but not withdraw from her physically. She would remain available for her during their special time together. Finally, Jackie would monitor Katie's preparations for bed and they would have a short bedtime ritual involving opportunities for quiet conversation and physical contact.

At times, Katie was receptive to Jackie rocking her during their time together. On a few occasions, she even asked to have Jackie give her a bottle as she was being rocked. Jackie gave the bottle to her only when Katie requested it and only when she was able to lie quietly in her arms, make some efforts at eye contact, and follow Jackie's leads. If Katie used the bottle in a demanding way, Jackie removed it.

Initially, Katie did not welcome these changes in her day-to-day living with open arms. She became more resistant and more complaining. Jackie could wait. Katie would simply sit near Jackie while she decided to engage in the activity that had been chosen for her. A few times Jackie had to sit with her and hold her in the chair when Katie wanted to run out of the room. Once in a while as she sat refusing to do anything, Jackie would give her a hug, a snack, a book to read, or a coloring book. She might also put on some music that she knew Katie enjoyed. At times, she caught Katie singing quietly to the music, only to stop when she became aware of what she was doing.

Throughout the days and weeks, opportunities for fun and free play were very structured. Jackie supplied them, but did not give them in response to Katie's "being good." Rather, Jackie dispensed them in ways that Katie could manage as part of the schedule. They simply reflected Jackie's belief that kids often needed an opportunity to have some fun. Since Jackie decided that such an experience would benefit her, Katie would get it. That simply reflected Jackie's love for her. A few times, she had casually told Katie how that process worked since Katie was struggling to convince herself that she somehow controlled when she got the "reward." It was hard for her to accept that Jackie controlled when she would have "fun" experiences and that Jackie presented them to her because they were good for her and because she loved her. She thought of sabotaging the fun but gave up that idea when it was quite obvious that Jackie would only be sad for her that she wasn't ready for even that limited amount of fun. Jackie would not get upset, so why do it?

As the weeks passed, Katie became calmer and less distressed by the tight supervision and few choices. She seemed to feel content about not having to make the routine daily choices that invariably had led her into so many difficulties. She seemed to feel content about being close to Jackie whenever she was not at school. She did not have to choose to be near Jackie, which would have suggested that Jackie was becoming special to her. Since she "had" to be near Jackie, she could allow herself to accept her presence without resistance. Jackie would chat with her as they both engaged in activities separately in the kitchen or living room. At times, she would walk past and run her hands through Katie's hair, rub her shoulders, or give her a "mom circle." She was not evaluating Katie; she was just accepting and enjoying her.

On October 24, Katie and Jackie had their weekly session with Allison. As she usually did early in each session, Allison was demonstrating considerable interest in Katie's daily life. Her comments included the following:

"You mean that you and your mom were together all day! Without one break?"

"Your mom says that she kissed the top of your head seven times yesterday and four of those times you didn't know she was going to! Is that right?"

"I hear that you were really mad at your mom on Sunday when she told you to rake the leaves with her when you wanted to go for a walk with Diane! Tell your mom that you didn't like raking those dumb old leaves."

"She brought you breakfast in bed and read you a story while you ate? Lucky! Is there an empty bedroom in your house for me?"

Allison asked Jackie to hold Katie in her lap in a way that they could look at each other and then she directed Katie toward being more aware of her ambivalence about spending so much time with Jackie.

"Tell your mom, 'I don't want to be with you all the time!'" Katie did.

"Now say, 'I want you to leave me alone!'"

"Leave me alone!"

"Again!"

"LEAVE ME ALONE!"

"Why can't I be alone?" Katie was responding immediately to her leads.

"I want to be alone!"

"I'm used to being alone!"

"When I was little I was always alone!"

"I liked being alone!"

"I was always so alone!" Allison now changed her voice tone so that it was quieter, with a slower rhythm and a touch of sadness.

"I felt so lonely!" Katie stopped repeating what Allison said and so Allison continued as if it were Katie speaking.

"Nobody was with me."

"Nobody wanted to be with me."

"Where are you, Mom?"

"Please come here."

"I'm a little girl and I need you."

"Why don't you hold me?"

"Little girls need to be held."

"And played with."

"And smiled at."

"Please hold me."

"Please hug me."

Jackie embraced Katie and Allison sat back and waited for a few minutes. Katie's emotions had followed the words. For a few moments, Katie responded nonverbally and was aware of her longing to be nurtured and played with by her mother. That was all Allison wanted now. A few moments at a time. Slowly building a new way of living for a seven-year-old girl. Sculpturing a life based on trust and relatedness. A few moments at a time.

After a time Allison said, "OK, Katie kiddo, enough of this snuggling stuff. Sit on this side of the couch. I have something that I'd like to show you and Jackie."

Allison went to the closet, brought out a multicolored shawl, and handed it to Katie. This fabric must have contained every color of the rainbow and a few more.

Allison then opened it up fully and draped it over Katie's shoulders.

"Did you ever see so many bright and lovely colors?"

"No. Can I have this?"

"No, Katie. It's a gift to me from a special friend. But I wanted you to see the colors." She let Katie feel and squeeze it for a time and they identified some of the incredible colors. Allison then took the shawl and placed it over the back of the rocking chair. She then went to the windows and pulled the drapes closed. It was an overcast Maine day and the colors of the shawl lost some of their brilliance. She directed Katie to look at the shawl while she turned out the lights. The colors were gone! She turned on the lights and the colors returned. She repeated the sequence twice more. Then, leaving the lights off she sat near Katie and said,

"In the dark, the world loses its colors. Even the parts of our life that are the most colorful become gray." Allison paused for a moment before continuing.

"Katie, when you were little, your world was like it is now in my office. It was dark, and you were alone, and there were no colors." Again, she paused, in the darkened space.

"Even in your life now, when you are really feeling alone and sad or scared or mad, you probably can not see any colors. Even . . . if . . . they . . . are . . . there."

Allison turned on the lights and the colors in the shawl returned. She opened the drapes and they were again radiant.

"Now, Katie, I'd like you to try something. Get in your mom's lap again."

Katie settled into Jackie's lap. Allison directed her to look at the shawl again, and really stare at it while Jackie held her. With the light still on, Allison said,

"Now Katie, with your mom holding you, I want you to stare extra hard at the shawl. I'm going to ask you to close your eyes and see if you can still see the colors."

"Close your eyes." Allison waited a moment. "Can you still see the colors?"

"Yes!" Katie exclaimed with surprise.

"Good, now open them again," Allison said. "Now I want you to try something even harder. I want you to keep your eyes open. I'm going to close the drapes again and turn off the lights. I want to see if you can still see the colors with Jackie holding you. Remember to stare real hard."

Allison closed the drapes, turned off the lights and the room was again dark.

"I can!" Katie shouted. "I can still see the colors!"

Before the afterimage went away, Allison congratulated Katie and turned on the lights. She took the shawl and playfully covered Jackie and Katie's heads with it.

"Well, you two. You've found another special thing that happens when you two are together. Colors in the dark. Colors in the sun. Colors that go away. And colors that come back. Katie, you're going to be noticing a new world of colors and I'm happy for you." Allison reclaimed her shawl and ended the session.

On October 15, Steven had stopped by unexpectedly after school.

"I was in the area visiting another kid and thought I might stop in, chat with Katie, and see how she's doing."

"Fine, Steven," Jackie said at the kitchen door. "As you can see, Katie is just sitting near me now. She just got home from school and had her snack. I've found that for now she does best when she sits for a short time without anything to do. It helps her with transitions. After a bit, I'll give her something to do. I'm not sure yet what is best to give her. It depends on how she's doing after a full day at school."

"When will she be done, Jackie?" Steven asked, "I thought that I might take her for a ride and stop for a snack if she wasn't getting a consequence for anything."

"I'm not sure when she'll be done, Steven," Jackie replied. "Maybe in a week or two, but maybe not for a month or two. She's been having a real hard time and she really needs to be close to me now."

Steven was puzzled. He could not think of what to say. He wanted to question Jackie but thought that he probably had better not do it in front of Katie. He engaged in small talk and then made an appointment to stop by and talk with Jackie when Katie was in school.

When Steven arrived two days later, Jackie greeted him with coffee and muffins and they sat at the table.

"I really don't understand what was happening the other day," Steven said after some discussion of practical matters that are always present in the foster care system. "I presumed that Katie was having a 'time out' for doing something and then you said that she was just 'sitting' and that she was sitting for an indefinite period of time. Why? What does that accomplish?"

"Katie needs to be closer to me," Jackie said. "Like I said the other day, she's having a hard time and needs my presence if she's going to be able to turn it around. Sitting is not a consequence. It simply is a means for enabling her to stay near me without getting herself in a lot of difficulty. She sits briefly during the transition from one activity to the next. She sits near me when she does not want to do one of her scheduled activities. She's come to accept it and actually is more relaxed sitting under my direction than if she had freedom to do things and get herself into trouble."

"How long has she been staying so close to you?" Steven asked.

"For significant amounts of time for about two weeks," Jackie said.

"Two weeks!" Steven said, as if he really didn't believe it. "That really sounds harsh. What does she have to look forward to? Why should she work to get anything if there is nothing to get?"

"Steven," Jackie replied, "I don't want her to work to 'get' something. Achieving external rewards will not get her to change in the way she needs to change. I want her to learn how to live well in my home. To do that, she has got to get the idea that it is best for her to be near me and to accept the decisions that I make for her. She also needs to see that I do enjoy her and to become comfortable with my enjoyment of her rather than becoming anxious and then trying to get me to stop enjoying her."

"How is she going to enjoy you by sitting?" Steven asked.

"She's accepting my decision that she sit, she's near me, and she's calmer and more receptive when she is not fussing so much about having to be in control all the time. I am in control so much that she almost doesn't notice it. There is simply no control issue, but only as long as she has no choices right now. She simply does what I say; there are no choices to mix her up. But she is not being punished, Steven. We have many enjoyable and fun activities together. She is not just doing chores."

"But she's over seven years old, Jackie. You're treating her like a baby."

"Good point. There are similarities with how I'm treating her and how a parent would treat a one- or two-year-old." Jackie said. "I need to be aware of her and to direct her. She helps me with a number of chores and she often sits for a brief time between activities. But I also need to spend a lot of time enjoying her, having fun with her, and keeping her central in my life, as a mother would do with her toddler. At times while she's 'sitting,' she might be working or playing quietly. Also, I'm often engaging her with songs, patty-cake, touching and laughing. We might sit quietly together and we might dance around the room. But we're together. "

"That doesn't sound so bad. I was afraid it was more punitive than it seems to be," Steven said.

"It's not punitive at all, Steven," Jackie said, "It nurturing and protective and it's meeting her most basic needs. In many ways she is not nearly mature enough to be treated like a seven-year-old. Emotionally, she is a toddler and she needs this degree of my taking charge of her life."

"What is punitive, Steven," Jackie continued, "is when parents are encouraged to give a consequence that minimizes the child's problems in order to avoid being 'negative.' A child might engage in destructive or disruptive behaviors over and over for days, and the consequence each time is a five-minute time out or losing a TV show or a dessert. Then the child engages in the same behaviors again and again. What a set up for repeated failure! And that's supposed to be positive? The child doesn't control his behaviors and the parents aren't encouraged to, either. The child is left with the conviction that his parents are not strong enough to help him to change. Or with the sense that his parents think that he's not strong enough to cope with serious consequences for serious misbehaviors. When we minimize the implications of these behaviors that occur over and over, we are supporting the child's efforts to minimize his behaviors, too. He thinks that he does not have to be responsible for his behaviors and we support his assumptions! When a child does not learn from his or her mistakes, we have to remove the opportunity to make more mistakes until the child is able to learn from them."

"But by having the consequence occur fast and be over with quickly, aren't we giving the kid a second chance?" Steven asked.

"What kind of a chance are we giving her when she just fails again to do what is asked of her? The parent has to make a judgment: 'Is the kid likely to make a good choice or isn't she?' If I'm fairly certain she's going to make another poor choice, I won't give her the option. I'll provide her with a lot of supervision, along with practice, chores, fun activities, or whatever, until I have some confidence that she is now more likely to make a choice that really is in her best interest. Or if I'm confident that if she makes the wrong choice she will learn from it."

"Well," Steven said, "I hope to hear you say that after another two or three weeks, Katie will be able to start making good choices so she'll be given more freedom again."

"I wish I could, Steven," Jackie said. "Believe me, this is not a picnic for me. It takes a lot of work to be with Katie all the time. I do know that if she can get the basic message that I'm communicating now, she's going to be in a lot better shape when I gradually 'turn her loose.'"

"And what is the basic message?" Steven asked.

"That being with mom brings security, love, and even fun, and those things feel good. Being with a mom also enables you to learn what you need to learn to have a good life. Once these truths become a fact to her, she'll be ready to make me a part of her, and then she'll feel secure and want to have fun and love with or without me."

"What you're saying is making more sense to me, Jackie," Steven said. "But it would help me in explaining this to my supervisor if you could give me actual examples of some typical days for Katie."

"Sure, Steven," Jackie said. "I keep a record of each day that I can bring with me to therapy. I'll expand on it somewhat and give you a copy."

"Great, Jackie. That would be helpful for me."

**Jackie's Journal:**

October 16, 1994: As usual, I stepped out of the kitchen for one minute to talk with Mark. Whimsy howled and barked. By the time I got back, Katie was calmly sitting at the table. Whimsy was in the corner staring at her and then me. He came toward me, with a slight limp. She had hurt his leg! She got my anger again. Every living being in my house was going to be safe! I thought I would gag when I told her of my love for her and my commitment to teaching her how to treat Whimsy right. Whimsy is totally off limits to her. If she's doing something nice in the family room and Whimsy comes in, she has to leave. She will not be in the same room with him unless someone is willing to supervise her 100 percent of the time. Whimsy's wishes have priority over hers now. Of course she also has to clean his poop from the yard and wash out his food and water bowls. I don't trust her with feeding him.

October 18, 1994: Turned my back for a moment and the Cheerios were all over the floor. Katie "didn't know" how they got there. I told her that since she was alone with them it was her responsibility to keep them from jumping out of the box. Thus, she needed to return them all to the box. After two hours, half were in the box. I scooped up some from the floor and dropped them down her shirt. Rage followed. In fairness, I told her to drop some down my shirt. She most certainly did. I put some in her hair; she reciprocated. We shared a glass of apple juice. She picked up remaining cheerios in 30 minutes. Took her to school two hours late. After school, she sorted the laundry to reimburse me for the car ride to school. She complained and threw some meat at the dinner table. Left the table and sat by the window. Before bedtime, I painted her face with erasable markers and she did mine. Mark got the Polaroid. She accepted snuggling at bedtime.

October 19, 1994: Home from school in cheerful and helpful mood. Soon asks to have girl from school visit this Saturday. No. She drops cheerful mood. Refuses to sweep floor. Throws broom. Sits in chair holding broom and dust pan until given permission to sweep. Whines when I say she's not ready to sweep yet. She has to ask to sweep while smiling a specific way. She eventually does. Her favorite meal—pizza. Complains about number of pepperonis on her piece. Grabs a pepperoni from Matthew. Has to give him three pepperonis from hers. Throws pizza. Leaves table—I am sad for her. Sits in chair by window. Before bedtime, we play "Mother, May I?" She laughs whenever I call her "mother." She accepts back rub and quiet lullaby.

October 20, 1994: Home from school, dropping school bag and papers on porch. Snack delayed until her school bag comes all the way home too. She makes valiant effort to get older kids to bring it in. Finally throws it in corner of kitchen. It needs to be on table by closet. Eventually gets there, but too close to dinner for snack. Angry at that. Eventually has cold dinner when the family is finished. Eats only small part, seemingly to punish me. I tell her that I enjoy being full and am surprised that she doesn't. At bedtime, she's not very verbal but does engage me in a friendly tug of war with old sheet. Calms down with rocking. Continually amazing how one emotional state often has no connection with prior one only minutes earlier.

October 22, 1994: Saturday chores fairly uneventful. "Misplace" her for five minutes after she uses bathroom. She steals Diane's teen magazine. I find parts of it under her bed. She doesn't know who put it there. She makes a picture book of five jobs that she will do for Diane. Whenever Diane gives her the picture of the particular job, she has to drop whatever she's doing and do it for her. I draw pictures that Katie can use, bowl of ice cream, hour of TV credit, and coloring book, and give them to her. This took her by surprise but she recovered fast and ate her ice cream while watching TV and coloring. Steps on crayons in carpet and spills some ice cream on couch. I give her bucket of soapy water and then vacuum. I hug her and the soapy water on her shirt gets on me. I fuss about that, put some more soapy water on my shirt and hug her again. We laugh and the sound seemed strange. She sits in kitchen, listening to me chatter with Diane until mealtime. Actually completes meal with family—first time in 10 days. The chair by the window was empty during the whole meal.

October 23, 1994: Leaves church in middle of service—yawning and burping during sermon. Spends Sunday afternoon taking nap and writing letter of apology to Pastor. Has cold Sunday dinner, after burping ("I didn't mean to") at table, but eats it all. Quiet time before bedtime. She and I play with two of Diane's old baby dolls. She actually makes one of the dolls sit for hitting the other doll. I rock one doll and she does not object when I rock her the same way.

October 24, 1994: After therapy this afternoon, she is more withdrawn. Focus on Mike's abuse of her seemed hard. At home while making muffins with me, actually asked why Sally didn't keep her safe. No eye contact. Then drops beans that I had her snapping. Able to laugh when she found two old cheerios under counter while picking up beans. After dinner, I catch her trying to take Mark's school papers that he had out to correct. Unusual that she would go after something of Mark's. Relate to anger at Mike? Letter of apology to Mark and then quiet time. Wants and accepts a bottle for fourth time.

October 25, 1994: Discovers at school that Halloween is next week. Shocked that she will not be getting a costume and not be "trick or treating." Finds an excuse to attack me and is held for over 40 minutes before she calms down. Actually has a few tears in response to my empathy for not having Halloween like the other kids do. After dinner, does a lot of laughing as we sing "Old Mc-Donald Had a Farm" and "The Wheels on the Bus."

October 26, 1994: Angry at breakfast—she screams for pancakes and she gets oatmeal. She won't get dressed for school and misses the bus. Wants me to drive her. I say that I'm too busy so she has chores and homework during the time that she should be in school. Very resistant so they continue until bedtime with breaks for meals and a brief game with me in which I pretend that she is a gingerbread cookie that I made and ate.

October 27, 1994: Goes to school quietly. I welcome her home, give her snack, and then lead her to finishing the chores that she had yesterday. Thirty minutes of anger but the chores were done before dinner. Ate most of her meal but had to sit in the chair by the window when she screamed at John for telling us a story about his day. I guess he needed her permission. Bedtime fine. We mimicked each other in a mirror. I traced her face while she watched in the mirror. She seemed fascinated with seeing my finger causing those sensations on her skin.

October 28, 1994: My light jacket was missing. I found it in her closet and while I was there I found some soiled and wet underwear. She did not know how they got there. She washed them twice. She removed everything from her closet to air it out. It would remain empty to make it easier for me to search. Clothing and toys were stored in the attic. She screamed over my "stealing" her stuff. I suggested that I was protecting them from being ruined by pee. Since I carried them to the attic she owed me a letter of thanks. The first sentence took 90 minutes. I wrote her a brief letter, thanking her for working so hard on the first sentence to get it perfect just for little old lovable me. At bedtime, I sang to her and then snuggled with her and read a book.

October 29, 1994: Saturday morning chores are not going well for Katie. While I do the dishes, she is sweeping the kitchen floor. When I direct her to sweep it for the third time because of the debris that is still there, she screams that it wasn't there a minute before. I ignore her but a minute later I start screaming that someone snuck another dirty bowl into my dishwater. I run into the living room and yell at Diane and then I run outside and yell at Mark. When I get back I scream that another bowl has been snuck into the water. I stomp on the floor and go to my bedroom and slam the door. Katie actually was quiet for a time and finished sweeping the floor. Diane suggested that one of them bring me a glass of water. Katie wants Diane to do it. Diane and I have a good laugh and at lunch I complain about having a sore throat from yelling so much.

## COMMENTARY

During the first therapy session in this chapter, Allison managed to build on the prior one in which Katie had been able to cry for the first time, in response to being able to let herself become aware of feeling worthless after peeing on the quilt. In this session, she worked to lead Katie into her past and to enable her to feel similar tears of worthlessness in response to her rejection by Sally. The very appropriate and visual wall-around-the-heart story elicited some empathy for "baby Katie" which served to enable her to tolerate reexperiencing, however briefly, her early years of despair.

By directing her anger and her subsequent sense of abandonment toward Sally, Katie was receptive to experiencing Jackie as being different from her first mother. She then was more able to allow Jackie to comfort her while she experienced the pain of her past. The act of being comforted, and accepting comfort, when experiencing distress is a core interaction for facilitating attachment.

In the other treatment session, Allison focused on increasing Katie's awareness of the ambivalent feelings that she had over being with Jackie most of the day. She wanted to help Katie to sense that her "freedom" when she lived with Sally and Mike was actually indifference and abandonment and the experience was very painful. She wanted Katie to have some initial awareness of the comfort and security that she might be able to experience through Jackie's continued presence and to contrast that reality with her daily life of isolation with Sally. The use of the colorful shawl served to give Katie a very visual and "magical" experience that might symbolize what might exist for her within her reach.

Allison frequently asks Katie to say certain words or phrases that are likely to reflect her inner life. This is necessary because many abused children have little ability to be aware of and express the thoughts, feelings, wishes, and intentions that lie under their behaviors. If the therapist waits for the child to spontaneously speak about her inner life the wait may be endless. The therapist does make it clear that his or her statements are guesses about what the child may be thinking or feeling. The therapist also makes it clear that if the child is aware of another thought or feeling, she should simply correct the therapist and say what she is feeling.

At times, the child will not repeat what the therapist says. In that case, it is helpful for the therapist to simply speak for the child unless such an intervention proves to be too upsetting for the child. Often the child accepts the therapist's voice as representing her own, and experiences the communication almost as if she had expressed it herself.

The days and weeks that Jackie structured for Katie to be able to manifest her actual affective level of maturity were crucial for her eventual progress, just as they are for many children who had a deficit of early experiences to facilitate affect development. By taking charge of Katie's life to that degree, she was able to care for her as if she were a toddler. She provided her with almost constant supervision and physical proximity, which Katie needed if she were to eventually look upon Jackie as being a figure of trust. Jackie made almost every choice for her, since her own ability to choose what was best for herself was so poorly developed. Katie's severe deficit in being aware of her inner life made it next to impossible to know what to decide for herself. Eventually, Katie was able to accept her need to have Jackie decide for her. Jackie structured the day closely to insure that Katie had the variety of active and quiet, fun and work, experiences that she needed.

For Katie, the "mom time" or the nurturing and fun experiences with Jackie that were available every day were a crucial part of the therapeutic benefit of her highly structured day. For that reason, it was necessary that Katie *not have to earn* her "mom time." To make them conditional on acceptable behavior would undermine their value in affirming Katie's unconditional worth. Regardless of her behavior, Katie received fun and love experiences from Jackie, just as a toddler in a good home always receives those experiences.

The affective self of the child with behaviors consistent with attachment disorganization is poorly integrated. She can move from rage, to pleasure, to feeling frightened, to feeling calm, in an instant. Thus, it often happened that Katie might be very angry with and oppositional to Jackie for much of the day, and then be very engaging and receptive to the nurturing experiences of "mom time" before bedtime. This reality does not make her "mom time" expressions and behaviors manipulative or less genuine. Her functioning during those times is as real as her functioning during her oppositional times. During the "mom time," Katie is able to manifest the "self" that is attuned with a nurturing and playful mother. At almost all other times, she is manifesting the "self" that is "out-of-synch," alone, resentful, and permeated with shame. Lacking integration, Katie is not able to maintain the "good self" when she is not experiencing attunement with Jackie. When Jackie is gone, her small and weakened "good self" quickly disappears under the intensity of the "bad self." Only through developing attachment security with Jackie—both the "good" and the "bad" Jackie, the nurturing and the structuring Jackie—will Katie be able to integrate the "good" and "bad" self. When she can eventually internalize this complete Jackie, she will then be able to maintain her sense of self as whole and worthwhile, and not require Jackie's continuing physical and psychological presence. If Jackie and Allison are going to be able to facilitate Katie's ability to develop attachment security with Jackie, it is crucial that they be able, regardless of Katie's barriers, to elicit her full engagement in those experiences of attunement, where the healthy self can begin to blossom.

# 12

## Thanksgiving Dinner

**B**y Thanksgiving, Katie had been in the Keller home for five and one-half months. It seemed to Jackie like five years. The only thing predictable about Katie was that she always wanted to be in control of every situation. She would do whatever she thought might achieve control over Jackie and the others in the family. At times, she seemed to be more peaceful due to Jackie's taking charge of every moment of her life. But her desire to resume control was never far from the surface. She still resisted, became enraged, destructive, and irritable. She might be cooperative with Jackie and seemingly content with her life for a number of days. The moment that Jackie gave her a bit of freedom, Katie would take the opportunity to try to be in control again and sabotage her efforts. Still, there was some progress, and Jackie decided that she would take the chance to bring Katie with the rest of the family to the traditional Thanksgiving Dinner. Besides, during the holidays, respite opportunities were nonexistent and Jackie did not intend to stay home for Thanksgiving with Katie while the rest of the family went to her mother's.

On Thanksgiving Day, the Keller family traveled to Brunswick to have the traditional dinner with Jackie's mother, Ruth. Jackie's siblings, Jane and John, and their families were also coming, just as they had all done for years. She did not see much of Jane, who lived with her family in Connecticut. John worked at the University of Maine in Farmington so she visited with him much more often. As a result, John had gotten to know Gabe, and now Katie, fairly well, and although he did not understand them, he knew how much work it was caring for foster children and how they often required a different way of child-rearing. Ruth tried to understand, but of course she had her opinions, which she freely gave to her daughter. Jane had her own life and never really understood what her sister was up to with her foster kids. Jackie did not expect to have her most relaxing Thanksgiving Dinner with her family. Still, she felt ready to deal with Katie's probable increase in oppositional behaviors. With an audience, Katie tended to experiment with new ways to irritate Jackie, seemingly to see if she could get away with more. Failing that, she would be content if she could embarrass Jackie.

Mark supervised Katie while Jackie was busy helping her mother prepare the meal. Katie was now used to John's kids, Nathan and Art, and they were used to her. They were careful with their toys and games around her. Jane's kids, Melinda and Bob, were not so well prepared. Katie asked to use Melinda's Gameboy. Mark began to suggest that they play something else but Melinda's dad, Robert, indicated that Katie certainly could play with Melinda's toy. When Katie was not able to win, she threw it on the floor. When it seemed to be broken, Robert remained understanding and forgiving, although Melinda did not. Mark indicated that Katie would be responsible to pay for its replacement if it could not be fixed. Katie screamed at that idea and she screamed even louder when Mark insisted that she sit next to him while the other kids remained playing on the floor. Jane came in from the kitchen to help and when she discovered the problem she assured Mark that it was not necessary for Katie to replace the Gameboy since she did not mean to break it. Mark indicated that Katie was responsible for replacing it if necessary. Jane was interested in helping Katie to get over her distress. She told her not to worry about it since Jane knew that she could fix it. She put her arm around Katie's shoulders and suggested that Katie help her in the kitchen putting the fruit appetizer into the dishes and carrying them to the table. Katie smiled and cheerfully went with her. She had found an ally.

Katie charmed Jane. Jackie looked at them with mild amusement and annoyance. Now her sister would never believe her when she described some of Katie's behaviors. She could anticipate more comments such as, "It can't be that bad," "She's just a little girl!" or "Aren't you just a little too hard on her?"

When it was time to sit at the table, Jackie discovered that Katie had managed to have her seat placed next to Jane's. She indicated that it would be best for Katie to sit next to her. Jane insisted that it was fine with her for Katie to remain next to her. In an effort not to be "unreasonable," Jackie consented. Jane agreed to select the right portions for Katie, although it was clear that she thought that Katie was old enough to do it for herself.

Jane prepared Katie's plate and the angelic child smiled and thanked her. When Jane put the gravy bowl down next to her, Katie quietly asked if she could put the gravy on her mashed potatoes herself. Jane smiled, gave her the ladle, and turned to talk with Ruth. Katie put one hand on the bowl and began to lower the ladle into the gravy. With the slightest smile, she tipped over the bowl, with the gravy pouring onto the table and into Jane's lap. Jackie, seeing the whole sequence, yelled, "Katie!" and Jane just yelled as she jumped up from her chair and headed for the kitchen sink. The rest of the relatives sat frozen, watching the river of gravy slowly making its way over the tablecloth toward the turkey. Ruth ran to the kitchen to be of help to Jane while Jackie hurried to Katie to escort her from the table into the living room.

"I saw what you did, Katie, and that makes me very angry at you!" Jackie yelled at her. "Jane was very nice to you and you repay her by doing such a mean thing to her." Katie only yelled, "I want my dinner!" in reply to Jackie.

Robert followed Jackie and Katie into the living room and said, "I'm sure it was an accident, Jackie. Don't be hard on her."

"It wasn't an accident," Jackie said. "Katie has lost her right to eat dinner with the rest of the family."

Robert did not know what to say, so he went to the kitchen to check on his wife. A few minutes later Jane and Ruth went into the living room.

"I'm OK, Katie," Jane said. "The gravy was hot but I wasn't burned. I had to change my skirt and I'm sure that I'll be able to get the stain out."

"I'm sorry for what happened, Jane," Jackie said. "Katie, tell Jane that you're sorry for what you did to her."

"I'm sorry, Jane," Katie said in her sweetest voice.

"It's fine, Katie. I know that you didn't mean to do it," Jane replied.

"She did mean to do it, Jane, and it's not fine," Jackie said, "Katie will be responsible for making enough money to pay the cleaning bill."

"I think we should just forget it, Jackie," Jane said, "I'm sure that it was an accident. Why don't we all go back and enjoy the meal."

"I'll be there in a few minutes, Jane," Jackie said. "Katie will be sitting here while the rest of us eat. I'll get her something later."

"That's not necessary, Jackie," Jane insisted. "I said that I'm fine and I'd rather just forget it."

"It is necessary for Katie, Jane." Jackie said. "It was not an accident and she needs to be accountable for what she did."

Jane looked at Jackie with growing annoyance. Ruth tried to resolve their conflict by saying to Jackie, "Honey, why not find a little punishment for her later. This is Thanksgiving Dinner and I want us all to enjoy it."

"I know you do, Mom. We all can still enjoy it. But Katie will have to eat by herself when the rest of us are done," Jackie said gently to her mother. She truly did not want to argue with her about this.

"You're becoming a bigger problem than Katie, Jackie. Why don't you just do what Mom asks." Jane was still annoyed.

"I can't. I need to do what is best for Katie," Jackie firmly replied.

"Well, maybe you're wrong. Maybe what's best is for all of us to just drop it and have a decent family meal." Jane's voice was becoming louder.

"I may be wrong, but I'm responsible for Katie and I have to do what I think is best for her," Jackie said.

"Why don't you think of the rest of the family, too? Not just what you want," Jane yelled.

"I'm not responsible for the rest of the family. But I am responsible for Katie and she's not eating with us!" Jackie's voice began to rise, too.

"If she's not eating, neither am I!" Jane yelled and turned and left the room.

Ruth looked sadly at Jackie, "Please, Jackie. It would mean a lot to me if we all could sit down together. We so seldom are together anymore. And I don't want you and Jane to fight."

Jackie felt the tears begin to roll down her cheeks. She took a deep breath. "I'm sorry, Mom. You don't know Katie. I've worked hard for her for the last five months. I can't give in on this or it will set her back too much."

Jackie stared at her mother, waiting for some acknowledgment of her words and acceptance for her decision. Her mother simply stood there, not saying anything. Jackie knew that she would not get the support that she was asking for.

"I'm sorry, Mom. I think that it's best for Mark and me to take the kids and leave now." Ruth still did not respond. Jackie took Katie by the hand and walked into the dining room. She looked at Mark.

"We better be going home now. I'm afraid that this just has not worked out today," Jackie said quietly.

"Let's go, kids, we'll get something to eat on the way home," Mark said as he got up from the table.

At the door Jackie turned again to her mother, "I'm really sorry, Mom, for how this turned out. I'll call you tomorrow." Ruth nodded as she stood by her chair. Jane was not in sight.

John got up from the table and came to the door. He hugged his sister. "It will work out OK, Sis. You got to do what you think is best. Mom and Jane will come around."

"Thanks, John." Jackie felt the tears coming again. "I know that you're right."

On the way home, Jackie sat in the front seat, staring at the road. She heard Diane make a few angry comments at Katie. Katie screamed at her. Diane yelled at Katie and Mark told her that her comments were not helping the situation. Jackie didn't have the energy to say anything. She could only think of her mother staring at her, condemning her decision. Eventually she imagined what Katie must have looked like while Jackie was arguing with Jane and Ruth. She knew that Katie would have been feeling excited and powerful then. Jackie would not let herself look at Katie now. She knew that if she did, Katie would smile at her. She also knew that if that happened she would truly hate her and she would not bother to hide her contempt.

That night Mark took care of Katie and got her to bed. Jackie kept her distance. She had no empathy for her. She could not interact with her. She wasn't going to try.

Later Mark sat next to her on the couch. He took her hand. She smiled at him and felt very tired and sad.

Slowly she began talking, "I think she might beat me, Mark. I did it with Gabe, but I don't know if I can continue to do it for her. I have given her so much. And she spilled that damn gravy to hurt me. She knew what would happen. I truly believe it. I feel that she's evil. She's just too much for me."

She leaned against him and sobbed. After a time she said, "I don't want to love that kid. Why do I still love her? 'Like the kid and dislike the behavior' is crap. I don't like that kid. I don't want to love her anymore. Why can't I stop?"

"Honey, that's who you are. That's one of the many reasons I love you so much. Whatever you decide to do, I know it will be for the best. I support you all the way. If you think that someone else has to raise Katie, then someone else will have to raise her. If you think that you need to continue with her, then she'll stay. If you want her to stay I will do my best to be of more help to you. You're in charge."

"Maybe I don't want to be in charge. Maybe I don't want the responsibility of bringing this kid into the human race. Maybe I don't want the responsibility for her life! Her problems and needs seem bottomless. I'm afraid she's going to pull me down with her and I'll be no good to anyone."

"I know you and I know me. No kid has that power and she'll never get it," Mark said. "But if you need to have her move somewhere else I understand and support you. I know that whatever you decide will be for the best."

Jackie looked at Mark. She smiled and kissed him. "Thanks for the vote of confidence." She laughed. "I wish that I could tell what was best. I can't now. Maybe I need to get some sleep."

When she awoke the next morning, Jackie felt more discouraged than she could remember. She had hoped, with the new day, to discover her usual enthusiasm for her life and her family. Not today, not now. Maybe she should give Allison a call and tell her about her Thanksgiving disaster. Maybe she and Mark should go out for breakfast. As she lay there she heard Mark begin to grumble and stretch. After so many years she knew that he was about to awaken within the next 30 seconds. A fringe benefit from marriage! You can predict to the very second how many and what type of groans your husband will make before he opens his eyes. On cue, Mark reached over and gave her a hug.

"Good morning, honey," Jackie said. "Would you mind taking care of Katie for breakfast? I need to lie here for a while and think over some things."

"Sure, sweetie," Mark said quickly. Jackie not getting up quickly was most unusual. "Anything you want to talk over with me?"

"Not now," Jackie responded. Mark got out of bed, dressed, and went directly to check on Katie. Nothing began in the Keller home until one was certain about Katie's whereabouts.

Jackie simply lay in bed. She looked at the picture of her mother and grandmother that she kept on the bureau. Her mother must have been 10 when the picture was taken and her grandmother was an attractive woman. She could imagine them standing there, under the old oak tree that Jackie herself had swung from when she was a kid. Her visits to Grannie's house were some of the most joy-filled moments of her childhood.

As Jackie's mind drifted, she began to pray. She hadn't intended to, but she was not surprised to find herself doing it. She generally did when she felt lost. Her faith in God often helped her to get through the hardest times as well as to find the direction that she needed to take. Her prayers led her through her numerous conflicting thoughts and feelings about Katie. From there she became aware of her sister's rejection of her and of her own shame over Katie's behavior at the Thanksgiving Dinner. Suddenly, she became aware of how she had needed to have Katie meet her needs to garner validation from her relatives about her work with Katie. That awareness seemed to begin to make a difference. Maybe she could talk with Allison about it. Maybe that would help her to know what she would do.

Jackie was not looking forward to talking with Katie about the dinner but it actually proved to be easier than she thought. She knew what Katie needed to hear so she said it.

"Katie," Jackie said over the breakfast table when she and Katie were alone, "you managed to really mess up the dinner for all of us yesterday. I'm sure you noticed how upset I was and how angry Jane and I were at each other. I was really mad at you and I'm sure you knew that, too."

Katie was listening, not sure where this conversation would be leading. Jackie continued, "After I calmed down, I realized that I should have made you sit next to me even if Jane didn't understand why. She just doesn't know you the way I do. Also, maybe I shouldn't have taken you with us to my mom's house. I could have found someone to watch you here. You weren't ready to enjoy the family holiday. It wasn't special to you at all. I know that it's hard for anything to be special to you. The next time you won't have to go if I think that you're not ready for it."

"Well, sweetie, you're still going to have to pay to have Jane's skirt cleaned. I'll be giving you some extra chores. And Mark and I are going to be making a special dinner here today for our family. We'll see if you can handle it sitting right next to me. If not, you can eat after we are done."

Jackie got up and kissed Katie on the top of her head. Katie's pouting continued, but she did not have a tantrum. Jackie's comments must have surprised her and she didn't know how to respond. Since Katie only wanted to do things that might put her in control, she'd just have to wait and figure it out before putting energy into a tantrum.

"You sure were put through a lot, Jackie," Allison said at the next therapy session on November 30. "You probably felt like covering Katie with gravy."

"I never want to see gravy again, Allison. Cranberry sauce yes, but no gravy."

"You seem to be doing better today."

"Yes, I am, Allison. I prayed and that seemed to help me to get some perspective again. But I am confused and not really sure what to do now."

"What do you think made it so hard for you, Jackie?" Allison wondered.

"It was just that she did it deliberately to upset me in front of my mom and Jane."

"And what about being with them made it more difficult for you?"

"I'm not sure, Allison, but at times it feels like I need my mom's approval for what I'm doing, and when I don't get it, it really bothers me."

Allison nodded and they sat quietly for a few moments until Jackie continued, "My mom is a good person and I know that she loves me. I really do . . . I never doubted that . . . I think . . . but sometimes I had a feeling that for some reason . . . she might be disappointed in me. It doesn't make sense in some ways . . . but I just didn't feel sure. I just never quite knew for sure."

"Could you give me an example, Jackie, of a time when you might have had doubts about your mom's acceptance and love for you?"

"Not love, Allison, I don't really think that I doubted her love. But acceptance, yes, that's the right word. . . . One time, I guess I was about 10. Jane would have been 13 or so. Mom left us home on a Saturday when she went to her mom's house to help her out with some things. She had asked me to be sure to clean my room and then do some work in the garden that afternoon. I ended up reading and watching TV and really forgot what she had asked. When she came home and saw that my chores were not done, she expressed annoyance but mostly it was how she looked at me. She just looked in a way that I felt that I had really let her down. I had hurt her. And I felt like . . . like she thought that I had done it deliberately. Like I wanted to hurt her. And I felt horrible that she would think that about me. And then I thought that maybe she was right. Maybe I was selfish and didn't really care if I hurt her or not. I just took care of myself and forgot about her. I know this sounds small, Allison, but it seems to be important. I think that I often had those thoughts. That she was disappointed in me because I was not sensitive enough to her. She had done so much for me, and I couldn't just do something small for her. She worked so hard and I didn't seem to care or notice."

Jackie had tears in her eyes now and her mind wandered over her childhood. She suddenly became more animated and said,

"Jane never seemed to get that look. It seemed like she always did what she was told. Mom always seemed to be pleased with her. She was like a younger version of my mother. I just could not compete with her. I wasn't ever going to get the place in my mom's heart that she had. I'd never be as good as her." More silence followed.

"That must have been so difficult for you, Jackie, if it seemed that your mom never really accepted you, or was proud of you, the way it seemed that she was proud of Jane. How do you think you handled that over the years?"

"I think that I just tried harder to please her, most of the time. But it never seemed to work. I always seemed to do something that wasn't right. And I'd do mean things to Jane. I really hated her some times. And then mom would be mad at me for being mean to Jane. She seemed to think that Jane was such a wonderful big sister! Why couldn't I appreciate her? After all she did for me?"

"So it seemed to you that your mom and Jane had a close bond, were similar in many ways. And you were outside of that. Your mom seemed disappointed in you, and Jane seemed angry with you."

"Yeah, but, don't get the wrong idea about them, Allison. They were not bad people. Mom really did love me, I know. And she worked hard and really did her best. And Jane did help me in a lot of ways."

"What do you think made you decide to tell me that, Jackie? You've mentioned a number of times now that you know that your mom loved you."

"Well, they were good . . . they are good . . . people. And saying these things about them to you. It just seems . . . that somehow it's not right."

"Because," Allison quietly said.

"Because it feels like I'm being selfish to say these things about them, especially Mom. Like I'm still putting myself first. Still not being grateful for all that she did for me."

"And maybe that she would still be disappointed in you if she knew that you were telling me these thoughts and feelings about her."

"Yes, Allison, she would." Tears were now flowing down Jackie's cheeks. "And she would have a right to be. Why aren't I more grateful for all that she did for me?"

Allison sat for a moment, staring into Jackie's eyes and the tears of shame that were flowing from them. She became aware of her own tears of empathy for Jackie and she could feel Jackie searching her eyes for the meaning of her tears. She then quietly said, "Jackie, to me, the question is not why you cannot be more grateful to your mom for what she did for you. My sense is that you are truly grateful to her. I think the question is more about what makes it so hard for you to accept that you feel some disappointment in how your mom related with you at times."

"But I have no right to be disappointed in her, Allison. She never was cruel to me. She was a good mother!"

"I don't think that we are exploring your mother so much as we are talking about your experience of your mother sometimes. Sometimes, Jackie, it seems that you experienced that your mother was disappointed in you . . . did not really accept you . . . thought that you were deliberately trying to make her life more difficult. . . . It seemed to you that she thought that you were not grateful to her for what she did for you . . . that you were selfish."

"But maybe she was right, Allison. Maybe I should have tried harder to make her life easier by doing what I was told."

"And maybe . . . ,"Allison said.

"Maybe . . . ," Jackie was puzzled. What other explanation could there be. More silence followed.

Finally Allison said, barely above a whisper, "Maybe you were a 10-year-old kid. . . . And maybe you were not trying to make her life more difficult . . . and maybe if your mom did think that you were selfish, she was wrong."

Jackie began to cry. After a few minutes, Allison reached over and held her hand. Jackie looked up and seemed to be pleading with her in her next question. "But why, Allison, why would she think that I was deliberately trying to make her unhappy, if I really wasn't?"

"I don't know, Jackie. I do know you were 10 years old. Maybe the answer lies somewhere in her childhood. Maybe in her relationship with her mother."

After a few minutes of thought, Jackie said, "Mom said once, Allison, that her mom taught her how to work, and then turned around and taught me how to play. She said that with a laugh while driving back home after I had spent a day at Grannie's house. But I thought that she also seemed sad when she told me that."

"Sounds like your grandmother did a good job of teaching your mom how to work. And I wonder if your mom ever really felt that her mom accepted her. I wonder if your mom had doubts about whether or not she was good enough. Or if she at times was selfish and did not work hard enough."

"Oh, my!" Jackie seemed startled by her emerging thoughts. "Mom thought that I was doing—being selfish and wanting to hurt her—the same things that Grannie thought that she was doing! I know that's true! That makes so much sense! That makes everything else make so much sense!"

"What sense does that make about who you were when you were a kid, Jackie?"

Jackie began crying again. She looked at Allison and replied, "It means that Mom was wrong. I didn't want to hurt her! I didn't want her to be unhappy! I was a 10-year-old kid. Mom was wrong! I wasn't selfish. I wasn't ungrateful!" Jackie stared deeply into Allison's eyes as she spoke. She was searching for something in her eyes. She was searching for confirmation that what was beginning to make sense to her, made sense to Allison. As she stared into Allison's eyes, the memories of her childhood seemed to deepen and to join together in easier ways. Things just seemed to make more sense!

"You know, Allison, Mom did love me. I know that. But I think that I felt that she loved me only when I was doing things that she approved of. At other times, like when I disappointed her, I knew that she loved me but I did not feel it. When I was with Grannie, I always felt that she loved me. No matter what I was doing. Even when she became impatient with me. I could still feel her love. It was not that way with Mom."

"Allison! I never really, really felt safe with Mom. Sure I was safe with her. But that feeling of love and acceptance . . . that really makes someone feel safe . . . I don't think I really felt that for just being myself, like when I was with Grannie. With Mom, I felt it when I was pleasing her." Jackie's thoughts were now racing through her mind.

"In some ways, Allison, I don't think I saw myself then the way I do now. I don't think I saw myself as a kid the way I do now. I wasn't selfish in a bad sense; I was a kid. I don't think my mom knew who I really was, inside. Or at least some of these parts of me. That's probably why I didn't know them either. I was . . . I am . . . a good person. There is nothing about me that I need to be ashamed of. There is nothing about me that I need to change. Sure I make mistakes. I make mistakes. And there is nothing about ME that needs to change! I just can correct my mistakes. My intentions are good. I never tried to make my mom unhappy! I never did! I know that now!"

Jackie smiled and stared into Allison's eyes.

"And you know it, too!"

"Yes, I know it, too," Allison replied and they smiled.

After a few moments, Allison asked, "How does Katie fit into this?"

"I think that on Thanksgiving, Katie's behavior made me again think that I was doing something to deliberately hurt my mom. And I felt that again, my sister and mom agreed, and I was the failure as a daughter and sister. And also I think now that I thought that Katie was deliberately doing something to hurt me, just like I was probably doing things to hurt my mom. But the difference was that mom and Jane did not see it. Now Katie was joined with them, too. They accepted Katie and were disappointed in me! No wonder I got so upset. No wonder I hated Katie. And Mom. And Jane. . . . And myself."

Tears and smiles and sighs of relief followed for Jackie as she stared inward while occasionally having eye contact with Allison.

"These things that you are working out. What do they mean about your continuing to raise Katie?"

"I think that they mean that I'm doing a damn good job. I think that they mean that pattern that seems to have been passed down from Grannie to Mom and from Mom to me, cannot be allowed to move on from me to Katie. If Mom is 'hurt' by my decisions regarding Katie, then Mom is 'hurt.' I am not deliberately hurting her. If Katie misbehaves toward me, or even actually does something to hurt me, her intentions are not toward me personally, but toward her own mother, her abuse, her life. I don't have to personalize her behaviors. They are much more about her past and her pain than they are about me. And my relationship with Katie is not about my relationship with my mom. Actually I am beginning to think that my relationship with Katie is forcing me to look at my relationship with my mom, too. And it needs to be done."

"I hear you saying that you are still committed to Katie."

"I am committed to her. More so than ever."

"Jackie, why don't you give some thought to asking your mom to come with you to meet with me. Why not think about Ruth, you, and me talking about what you've been discovering and saying to me?"

An anxious look appeared in Jackie's face. "Is that necessary?"

"No, Jackie, it's not necessary and it is entirely up to you, and of course, Ruth if you decide to invite her. It's just an idea that I got when you mentioned that you thought that your mom would be disappointed in you if she knew you were saying those things about her. I thought that if you talked with her here, you would discover if she is disappointed or not. Either way it might be helpful to you in your efforts to make sense of who you are and how you want your relationship with your mom to be in the future."

"Wow! Actually telling my mom some of the things that I just said to you! Wow! Actually telling her!"

"Think about it."

"I will, Allison. Thanks for offering to do that for me. I think." Jackie laughed.

"Should I get Katie now?"

"Yes!"

As Allison rose from her chair she gave Jackie's hand one last squeeze and she dabbed her remaining tears with a tissue.

Allison brought Katie into the room with her usual, "Well, it's Katie kiddo. Good to see you again, kiddo!" She smiled at her while Katie took her usual spot between Jackie and Allison on the couch.

"Well, kiddo, you don't look your usual cheerful self. What's up?"

"Nothing."

"Wow, Katie, it sounds to me like something is up, that if you were to tell me what it is you might say something like, 'I don't want to be in dumb therapy today, Allison, and I'm not talking to you!' Is that about right, Katie?"

"I don't want to be here and therapy is dumb!"

"Wow! I guessed right! Thanks for telling me Katie, thanks for letting me know that you really don't want to be here today! Well, if you don't want to talk, I'm just going to have to count your fingers. Let's see . . . 1, 2, 3, 4, 5 over there . . . 10, 9, 8, 7, 6. There, 5 and 6, that's 11. What! You have 11 fingers! You gotta be kidding! How could that be? Let me do it again . . . 1, 2, 3, 4, 5 on that hand. Now, 10, 9, 8, 7, 6! 6 and 5, wow, you do have 11 fingers! That's incredible! You're incredible! See, that's proof that you're just an incredible kid, kiddo."

"I don't have six on that hand," Katie said. She wasn't laughing and her eye contact was poor. Allison immediately knew that engaging Katie today would not be as easy as it usually was.

"Of course you only have five fingers on your hand."

"Five and five are ten." Katie said.

"You sure know your numbers, kiddo, I'm sure not going to trick you."

Katie appeared passively resigned to being with Allison and Jackie. This contrasted noticeably with her general air of expectant uncertainty about what would be occurring. If she wanted to convey the idea that she was bored and annoyed at wasting her time there she was doing a good job.

"My goodness, Katie," Allison began, "you sure don't seem to want to be here. It seems to me that you want to say, 'I want to leave. I don't like it here. I don't want to talk about anything! I don't want to think about anything! I don't want to feel anything! I don't want to do anything! Let me go. I want to leave!' My guess is that those are some of the things that you would be saying if you wanted to tell me something."

Katie remained quiet and sullen.

"That's it, Katie. See how quiet and annoyed you can be while I talk with your mom." Allison said casually and then looked over at Jackie.

"Jackie, Katie seems to be very unhappy about being here now. Do you have any idea what is bothering her?"

"She didn't seem upset when we drove over here, Allison. I'm not sure what's on her mind now," Jackie said.

"Well, something is getting to her." Allison said. "Did anything happen since I saw her last?"

"It was a hard Thanksgiving for the whole family, Allison. Maybe that's bothering her," Jackie said.

"Nothing's bothering me!" Katie screamed.

"Wow, you yelled that loudly, kiddo. Maybe something about Thanksgiving is on your mind," Allison said.

"No it's not!" Katie yelled.

"What happened, Jackie, that might be upsetting Katie now?"

"Well, Allison, we went down to my mother's house for Thanksgiving Dinner. When we sat down to eat, Katie spilled the gravy on my sister's lap so she had to leave the table."

"It was an accident!" Katie screamed.

"Katie had my sister and mother thinking it was an accident but I saw her smile before she did it and I knew it was on purpose," Jackie said.

"I did not! You're lying! You're lying!" Katie yelled at Jackie.

"You sure are mad at your mom, Katie. Tell her. Say, 'I'm mad at you, Mom!'"

"I'm mad at you!"

"Wow, Jackie, she really is angry with you, she won't say 'Mom,'" Allison said.

"Say, 'You're a mean mom!'"

"You're mean!"

"Why do you think she's so mad at you, Jackie?" Allison asked.

"Well, she has had to do chores to pay to get Jane's skirt cleaned. And she was so upset that she ended up missing the family Thanksgiving dinner that we had at home the next day," Jackie said.

"But she's always getting annoyed at you for giving her some consequence. Generally she doesn't get nearly so mad at you."

"You're right, Allison. Maybe it's because of my reaction to what she did."

"What was your reaction, Jackie?" Allison asked.

"I was very mad at her for what she did. You see, my mother and sister got angry with me and we all left early. I was crying a lot and Diane yelled at Katie. All the way home and that night I didn't talk to Katie. That's the only time I ever stopped talking to her when she did something wrong."

"Jackie, I'll bet you're right. Katie is probably mad at you because of how mad you got at her," Allison said.

She turned to Katie, "I'll bet you were saying to yourself, 'Why is she so mad at me. Good moms aren't supposed to get so mad! She's not allowed to get mad at me that much!' Right, Katie?"

Katie did not say anything. She looked toward the couch.

"Oh, Katie, now I understand. No wonder you got so mad at your mom! You could tell that she was more mad at you than she ever was before! You didn't know what that meant! Maybe she was so mad she'd never stop being mad! Maybe she would become like Sally!" Allison sat motionless for a moment and then leaned forward and said quietly, "You thought that she might be hating you. . . . You thought that she might not love you anymore. . . . You thought that she . . . might not . . . want to be your mom anymore."

Katie remained motionless. Allison then said even more quietly, "You must have started to feel . . . sad . . . and scared . . . no wonder you're mad at . . . your mom."

Allison began to stroke Katie's hair.

"Don't do that!" Katie screamed at Allison.

"Would you get closer to Katie now, Jackie, she's mad at me now for talking to her and you about how hard it was when you were so mad at her."

Jackie moved closer to Katie, putting her arm around her and holding her hand. Katie did not move—either toward her or away from her.

Allison whispered, "Katie, Katie, it was so hard, so sad, so scared . . . Katie, Katie, so hard, so sad . . . Katie . . . ."

"DON'T SAY THAT!" Katie screamed. "DON'T SAY THAT!"

Jackie continued to gently rock her, rest her chin on her hair and Allison repeated the words that reached into Katie's soul a second time. Katie screamed again. Jackie sat holding her daughter, wanting it to stop, wanting it to never stop.

The screams continued, "Shut up! Shut up! Shut up!" though Allison was no longer speaking. As the moments passed, they changed. They originally were filled with rage. Now they were more and more permeated with despair. Her screams became cries of one abandoned to the night, forever alone.

Allison whispered once again, "Katie . . . Katie . . . so sad . . . Katie . . . Katie . . . so scared."

Katie's cries continued; seemingly, they would continue forever.

Jackie pulled Katie up onto her lap and held her as one would hold a crying toddler. Katie buried her face in Jackie's chest.

"My Katie . . . My Katie . . . you're safe . . . you're with Mom. I love you, Katie . . . I love My Katie." Jackie whispered. Katie clung to her. Jackie felt Katie's fingers dig into her sides. She clung to her as a baby would. A terrified, despairing, baby.

Allison went to the corner shelf and turned on the tape player. She always kept a tape in the player that would be suitable for times like this one. This tape contained Irish lullabies, with gentle and loving tones. Allison hesitated to play it because she thought that she might be encouraging Katie's feelings of being an infant too much, causing her to resist. Katie accepted it.

Jackie stopped talking. She began to move slowly and hum in time with the lullabies. Allison simply watched. She didn't exist to Jackie and Katie. They were in their own world now. This world would heal and reach Katie much more than anything that Allison might say or do.

Eventually, Allison turned off the music and indicated that the session would have to stop. There was nothing that she wanted to say. Nothing that she should say. When Jackie and Katie got up to leave, she stared at them for a moment and then she went over and hugged them both.

## COMMENTARY

When Katie spilled the gravy on Jackie's sister, she was engaging in a behavior that is very common among children with trauma/attachment problems. She was ruining a family celebration for all, splitting Jackie from her relatives, eliciting anger and rejection from her, and taking pleasure in the shambles that she created, all from one action. Children similar to Katie are inevitably on their worst behavior during moments like the Thanksgiving Dinner. They cannot tolerate such mutual enjoyment and support and they cannot tolerate allowing others to have that experience. To them, it is much more desirable to experience the power of destroying the experience for all and confirming their self-perception as being isolated and evil.

Jackie's response to Katie's behavior can best be understood by the dynamics of shame, similar to, but much less profound, than is its meaning in Katie's life. Central to Jackie's identity is her ability to be a good therapeutic foster parent. Since Katie's behavior so infrequently confirmed her view that she was good at her work, Jackie was more vulnerable to the need for confirmation from those important to her that she was actually good at what she did. She was seeking that confirmation from her sister and mother. Katie sensed this and took advantage of the opportunity to hurt Jackie and test her commitment. The criticism from her sister and mother elicited Jackie's doubts and triggered shame, which in turn, led to rage at Katie. Jackie was not able to integrate the rage at the time, and she distanced herself from her.

Jackie's shame is not an uncommon response among parents who attempt to raise children who continuously reject them. Their children seldom confirm that they are good parents. Their child's oppositional behaviors constantly suggest that they are failing her in some fundamental ways. They give and give to their child and the response that they most often receive is "Is that all? I want more!" or "I don't want that, I want this!" In the face of their child's rejection, they turn to friends and relatives for support and confirmation that the ordeal that they are living has meaning and their efforts are worthwhile. Often, they receive skepticism, advice, and criticism that they are being either too harsh or too easy and either way they are not meeting this poor child's needs. When professionals, therapists, teachers, and social workers concur with the opinions of their relatives and friends, these parents are extremely vulnerable to experiencing shame. From such a position, it is extremely hard for these parents to then attempt to reduce the pervasive shame experienced by their child. When Jackie experienced herself as a failure as Katie's parent, she had little energy or skill to continue to parent her.

Therapists need to acknowledge and address parental shame from raising children such as Katie. If there are two parents, the two need to be solidly in support of each other in the face of their child's rejection. The best source of support is often other parents who truly understand what it is like to raise children who have behaviors secondary to unresolved trauma and attachment disorganization. These peers are in the best position to know what support might be the most beneficial. Also important is the understanding and support of a therapist who knows the symptoms and needs of this child as well as the various parenting strategies and support that parents need in order to have a chance to raise their child adequately.

Jackie's response to Katie's behavior intensified because it activated aspects of her own attachment history with her mother, Ruth. When Jackie had been a child, she often had doubts about whether Ruth accepted her as she was. She felt love when she was pleasing Ruth, but felt isolated from her if she did something that displeased her. They did not regularly repair these breaks in their relationship. Jackie's doubts intensified because she experienced Ruth as perceiving her as deliberately doing things to cause Ruth distress. This perception—of Ruth's perception of her—activated shame rather than guilt in response to her misbehavior. Often an act becomes associated with shame or trauma because of the meaning that we give to the intentions of the other or the meaning that we think that they give to our intentions rather than to the act itself.

Studies are now showing that the attachment classification of the foster or adoptive parent is an important—though not the only—factor in whether or not their foster/adoptive child will attain attachment security with them. These findings "make sense" since attachment patterns of behavior are reciprocal and, just as they routinely pass from parent to child, they may also pass from child to parent. Katie's behaviors "with respect to attachment" are certain to activate similar patterns in Jackie. If Jackie's patterns are "secure" (or "autonomous" as this classification is known as when applied to adults) she is more likely to be able to remain psychologically safe, stay emotionally present to Katie's distress, and respond in a reflective, flexible manner that facilitates Katie's ability to integrate the experience. However, if similar patterns within Jackie are to some extent "insecure" (or "unresolved") then she is not likely to feel psychologically safe, and she is at risk to react to Katie without sufficient affect regulation or reflection.

By speaking with Allison about her reaction to Katie's Thanksgiving Dinner behaviors, Jackie was able to better regulate the affect associated with that event. She then was able to reflect upon its meaning to her in a manner that led to a greater sense of safety and resolution of similar experiences during her childhood in her relationship with her own mother. Allison could engage Jackie in a manner sufficient to co-regulate the affect of shame and co-create new meanings regarding her misbehaviors toward Ruth. Jackie was then able to be more present with Katie with regard to the Dinner event and similar events likely to occur in the future.

Sometimes, only one such dialogue is necessary to facilitate such important intersubjective experiences of resolution and integration. At times, these insecure attachment patterns are more extensive and greater exploration of them within a trusting relationship may well be necessary. At other times, these patterns are so pervasive that they may preclude someone who has her own pervasive difficulties engaging in patterns of attachment security from parenting a child. Whether the adoptive or foster parents' areas of attachment insecurity are limited and mild or more extensive, therapists must openly address these issues within a safe relationship if the parents are to become more able to parent their children well.

In therapy with Katie, Allison focused more on Jackie's response to Katie's behavior than on the behavior itself. She took her cue from Katie's initial resistance to therapy, something that was not usually present. Katie was defending herself against intense affective experience that seemed to go beyond her usual affective response associated with her own behavior. What was the most unusual about the Thanksgiving Dinner event was not Katie's behavior, but rather, Jackie's. Her emotional withdrawal from Katie for the rest of the day triggered an affective response in Katie that was similar to her response to Sally's extended periods of rejection of her. Jackie left Katie feeling terrified that whatever relationship might have existed with Jackie had now ended. Jackie would now most certainly insist that she move. She had finally revealed that part of herself that Jackie would find disgusting and which would cause her to throw her away.

By allowing Katie to recognize and acknowledge her fear that she was finally being rejected by Jackie, Allison was able to lead her to expressing the depth of despair into which she was now falling. Through rage, Katie initially rejected Allison's lead. Soon she began to respond to Allison and Jackie's empathy and loving attitude and she allowed herself to express her affect fully and then accept Jackie's reassurance and continuing commitment.

# 13

## Jackie and Ruth

Following her meeting with Allison, Jackie felt a sense of lightness and freedom that left her elated. That evening she spoke excitedly to Mark about her insights into her relationship with her mother and how it affected her own parenting behavior. Upon recalling Diane's early years, she began to see how some of her early interactions with her daughter had parallels with her current, though much more intense, difficulties with Katie. She had been determined to provide her daughter with an involved, accepting, playful, and responsive relationship with her and for the most part she had succeeded. Now she understood why it had been so difficult at times in those early years. It took a great deal of self-reflection and talks with Mark to be able to understand and accept Diane's normal childhood anger and defiance toward her.

With Katie, Jackie was beginning again her long journey as a parent. Katie's rage at her did often leave Jackie thinking that she had failed this child, in spite of Allison and Mark's comments to the contrary. At times, she could not left go of a sense that she just was not giving enough. At times, she wanted to scream at her that she was an excellent mother and Katie would just have to learn to appreciate her.

Within a few days, Jackie became aware of some regrets about her conversation with Allison. She had a sense that she had been too critical of her mother. She felt shame over having told Allison about the distress that she felt regarding her perceptions of her relationship with Ruth. Over the following two days, Jackie obsessed about her relationship with her mother. She returned continually to Allison's suggestion that Jackie and Ruth meet with her. The idea terrified her but at the same time made her aware of a deep desire to try to share her thoughts with her mother and possibly move their relationship into a new realm. Over the next few days, she managed to call Allison, get an appointment, call her mother, and get her agreement to meet with her the next week at Allison's office. It seemed to her that she had no choice.

On December 10, Ruth came to Jackie's home and the two of them drove to Allison's. Jackie anxiously thanked her mother for being willing to come with her, at one point apologizing for taking her away from her own activities. Finally, with an expression of mild impatience Ruth said, "Jackie, you asked me to come so I want to be here. I'm not sure what it is about, but that's not the point. I want to be here so there's no need to be sorry for asking me." Small talk filled the final minutes before Allison welcomed them both.

"Thanks, so much for coming, Ruth. It was my idea for the meeting actually, and Jackie agreed after thinking about it for a while. As you might guess, the idea for me to meet with you both came after the trouble at your home at Thanksgiving, when Jackie decided that it was best for Katie to leave before finishing the dinner. It seemed to me that it was a very difficult experience for you both. I thought it might be helpful if we talked about that a bit, but more importantly talked about some of the thoughts and worries that it seemed to awaken in Jackie."

"That's fine with me, Allison, though I've almost forgotten about it myself. I'm not upset about it. I realize that I don't really understand what Katie needs. After it was over, I knew that Jackie must be right. Or if not right, at least that Jackie is the one who had to make the decision. I shouldn't have tried to change her mind."

"I can understand, Mom. It was your home and you worked so hard to have a nice Thanksgiving. I got over it soon and understood your feelings."

After a short silence, Ruth smiled and said, "Then why are we here?"

Jackie felt more anxious that she had ever before felt in Allison's office. Dealing with Katie was nothing like trying to talk with her mother.

"Mom, it's not about Katie and Thanksgiving, though in a way it is about Katie and me. And me and you. . . . Mom, when I was talking about Thanksgiving with Allison I just became aware of how much I want your approval. How much I want you to think good thoughts about me. How hard it is for me when you disagree with me."

"Jackie, I do approve of you. Of course I do. You're my daughter! Whatever you do is fine with me.

"Mom, it often doesn't feel that way to me."

"What do you mean? I've never criticized what you've decided to do in your life?" Ruth seemed puzzled and somewhat hurt at what her daughter was telling her.

"I know you haven't, Mom, but . . . in some ways it seemed to me that . . . you just did not . . . that I was never quite . . . that you were more pleased with Jane than you were with me."

"Oh, Jackie, how could you say that? I always loved you as much as I loved your sister. And I still do!"

"But, Mom, it seemed that she always was able to do what you wanted and I always got into trouble."

"But she was older than you. And you were always more active than her. I might have had to correct you more but I felt no differently toward you than toward her."

Allison tried to help, "Ruth, would it be OK if I give my thoughts about what Jackie might be trying to say?"

"OK."

"I think Jackie knows that you love her and always loved her as much as you loved Jane. I think, at times, for whatever reason, she felt less approval, or less acceptance. That does not mean that you felt less. She experienced less.

"But I did love her . . . or accept her as much. . . . I always did. She has to believe me!" Ruth was becoming distressed.

"Ruth, I can hear your distress over your daughter's experience of part of your relationship with her over the years. I can understand why you want so much . . . so much to reassure her that you did not have those thoughts . . . that you were not disappointed in her. . . ."

"I wasn't!"

"Ruth, would you be able—if it would help your daughter—and I believe that it would—not to reassure her right now. Right now, just try to imagine what her experience must have been—and I know that this is painful for you as it would be for any mother—how hard her experience must have been if she often thought that you were disappointed in her. Whether or not you actually were is not so important right now. If she thought that you were. What her experience must have been."

"But! . . ."

"I know that we are asking something now from you that is hard to . . . . If she thought that you were disappointed. . . ."

Ruth sat motionless, at first stunned, tense, troubled. Then she looked into Jackie's eyes and saw her daughter's tears. She wanted to say that it wasn't so. She did accept her! And then she heard Allison's words in her mind again, "If she thought that you were disappointed . . . how hard . . . for her." Ruth reached out and took her daughter's hand. She spoke, though Jackie hardly heard the words,

"I'm so sorry . . . I'm so sorry . . . I didn't mean to . . . I'm so sorry."

"Thanks, Mom." Jackie became anxious for her mom, for herself. "I don't feel that now."

Allison quietly joined their dialogue, "Jackie, your mom is really, really with you now in the pain that you felt for so long. Let her help you with it.

It is not too hard for her. Let her be there for you now. Let her be with you now."

Jackie and Ruth silently stared at each other, both now crying. And they embraced.

After a few minutes they moved apart and Jackie quietly said, "Thanks, Mom."

Allison again quietly inserted herself into their joined presence, "Jackie, tell your mom more now about your experiences with her over the years. She wants to help you with this. It is hard for her but she is being so strong for you. Let her know so that she can understand."

Jackie's anxiety returned. Hadn't she said enough! She didn't need to ask her mom for more! She looked at Allison's calm and caring face. She had trusted her before with Gabe and Katie. She would trust her again. She went back into her experience.

"Mom, I know that at times I wasn't the easiest kid to raise. And I do know that Jane really did not make the mistakes that I made. I know that." She struggled over how to go further with her thoughts. She did not want to hurt her mother. Then the words seemed to decide for her.

"What was hardest for me, Mom . . . I think . . . is that sometimes I thought that you thought that I was selfish. That you were more disappointed in what you thought was why I did something wrong than in what I actually did. I felt I . . . really did . . . that you thought that I was selfish."

"I'm sorry, honey. I'm so sorry."

"And then . . . sometimes I so much wished that I were Jane . . . or like Jane. And other times I hated her. You didn't seem to think that she was selfish. Just me. . . . And then I hated myself."

Mother and daughter continued to stare at each other. Ruth's unwavering compassion for her daughter's pain gave Jackie the courage to continue.

"Mom, I never hated you. . . . I really didn't. . . . And I know that you didn't hate me. . . . It was just . . . just . . . that . . . you were a bit disappointed with me . . . and I often thought that I would never . . . never be as special to you as Jane is."

"Oh, honey." Ruth started to move toward Jackie but her daughter held out her hand.

"Please, Mom. This is so hard. But I need to finish. . . . On Thanksgiving, I disappointed you again. And I hated myself again. And this time I hated Katie, too. I again caused you to be unhappy . . . and Mom, right now . . . right now . . . I feel that I might be disappointing you by telling you these things . . . by making you unhappy again . . . by being selfish . . . by bothering you about things that I should have let go of years ago. That I'm only considering me and not realizing that you did the best you could."

Jackie and Ruth stared at each other. Jackie wanted Ruth to talk, but she feared what she would hear. Ruth wanted to talk but hesitated, not knowing if Jackie had more that she needed to say first.

Finally, Ruth could wait no longer, "Honey, I have never been so proud of you as I am now. You have the courage. . . ." Ruth began to cry. Jackie and Allison waited quietly. Jackie reached out and took her mother's hand. Ruth continued, "You have the courage . . . that I never had to tell my feelings to my mother. . . . And my feelings were so much like yours! I was convinced that I was never good enough. I was convinced that I was selfish. And I never was able to tell her. And you did . . . and you are . . . and I'm just so proud . . . of who you are . . . of who you have become. I am so lucky to be able to call you my daughter . . . so lucky that you never gave up on me to be your mother when you needed your mother."

They embraced again. Jackie began to shake as she cried. Ruth stroked her back and hair and then held her tight and rocked back and forth with her daughter in her arms. After a moment she kissed her face and then pulled her close again.

Minutes later they moved away a bit though their hands remained together.

When they looked at Allison together and smiled, she spoke, "I am honored to have been present just now with you both. I so admire what you both have been able to do. I feel joy for you . . . and with you . . . right now."

## COMMENTARY

When Jackie first spoke with Allison about her doubts about her relationship with her mother, she became aware that it was affecting her relationship with Katie. She became increasingly able to see how some of Katie's behaviors elicited a response in her that probably had as much to do with her past interactions with Ruth as it had to do with Katie's actual behavior. She became more aware that if she could make sense of her relationship with her mother, she might be able to better parent Katie. Most likely her initial motivation in doing the difficult work of addressing her relationship with Ruth was to help Katie. Frequently, this is the case. Many parents would be unlikely to try to resolve and integrate difficult experiences that they had had with their own parents if it were it not for the desire to better meet their child's needs. This motivated Jackie to first speak with Allison. As the days went by, Jackie increasingly wanted to address those experiences for her own sake as well as for her relationship with Ruth, not Katie.

In this story, Ruth's response to Jackie proved to be excellent and facilitated a strengthening of their relationship. If Ruth were not able to "hear"

Jackie and have empathy for her, the experience in Allison's office would have been very stressful for them both and unsettled the overall stability of their ongoing relationship. Allison would have made Jackie aware of the risks that she was taking in addressing those unresolved experiences. Since Jackie was an adult who was functioning quite well in her life and had the strong support of her husband and others, Allison was confident that Jackie would be able to integrate the experience even if Ruth rejected her efforts to obtain understanding and validation. When Allison worked with children like Katie, she needed to be more certain about the ability and willingness of the parent to "hear" and have empathy for the child's experience before asking the child to communicate their vulnerabilities to her parent.

Frequently, a child with significant difficulties due to trauma and attachment problems such as Katie activates the foster or adoptive parents' own attachment histories. When they are able to successfully address and integrate those experiences through the help of their partner, friend, or therapist, they often see an immediate improvement in their ability to maintain The Attitude with their child. When they are able to openly discuss and integrate these experiences with one or both of their parents, the improvements are even more obvious and easy to attain. Even when their parent is not able to join them in revisiting their early family years, this exploration into their own life story is likely to facilitate their social and emotional development, including their parenting abilities. When the parents are willing and able to do what they ask their struggling child to do, all benefit from the journey.

# 14

## Winter in Maine

The next few months were a roller coaster ride with each hill bigger than the last. At each summit, Katie's rage outbursts were something to experience. She would hurl herself to the floor, bruising her body and knocking over anything nearby. Anger seemed to be her only way to enter into a relationship. Katie was here! So alive! With such passion! And so much hate! And always under the hate, always—the shame!

At the foot of each hill, she would seem to be miles away, lost somewhere in a reality that she could not share. Katie would express no affect through which one could sense her inner life. At these times, Jackie almost wished for her anger.

But Jackie first noticed another quality in Katie early in January, a few weeks after the holiday season. Katie might laugh spontaneously and begin to enjoy talking with Jackie and Mark. There was a genuineness to her interactions which had never before been evident. She seemed to be able to briefly recreate how she was during "mom time" outside of those structured times that were maintained by Jackie's intersubjective presence. At these times, she did not convey her usual obsessive and controlling qualities, nor did she talk in her typical chattering monologues. Katie seemed to be "an ordinary kid" at these moments. Jackie did not mention these observations to her. Often they would end suddenly with Katie saying or doing something that was certain to cause a break in any comfortable emotional reciprocity in their time together. Jackie counted these moments in minutes, not hours. She told Allison about it and they both smiled in hope. They were careful not to expect it to continue. They needed to guard against disappointment. Also, their very expectation would probably be sensed by Katie and would certainly drive her further away again. They would not expect these moments—they would be open to them, discover them, respond to them, and accept them.

Katie had now been with Jackie for seven months. To most outsiders, Katie had not changed at all. Allison and Jackie knew that she had. They had seen moments of reciprocal enjoyment where the need to control seemed to dissipate. They saw a child who might be told something to do, and who actually, calmly, did it! They saw a child who seemed to be expressing — at times — a sense of inner safety and contentment. They did not know if these moments would ever become a significant part of her life.

On January 27, 1995, Allison and Jackie met with Steven and his supervisor, Kathy. Kathy had told them last June that she would review their progress in six months and she had actually given them an extra month. Steven had not been able to attend many therapy sessions over the last two months, either, so the meeting would serve to give him an update.

Jackie summarized Katie's typical days with their rage and defiance, lies and destruction. She went on to describe how Katie spent a lot of time sitting quietly, working, or playing with a few toys in whatever room that Jackie happened to be in. She mentioned how Katie frequently ate her meal alone after everyone else had finished because she would often try to disrupt the meal by saying something mean to someone or by eating her food in some gross way. She indicated that Katie had only received a few small gifts for both her birthday and Christmas since anything more would only disrupt her functioning and ruin the day for her, and possibly other members of the family, too. Katie did seem to accept Jackie's hugs and she even asked to be rocked and sung to on occasion. Jackie was excited by those moments of shared enjoyment. She explained to Kathy and Steven what her "mom times" with Katie were like and how she hoped that they would serve to open the door for Katie to experience having a mother in a new way. Katie now had another way of living in the home besides being motivated only by her pervasive needs for control. Of course, apart from the bedtime ritual, she did not choose that "other way" very often.

Allison spoke of how Katie was generally quite engaged during the treatment sessions, even though Allison directed the session and related with her in a close, intersubjective, manner. Allison noted that Katie still had a great deal of difficulty exploring her misbehaviors without falling into seemingly endless shame. This led to defensiveness, denial, and rage. Allison said that Katie seemed to be able to manage her shame-experiences more openly, but not consistently so. She indicated that these explorations would remain central to Katie's therapy since they were central to both the integration of her sense of self and also to her readiness to form a secure attachment to Jackie. Allison also described those therapeutic experiences of special affect and intimacy, which she took to be indicative of Katie's potential for a more significant and lasting developmental attachment security.

"So far she doesn't seem to have made any significant improvements that last on their own," Kathy suggested. "She sounds just as angry and defiant as she was when she first came into foster care over two years ago. Will she ever really be able to live a normal life in a family?"

"That's our goal or we wouldn't be pushing her and ourselves so hard," Allison said. "She's still only seven years old. She's bright and she's a fighter. We're just teaching her that she doesn't need to fight with Jackie, especially when she's having a hard time and needs her the most. If she can learn that, she'll have quite a future. Also, I really don't agree with you about her not having made any significant improvements. Certainly, there are no major external changes. However, she has demonstrated more subtle changes in her ability to tolerate intense affect and closeness with Jackie and me. I think that for the first time she is beginning to notice the world of trust, affection, and reciprocal enjoyment. She hasn't stepped fully into that world but she has noticed it and maybe gotten her toes wet."

"But will she ever do that, I mean really do it?" Kathy asked.

"I don't know. But I know that she deserves a shot at it. I also don't know anyone who could encourage her to do it better than Jackie. She's doing a great deal for this kid and I think that someday we'll see the results."

"What do you think, Jackie?" Steven asked.

"I agree with Allison," Jackie replied. "I can't read into the future but I know that Katie has spunk. She works hard at what she thinks is best for her. The problem is that what we think and know is best for her is almost always something different from what she works for. She just has to discover that she needs a mother, not a servant. She needs to learn how to have fun with me, rely on me, and listen to me, not control me and get me to reject her."

"She seems to have come pretty close to getting you to reject her on Thanksgiving," Steven said.

"Yes, she did. But not since then and I feel like I'm on a roll. The little turkey has met her match," Jackie smiled.

"Well," Kathy said, "this brings us to our next big question. We need to decide if we should proceed with asking the court to terminate Sally and Mike's parental rights. She has been in foster care for almost two and one-half years now, and her parents have done very little toward reunification with her. As you know, her mother is not really interested in seeing her more than every few months and she has done little work in her own psychotherapy. Her father has done nothing and they continue to live together. Neither parent has accepted responsibility for their acts of abuse or neglect. They actually are not seeing a therapist now because they failed to keep some sessions and they need to make a payment for the missed appointments."

"It has seemed to me ever since I first saw her that this kid is not going to be reunited with her parents," Allison said, "Not only are they not doing their work but they have left her so damaged that they could never adequately raise her again. If she went back to them she wouldn't last a week and she'd leave there so damaged that there would be a big risk that she never would be able to make it."

"You're right about that," Kathy said, "but another important question that the court will be asking is whether or not she is adoptable. If we cannot say that we can successfully place her for adoption, I doubt if the judge will terminate her parents' rights. The court does not like to create legal orphans, no matter how improbable it is that she will ever have a meaningful relationship with her parents."

"I understand your problem," Allison said. "At this time, even if you found an adoptive home willing to try to raise her, the risk is there that the adoption would eventually disrupt. Even if the adoptive parents maintained their commitment to her, she is likely to need major services in the years ahead unless she can make significant changes. Her chances of making those changes are much greater if she can continue her work with Jackie and me."

"But the question is, will this kid be able to be adopted at some point down the road?" asked Kathy.

"I strongly believe that Katie should have the opportunity to be adopted. And I'm more than willing to recommend that to a Judge," Allison said. "You know that even if the Judge agrees to terminate her parents' rights three months from now, it will still be another nine to twelve months before an adoption worker has gotten to know Katie and found the right home for her. That will give Jackie and me a lot of time to continue working with her and help her to be as healthy as possible before adoption. She is still only seven. She deserves a shot at a permanent home, although we will have to be very careful to match her up with the right family."

"Since we're still mandated to do reunification, Jackie, I have to be careful how I word this," Kathy said. "If her parents' rights were terminated in the future, do you think that you would apply to adopt Katie?"

There was silence and Jackie seemed to have trouble breathing for a moment. Finally she said, "That idea has crossed my mind any number of times, Kathy. The thought of getting her to finally trust me and then telling her that she is going to be adopted by someone else sure doesn't feel good. I had the same situation with Gabe. I cried a lot before deciding that I could not adopt him. There are various reasons, none of which made me feel any better in making my decision with him. The main reason is that I truly want to continue my work as a foster parent who can help these troubled kids really learn about maternal love. I think that I'd like to do it for another 20 years or so, which means another 10 or 15 kids. I couldn't do that if I had adopted Gabe. If I had, I wouldn't be working with Katie now."

"I hadn't really thought through what you're doing with Katie," said Steven. "Now I'm wondering if this is right. Should we be setting it up so that she attaches to Jackie only to have her move to another home a year later? Is that fair to her? Are we being deceitful?"

"That's a hard question to answer," Allison said. "Over the years I have come up with three responses. First, what other options do we have? With a kid as unable to form attachment security with caregivers as Katie is, I am convinced that the odds that she could do it with adoptive parents are not good. Most adoptive parents are not interested in adopting in order to become foster parents. They want to give their love and home to a kid who can accept what they have to offer to a reasonable degree and benefit from living with them. Katie would be unlikely to respond to such a home unless the parents were able and committed to learn to parent her in a way similar to the way Jackie is doing. It takes a certain kind of person to parent a kid like Katie. If we are truly honest with prospective adoptive parents about what really is involved in parenting a child with severe difficulties secondary to trauma and attachment disruptions, I don't think that we'll find nearly enough families who sign up for the duration. Also, the types of interventions offered by me and Jackie are not available in many parts of the state and country. This is a fairly new area of knowledge that is not yet understood well enough by mental health and social services professionals."

"Second, since it usually takes at least two or more years from the time a child enters foster care until she is placed into an adoptive home when reunification with the parents is not successful, is it really in the child's best interest to be discouraged in her need to develop attachment security? Can we—should we—ask a child to rely on herself while living in foster care, rather than on her foster parents? Tell her that her foster parents should not mean much to her? Tell her foster parents not to let the child into their hearts? I would consider such a stance to be emotionally neglectful. Those children would be less able to respond to an adoptive placement than would those children who are able to form a secure attachment with their foster parents."

"Third," Allison continued, "it has been my experience that Katie will be able to form an attachment with adoptive parents after first learning how to do it with Jackie. When Gabe learned that he would not be staying with Jackie and that he would have his own adoptive family, he cried and screamed for days. But this was healthy grief over his anticipated loss of the first person whom he ever trusted. Yet throughout the grieving, he was able to turn to Jackie for comfort! When he was ready to face the adoption itself, he talked with her for hours about his hopes and fears about his new family! When he finally got the photos of his new parents, he was excited and he shared his excitement with Jackie.

He did not retreat into his life prior to learning how to show attachment security. He did not lose his trust for Jackie. He knew that she still loved him and wanted what was best for him. It is important that the child be told clearly that the foster placement is temporary and that when they do develop attachment security, they be supported in their grief. Katie has been told that her placement in Jackie's home is temporary."

"How is Gabe doing in his adoptive home?" Steven asked.

"Well, he's been living with his family for about 12 months now and it is going well," Jackie said. "He was sad for a while but now he seems to feel secure in his home. He calls me and sends me letters. It's obvious that I'm still important to him. I think I've become a special aunt to him. Most importantly, his attachment to his adoptive mom seems to be strong. I wouldn't be surprised if by now she is more important to him psychologically than I am."

"It's sad that Katie will have to move someday," Allison added. "I am convinced, however, that adoption and not long-term foster care is the most likely to meet her needs. It would not serve her interests if we discouraged her from learning to develop attachment security until her parents' rights were terminated and she were placed in an adoptive home. And she would have wasted two or three years of her early life when she is more receptive to learning how to attach. And she most likely would have had another three or four placements. And after all that, there's a fair chance that a suitable adoptive home could not be found. I don't have to tell you about the many adolescents in foster care who do not have a permanent home and who are not likely to form a secure attachment with anyone who really loves them and is committed to their care."

"No, you don't," Kathy said. "Thanks for explaining your reasoning and your experiences with kids who are able to learn to develop a secure attachment to their foster parents and then are adopted by someone else. That's certainly an important issue if a child is not adopted by his foster parents. We'll be discussing this back at the office, but there's a good chance that when we go to court in the spring we will be seeking to terminate Mike and Sally's parental rights."

On February 20, 1995, Katie's one-week school vacation started. She was doing fairly well at school, compared to her home difficulties. Her teacher, Mrs. Robinson, said that she was keeping up with her class in her academics and might even be reading at a higher level. However, she really did not seem to comprehend what she read as well as did the other kids in the class. She had a hard time discussing the stories and her teacher thought that she often did not seem to understand the main theme and the wishes and motives of the characters.

With her peers at school, Katie tended to be controlling and domineering. She did not seem to have formed any special friends. The other kids were not sure how she would react and they tended to give her some distance. Mrs. Robinson thought that she was socially immature compared to her peers. She also had initiated a reward system to see if she could increase Katie's on-task behaviors and reduce some of her disruptive behaviors. When she talked with Jackie about implementing a similar system at home in order to have greater consistency, Jackie declined and indicated that she already had a very comprehensive and structured program in place that did not rely on concrete rewards to motivate her. Mrs. Robinson then tactfully told Jackie that Katie had told her of some of the consequences that she got at home. She went on to add that Jackie might attain greater results if she adopted a more positive approach to Katie's problems, rather than emphasizing her misbehaviors. She suggested that Jackie consult with the school behavioral specialist for ideas that would focus on the positive. Jackie explained why she doubted that such a behavioral plan would work, given Katie's significant difficulty tolerating the more basic "rewards" of fun and love. She indicated that she did not regard the structure and supervision that she was giving to Katie to be "negative," but rather were giving Katie a greater opportunity to engage in positive behaviors. Mrs. Robinson became aware of the fact that she and Jackie really were not speaking the same language. Jackie was grateful when Katie's teacher changed the conversation to academics.

Katie continued to show the intensity of her rage at Jackie in every way imaginable. She was indiscriminate in her choice of time, place, and circumstance, to unveil her hatred. She would be angry at whatever Jackie said or did, simply because she needed to be. The question that Allison posed was, What did she actually seek to attain by her outrage? Rejection by Jackie? Proof of her own worthlessness? Matching rage from Jackie? Denial of her own despair? Confirmation of her expectations that the world would never meet her needs? That the world, namely Jackie, really didn't care? Allison thought that at times Katie was motivated by any or all of these factors. Jackie agreed.

Why then did she seem to appropriately engage Jackie at times? Why did she seem to be genuinely interested in something happening in the family that did not relate to her? Why did she seem to actually enjoy herself? Yes, these times lasted 10 minutes, tops, but they still counted. They counted a lot.

Without having the structure provided by school, Katie needed to have a fairly tight schedule at home if she were to function at all appropriately during the vacation week. Jackie planned some arts and crafts activities along with the usual routines. She also intended to get Katie out in the snow for a time every day although Katie would most certainly complain about being cold and quickly begin to whine about wanting to come inside.

Jackie decided after lunch to take Katie outside to build a snow horse in the back yard. After the usual grumbling, Katie did manage to find and put on both of her boots along with her snowsuit—not a small accomplishment. The snow was wet, heavy, and sticky—great to work with. In little time at all, they managed to roll together two large snowballs that would form the body of the horse. They struggled to raise a smaller ball on top of one of the large ones. This would somehow be fashioned into the neck and head. The tail would come last, if they could get it to stick to the other ball. Then they would shape the four legs and cut out an opening between the front and back legs. Surprisingly, Katie involved herself in the activity and complained little. After finally shaping it to their satisfaction, Katie backed up to look at it while Jackie began digging out the space under the body.

"It doesn't look like a horse!" Katie yelled.

"Sure it does!" Jackie hollered back. "You just have to use your imagination a bit."

"It looks like a big dog!" Katie yelled again and laughed.

"A big dog! What are you talking about?" Jackie smiled and got up and walked over to Katie.

"That's no dog!" Jackie said. They both continued to stare at it. "It's more like a bear!" They both laughed.

"No, it's a little elephant!" Katie said. They laughed even harder.

"I think it's a giant frog!" Katie continued to laugh.

"Katie, don't call our horse a frog! A dog or elephant is one thing, but not a frog!" Jackie teased.

"It's a goat!" Katie added as she howled.

"Katie, cut it out!" Jackie pretended annoyance at her descriptions of their work.

"It's a goat!" Katie repeated.

"You're asking for it!" Jackie took a handful of snow and threw it at Katie, hitting her on the chest with some of it going on her face. Jackie held her breath.

Katie screamed. This scream was different. It was permeated with laughter. Katie took snow into her hand and ran at Jackie. Jackie fell backwards and Katie pushed the snow into her face. Jackie then screamed and grabbed Katie and they both rolled in the snow until they were wet with snow and sweat.

"Katie, why don't you sit on our 'goat' and you'll discover that it feels like a horse." Jackie finally said. They ran to their snow figure and Jackie lifted Katie up onto it. She then knelt down and continued to dig an opening under it.

Katie finally got into the spirit of their "horse." She pretended that she was riding it, holding on tight as she galloped "across the plain." Katie yelled to her horse and bounced on its back. Jackie dug further and further under the horse until she made a hole to the other side. She started to back out when Katie's final bounce broke the back of their horse and what felt like an elephant and Katie fell on top of the shocked Jackie. Katie was scared at the sudden fall and the sight of Jackie's legs sticking out of the snow under her. Jackie was frightened over Katie's fall, especially since she could not see her or anything else until she dug her way from under their fallen steed.

"Are you OK?" Jackie asked as she struggled from under the avalanche.

"I'm fine," Katie replied and sat motionless, not knowing what to do next.

Slowly, and then with increasing momentum, they both began to laugh again, totally taken over by their wild adventures in the snow. There was little to show for their hour of labor to build the white horse.

"Well, Katie, I guess our horse doesn't much look like anything now. But I think we must look like two soggy ducks," Jackie said while still reclining among the ruins.

"Two soggy ducks!" Katie repeated and laughed again. Then she added without thinking, "A mama duck and her baby. Stuck in the snow away from their nest."

"Well, Katie," Jackie said, taking that comment as casually as she could, "this mama duck and her baby had better get into their nest right away or they're going to get sick." Jackie got up and helped Katie to her feet.

As they walked toward the house, they took one last look at their piles of snow.

"Katie," Jackie said, "now we can tell everyone that we made a beautiful horse and no one will ever know that it looked more like a goat."

Katie liked that idea. In the kitchen, she told Diane about their beautiful horse that sadly collapsed. She looked at Jackie, smiled, and almost winked.

Jackie decided to give Katie a snack with hot chocolate and crackers. They both fussed about being cold and enjoying the warmth of the kitchen. Jackie wondered when Katie would do something to try to ruin the atmosphere. She had never spent so long with her when they both were having fun. The old record was about 10 minutes. She was entering new territory. It could not last.

After the snack, Katie took her plate and cup to the sink. She turned to Jackie and asked, "Can I watch the movie *Aladdin* on TV now?"

Jackie knew this was the moment for the outburst. Katie had found a great reason to be angry and she just needed Jackie's cooperation.

"Not this afternoon, sweetie. I'd like you to sweep the kitchen floor while I do the dishes and then you can play in the dining room while I do some paperwork that I have to get done. I know you've had a lot of fun and it's hard to stop. Kinda sad that fun can't go on forever, isn't it? Oh well, *Aladdin* will be there some other day."

Jackie looked at Katie. She wasn't screaming of throwing herself on the floor. Neither did she reach for something to throw, nor try to run from the room. She just stood there. And she looked sad. Sad! She looked right into Jackie's eyes with nothing but sadness in her expression. Jackie did not know what to say. She patted her head and commented again about it being hard when fun stops.

"OK, Mom," Katie said quietly and walked to the closet to get the broom and dustpan. Jackie turned to the sink and almost dropped her cup. She forced herself to stay there, splashing in the water and trying to wash the dishes. She didn't want to do anything that would confuse the situation and interfere with whatever was going on inside Katie's head.

The rest of the day and evening were fairly uneventful. Katie complained a bit and tried to get Matthew upset with her. She went to bed without a fuss and seemed to enjoy Jackie's reading to her and tucking her in.

As Jackie turned to leave her room, Katie asked, "Mom, can we make another horse tomorrow. I'd like everyone to see it and draw a picture of it."

"That sounds like a plan, Katie. I'd enjoy it, too. We should have some time after lunch just like today."

"Good night, Mom."

"Good night, Katie kiddo."

The next day the horse never got made. When Katie came down for breakfast, she refused to eat the eggs, toast, and juice that Jackie gave her and she insisted on having pancakes. That disagreement led to her refusing to eat, refusing to wash herself and brush her teeth, refusing to "pick up" the downstairs rooms, refusing to sit and think about her choices, and generally just being disagreeable and a pain to be around. This led to Katie spitting at Jackie and then needing restraint. Katie's gloomy and cross attitude continued throughout the day.

"But why didn't you tell her how great it was that she was able to have fun with you and also that she was able to accept it when you told her 'no?'" Steven asked at the next therapy session after hearing about the snow horse.

"If I had," Jackie replied, "she never would have finished the day OK and she probably wouldn't have another time like that for quite some time."

"But if she's not going to be praised for that, when will you praise her? How will she ever know that she's doing a good job?"

"Steven, you're assuming that if Jackie shows pleasure in what she did, Katie will be more likely to do it again," Allison said, "But that's not Katie. She's not going to be motivated to act that way because Jackie's getting something out of it. If Jackie is really pleased, Katie won't be able to see that this is benefiting her, not Jackie. She'll think that Jackie wants her to act that way for her own benefit, not for Katie's. The best praise for Katie now is simply Jackie's enjoyment during the activity—expressed nonverbally and spontaneously—that reflects their reciprocal fun and Jackie's happiness *for and with* Katie's happiness. She can't yet imagine that Jackie really is happy *for her*, and not for her own benefit. Finally, if she thinks that Jackie is pleased when she acts this way, she'll think that this is a new way to frustrate Jackie. She'll resist having fun with Jackie and instead be motivated to bug Jackie, without any focus on whether or not having fun with Jackie is of benefit to herself."

"I still don't see why it will hurt her progress if we just tell her that she's finally doing what we have wanted her to do for so long." Steven was not convinced.

"She's only going to do it when she wants to," Allison said. "She'll continue to do it, *if* she wants to. This is *her* experiment to decide if *she* wants a life based on attachment with Jackie. Stating our preference for her, *at the time that she's trying it out*, will distract her from the inner feedback that I want her to notice. Namely: 'This is good.' 'I like this.' 'This isn't anything to be scared of.'"

"So when can she handle praise?" Steven asked.

"Praise is overrated as a way to raise kids generally," Allison said. "Praising kids has at least as many disadvantages to their development as advantages, if not more. Parents need to foster intrinsic motivation for the child to do what is in his long-term best interests. Intrinsic motivation is not based on external factors, whether they are rewards or personal evaluations that we call praise. Intrinsic motivation comes from parents loving their kid a lot, being good models about how to live, and communicating the need to learn to make choices and to live with the consequences of the choices that we make. Intrinsic motivation comes from feeling good inside over the consequences of one's own actions. It needs to be her judgment, not ours. Showing our kid how special she is and being interested in how she is learning to manage her life goes a lot further in fostering her development than making comments such as 'good girl.' I want her, and *only* her, to ever decide if she's a good person."

"Saying that she did a 'good job' is OK, but overdone, I believe," Allison continued. "Kids are often told that a hundred times a day. They know when it really is a good job and when it's routine or mediocre. When we use it too much they probably get the idea that we think they really are not very capable. And they cannot escape the feeling that we are always evaluating them. They need to feel that we enjoy and accept their behavior most of the time, accept them all of the time and evaluate their behavior infrequently, and evaluate them—never. Sure, give specific recognition for something that your kid

is proud about. You are sharing her joy. You are affirming her inner experiences. You are loving her, not evaluating her. But don't think that your praise
is what motivates and maintains a child's interests and accomplishments
while traveling on his life's path."

"But Katie gets into trouble dozens of times each day," Steven said.
"Aren't we evaluating her each time and doing it negatively. Shouldn't we
balance it with dozens of positive evaluations, no matter how small they are?"

"When Katie is getting into 'trouble' dozens of times, we are not evaluating her at those times," Allison said. "We are accepting her. We are evaluating her choices when we are connecting consequences to them. We might be
puzzled at her choice because it leads to a seemingly undesirable consequence, but we are not evaluating it. We might even say something like,
'Well, Katie, I hope that you'll be happy with your choice.' Or, 'If you change
your mind, you'll probably have another chance, tomorrow, or next week, or
whenever.' Or 'Maybe you do like this consequence, or maybe you'll like the
other one.' Or 'Oh, well, there are other days.' And we make those comments
without sarcasm or an 'I know better than you' attitude. We do want her to
choose what is best for her, and we will expect her to manage whatever consequence her choice brings her. If she becomes upset by the consequence,
that's fine. We'll support her through her distress, but we will not eliminate
the consequence."

"Sure, at times we need to evaluate her negative behaviors—and do so in
a strong, clear manner. If she tries to hurt the dog, she does need a strong response that such behaviors are not acceptable. But those behaviors are less
frequent than we think with most children. They need acceptance for their inner lives and for most of their behaviors—with the associated consequences,
with our few strong evaluations being directed toward specific serious behaviors."

"As usual," Steven said, "I hear you and might eventually come to agree
with you. Right now, I need to give that some thought."

"Fine with me," Allison replied. "Well, it's time for me to get the kid
again."

Once settled on the couch between Jackie and Allison, Katie demonstrated
her usual curious and mildly playful attitude that suggested that she would
probably be fairly receptive to Allison's interventions.

"Katie, your mom tells me that you and she made a beautiful snow horse.
It must have been so sad when it broke and fell on her," Allison said inno-
cently.

Katie looked at Jackie and smiled. "We really were *so* sad. Mom said that
she had never made one so pretty," Katie said quietly before exploding in
laughter.

"What's so funny?" Allison asked. "What are you two laughing about?"

"Oh, nothing," Jackie said.

"Nothing!" Katie said and laughed some more.

"Something is not right here!" Allison exclaimed. "What really happened?"

"Nothing!" Katie yelled again. Then she looked at Jackie again.

"Tell me, Katie, or you're in trouble." Allison smiled.

"It's true!" She laughed.

"You asked for it!" Allison said as she tickled her and playfully pushed her head against the pillow. "Now tell me!"

"OK!" Katie yelled. "It was ugly and looked like a goat. Or a dog."

"Katie even said that it looked like a frog, too!" Jackie added.

"We weren't sad when it broke. We laughed until I almost peed!" Katie shouted.

"So that's it. An ugly horse. And you almost peed in the snow. If you had peed, you probably would have told everyone that the ugly horse had done it!" Allison suggested.

They chatted some more about the great deal of snow that was falling on Maine that winter. Allison suggested that they make a snow dinosaur next. Jackie grumbled when she thanked her for the suggestion while Katie got excited about the idea.

"It will probably end up looking like a whale," Steven added.

After discussing a few more minor events of the week, Allison directed Katie's attention to her past, "Katie, we haven't talked much about Sally and Mike lately. You were hurt a lot when you lived with them in many ways. We need to talk about that part of your life more so that it doesn't hurt your life now so much."

"It doesn't hurt me," Katie said.

"I wish it didn't, sweetie," Allison said, "I think it does though. It makes it hard for you to live with your new family without having so many troubles. I think that Sally and Mike are still mixing you up inside and you don't know how to trust Jackie and Mark very well."

When Katie did not reply, Allison continued, "Today I'd like to make a play. You will be Katie and Jackie will be Jackie. But I am going to pretend to be Sally. I'll be guessing what Sally might say to you and your mom as if she were here and I'll say those things. You pretend that I'm Sally and say whatever you want to me. OK?"

Katie looked at Jackie and then nodded.

"Your mom, Jackie, will be sitting next to you on the couch. I'll leave the room and when I come back, I'll be pretending that I'm Sally. I'll sit in that chair and begin to talk with you both. Remember, the things that I say are not what I think or feel but what I am guessing that Sally might think or feel be-cause of how she treated you. If it gets too hard for you, let us know and we'll stop."

Allison waited for Katie to ask questions. When none came, she added, "If you can't think of something to say, Jackie will whisper something into your ear and you can say that. Jackie's job will be to help you to feel safe and to give you things to say if you get stuck. OK?"

"Yeah," Katie said, almost looking excited, but showing anxiety, too. Allison got up and left the room. Jackie sat on the couch next to Katie with her arm around her. Jackie asked her if there were things that she wanted to say to Sally. Katie couldn't think of anything so Jackie gave a few suggestions. Katie added another and they sat and waited for Allison's return.

There was a knock on the door and Allison entered. Katie laughed when she saw her. She was wearing a long dark coat, and had a scarf over her hair. Katie had never seen those clothes before. Allison also held a cigarette in her hand. She had learned that Sally smoked a lot.

Katie laughed and yelled, "You don't look like Sally!"

Allison ignored what she said and then spoke to her, more rapidly than she usually spoke and with a higher pitch to her voice, "Hello, Katie, I haven't seen you in a long time. How are you doing?"

"OK," Katie replied, still laughing.

"Who is that lady, Katie? You living with her?"

"Yeah, she's my mom, Jackie," Katie replied with a smile.

"She's not your mom!" "Sally" yelled. "I'm your mom and you only have one, so don't you call her mom!"

"She's my mom now," Katie said, no longer smiling.

"She is *not* your mom, I said," "Sally" yelled. "So call her Jackie!"

"I'll call her mom if I want to," Katie said.

"Well, you're still the brat that you where when you lived with me," "Sally" said. "I can see that they have not helped you any!"

"I'm not a brat!" Katie said. "You're a brat!"

"Don't talk to me that way, little girl!" "Sally" yelled. Then she turned to Jackie and said in a grouchy tone, "Is she bad most of the time like she was with me?"

"Katie is not a bad girl, Sally," Jackie said firmly. "Sometimes she might make a poor choice about something, but she is *not* bad!"

"I don't believe you!" "Sally" said. "You probably spoil her and don't make her mind! No wonder she hasn't changed."

"You don't have to believe me, Sally," Jackie said, "but I'm telling the truth. Katie is a good kid, a special kid. And I don't spoil her. I love her and teach her how to live a good life in a good home."

"Yeah, right," "Sally" said with annoyance, "and you probably blame me for her problems, too, don't you?"

"I don't blame you, Sally, but I know that you and Mike did not raise her the way she needed to be raised. Whatever your reasons, you didn't love her enough in ways that she needed to be loved when she was a baby and little girl."

"Right, you know everything," "Sally" said loudly, "I was a better mother for her than you are!"

"You were not!" Katie yelled. "Jackie is a good mom! She never hits me and calls me names like you did. And you didn't care when Mike hit me hard. She'd never let anyone hurt me!"

"Shut up, kid, I wasn't talking to you!" "Sally" said.

"I will not shut up! You said something mean to my mom!" Katie yelled.

"Why did I bother coming to see you? You're bad and I'm wasting my time!" "Sally" said with disgust.

"You were bad, not me!" Katie yelled. "You never held me or played with me. You always told me to go to my room. You didn't want to be with me! And you slapped me just because I dropped something!"

"You don't remember how I raised you." "Sally" said. "You're just saying what other people told you and they're lying."

"I do remember!" Katie said forcefully. "I know you did those things to me. I don't forget how mad you were at me. You never wanted me with you!"

"I'm wasting my time as long as you're living with this lady who is lying to you about me! If I got you home again you'd start acting better or I'd know the reason why," "Sally" said.

"I'm not living with you again!" Katie yelled.

"Oh, yeah, you're not the boss!" "Sally" yelled. "I think I might just take you with me now!"

Katie leaned closer to Jackie and Jackie embraced her more tightly. "I'm not going with you! I'm staying with my new mom!"

"That's what you think, kid!" "Sally" yelled as she stood up and moved toward the couch. She reached for Katie's ankle. Just as she was about to touch it, Katie pulled her foot back up onto the couch.

"Don't you touch her!" Jackie yelled.

"Don't touch me!" Katie joined in.

"Come on, Katie, you're coming with me!" "Sally" yelled.

"No she's not, Sally, it's time for you to go!" Jackie said firmly.

"Leave!" Katie yelled.

"I don't have to do what you say!" "Sally" said.

"We're both telling you, Sally, it's time for you to go now!" Jackie said again.

"Go!" Katie said and pointed toward the door.

"Sally" turned toward the door, opened it quickly, and slammed it behind her.

There was silence in the office. Katie and Jackie remained in a tight embrace. Katie was breathing heavily. She was clearly upset.

"You sure didn't need much help from me, Katie," Jackie said quietly. "How do you feel about it?"

"I feel good. I told her that she did bad things. I wasn't a bad baby. How can a baby be bad?" Katie said.

"That's right, kiddo," Jackie said. "You told her the truth!"

"She said that she was a better mom than you are!" Katie said, almost in surprise at the idea. "I told her that you were a better mom!"

"I'm glad that you think and feel that way, sweetie!" Jackie said.

"I told her that I wasn't bad!" Katie said, as if surprised at herself.

"Yes, you did, Katie, yes, you did!" Jackie hugged her even tighter. They were quiet for a while. Then Jackie added, "That was hard work! I think that we both did a good job. Do you agree?"

"Yeah," Katie said slowly and quietly. They continued their embrace for a few minutes in silence.

Allison then entered, no longer wearing the coat and scarf. She sat in her usual chair and talked as if she had not been present. "Wow, you two look like you've been through a lot. How did it go?"

"I told her that I wasn't bad!" Katie exclaimed. "She said that I was a brat and I was bad and I said that she was a bad mom and I was not a bad baby."

"You did! It sounds like you really were able to tell her what you're learning about yourself and your past, Katie. I'll bet that feels great for you!" Allison said.

"Yeah! And she said that Jackie is a bad mom and that she was a better mom! And I told her that Jackie was the better mom, not her! And she got mad at me!" Katie spoke rapidly, talking as if Allison really did not know what had been said. She then continued, "And she tried to make me go with her! But I wouldn't let her take me! I held onto Mom and we told her to leave!"

"Wow, you two really went through a lot and it sounds like you really handled it well!" Allison said. "What do you think, Jackie?"

"We sure did, Allison. But we had to work really hard. It was scary the way that she yelled at us and said mean things about us. We held each other tight and that probably helped us to tell her that she was wrong in what she said!" Jackie said with satisfaction.

"Yeah!" Katie said, "We told her that she was wrong!"

"I like the work you two did!" Allison said, "What do you think, Steven? You heard them and 'Sally.'"

"It was something, Allison," Steven said. "It was a little scary, and Sally said some mean things. She also didn't tell the truth about how she and Mike raised Katie. I was glad when Katie told her that *she* was telling the truth. I also was glad that Katie told her that Jackie was a good mom!"

"I am, too," Allison added, "I sometimes have thought that Katie might have trouble telling the difference between Sally and Jackie. But it sounds like she really is learning to see the differences real well."

All four of them smiled and sat quietly for a few moments. Jackie and Katie were still hugging each other.

"I guess that there's not much more to say," Allison said. "Let's stop now."

When Jackie and Katie left, Steven stayed a moment to talk with Allison. "That was powerful, Allison. For a while I thought that it was going to be too much for Katie."

"Yes, Steven, it was hard for her. I was watching her closely and she seemed to be managing it well, though. If it had seemed to be too much to her I would have reduced the intensity or even stopped. She seemed almost driven to respond to 'Sally' and I sensed that she was doing what she needed to do."

"Is that enough or will you have to be 'Sally' again?" Steven asked.

"Well, that depends on a lot of things about Katie's functioning in the weeks ahead. Most likely, though, we will at least do it once again and this time try to elicit Katie's sense of loss over Sally's abandonment of her. Sally most certainly was nurturing, caring, and responsive to Katie sometimes. I need to give Katie the opportunity to be aware of that and to feel sad, if she has that feeling, over the fact that Sally was not able to be a better mom for her. If she can do that she might be able to accept and integrate the parts of herself that are sad, scared, and vulnerable, along with the angry and shameful parts just as she was when she was an infant and toddler."

"If she can do that," Steven said, "I guess we'll be home free."

"If she can do that," Allison added, "I guess Katie will have a decent chance to begin to learn what a home can really feel like."

**Jackie's Journal:**

February 28, 1995: Katie seemed more withdrawn today. I suggested that she still might be thinking about "Sally" from Allison's session yesterday. She would have none of that. At school, Katie apparently managed to get a toy reward for having a good day. She immediately threw it at another girl who was simply looking at her. When she was corrected for that, she looked at Mrs. Robinson, stepped on the toy, and smiled. I probably shouldn't feel pleased with that but I had a hard time not smiling when I read the note. Maybe they will gradually begin to understand Katie. Bedtime went well. She accepted my playing "Eeny Meeny Miny Mo" with her 10 toes and she giggled when I was being funny. She got a few hugs, too.

March 1, 1995: Katie seems to have found a new source of pleasure. Before dinner, I gave her markers to draw with at the table while I prepared the meal. I looked away for a moment. She had stepped on the felt tip of two markers lying on the floor. What a mess! And she looked at me and smiled! I guess it was something that she just had to find out for herself. It had rattled Mrs. Robinson, would it work on me? Well, not really. I was sad that she now had no markers to draw with since she so liked them. She got a bucket with soap water to clean up the floor. Of course, she was slow, thinking that she would be saved by dinner. Wrong! The rest of us ate at the dining room table while she continued her solitary cleaning. The teenagers were extra hungry and had extras. When Katie finally finished she had her meal but there weren't any extras. Bedtime went well. She even enjoyed our feeding each other slices of banana on toothpicks. After her dinner, I wasn't sure how that would go over but the bananas were getting old and I took the chance. I rocked her a bit too.

March 4, 1995: Katie actually did her chores this morning in an hour. Usually it takes her two or three on Saturday mornings. I found out why. She and Diane went outside in the middle of the snowstorm. To me, at this time of year, there is no snow that is good snow. To them, it was an opportunity to be kids. Imagine that. Katie actually choosing to be a kid. Diane seems to feel that she has permission to act younger and silly when she is playing with Katie. Katie doesn't mind. So they both were being silly and wild in the storm. Looking at them, who would know what a monumental task Katie was performing in front of my eyes. She was having fun. Really having fun! Maybe Katie is teaching us the value of "snow therapy." If so, I might move to northern Alaska. Sure enough, when she came in she left her wet snowsuit on the kitchen floor. And she ordered me to make them some hot chocolate. I told her to sit until she calmed down. Then she picked up her snowsuit and cleaned up the puddle on the floor. She got no hot chocolate but I offered her a choice of milk or orange juice. She said that I ruined her day. To her, I seem to make a habit of that. At bedtime we played "Pop Goes the Weasel." Each of her stuffed animals had a turn popping up from under the covers and in so doing knocking most of the other animals off the bed. Soft circles on her face helped her to sleep.

March 5, 1995: Church, as usual, did not impress Katie. She finds the entire service quite boring. Since, when she is noisy during the service, she spends some time later in the day being quiet to make up for the "thinking time" that she missed, she generally now chooses to have her "thinking time" at church to get it over with. Although today after lunch, she sat with Mark and looked at the Children's Bible together. She seems to like the Old Testament stories better than the New Testament. Why am I not surprised? I have noticed that by late Sunday afternoon Katie tends to be quite irritable and restless. Maybe spending the weekend with a fairly relaxed, friendly, and active family is hard on her. She needs school to get a break from the mental stress of family life. And summer is only about 15 weeks away! Bedtime, as usual, was our main time for some enjoyment. It's as if she calls a truce during our special time each night. The rest of the day—forget it.

March 10, 1995: Katie is furious that her teacher made her write an apology for breaking Erica's lunch box handle. She says that she did not do it and her teacher would not believe her! Imagine that! She says that her friend Sandy really did it but lied and said that she had done it! She apparently had to be restrained by Mrs. Robinson. Oh, well. The fruits of a lifetime of lying. Being blamed for something that you did not do. I told her that she could solve the problem easily by starting to tell the truth. She looked at me like I needed brain surgery. I suggested that if she ever changes her mind I might be available to help her to practice her truth telling. In the mean time, she was on her own among the hazards of being falsely accused.

March 11, 1995: What a wild Saturday. Katie was horrible when she awoke. By 10:00 a.m., she was friendly and cooperative. At lunch, she had to be sent from the table. By 2:00 p.m., she seemed to be content to do what was on the schedule. By 5:00 p.m., she was outrageous with John and not much better with me when I interceded, if only to save her life. At bedtime, she was loving and laughing and just a joy to be near. Why am I going crazy?

March 12, 1995: Today was a dream. She was cooperative in Church, helpful at lunch, a jolly companion while we explored the winter woods, and the same loving daughter that I saw last night, at bedtime. What does this mean? She must be setting me up prior to springing on me.

March 19, 1995: The whole week has gone well. Sure she has had her troubles, but she is managing her consequences OK and she is actually fun to be around. Maybe something is starting to sink in. Maybe Allison is right though, when she says, "Trust nothing until you have seen it for three months." We'll see.

## COMMENTARY

Katie had no idea what was happening deep within her brain. Actually none of us really does. Were connections between the "old brain" and the "new brain" that should have been developing during the first two years of her life now sprouting at the age of seven? Was she beginning to notice, and experience, the pleasure of reciprocal smiles and expressions? Was she starting to experience comfort, excitement, affection, and fun from being held, touched, grabbed, and at times, swung in a blanket by Jackie and Mark? Was she noticing the pleasure and security that came from reconnecting to her mom after a conflict? How and when did she first notice that others have feelings? She seemed to be worried when Whimsy did not get up one morning and Jackie took him to the vet. Was she feeling empathy? For Whimsy? For Jackie?

Katie was beginning to notice the interpersonal world of the Keller home. And she was a part of it. The other family members were not simply "living objects" to manipulate, deceive, intimidate, or attack. Jackie did not talk with her, listen to her, feed her, comb her hair, and giggle or snuggle with her at night because she had to. Steven, Allison, Mark, and Katie herself did not make Jackie do those things. Jackie wanted to. Why? Now that was a question that still stumped Katie. It had never occurred to her that anyone would take pleasure in being with her, keeping her safe, playing with her, and helping her. Jackie did. Why?

The questions were appearing and her mind was struggling with them. Katie tried to avoid them. Hence, her roller coaster ride of January, February, and March. If she could manage to avoid those questions, she could preserve the map of her world that she had patched together with Sally and Mike. She could base her life on charm and rage, excuses and blaming others, and above all, controlling everything in order to try to keep herself safe and meet her basic needs. These new questions disrupted her first assumptions, which were the fruits of her first efforts to make sense of her life. Jackie and Allison constantly raised these questions and it was increasingly hard to avoid them. Within and without, Katie was in turmoil.

The psychodrama in which Allison played the role of Katie's birth mother, Sally, proved to assist Katie in her efforts to redefine herself and her respective relationships with both Sally and Jackie. Using psychodrama in this was is a very intense experience that can facilitate a great deal of reorganization of a child's early working models of self and others. Allison chose not to employ psychodrama in Katie's therapy until she had worked with her for a number of months. She wanted to increase that probability that Katie would be able to assert herself, contrast Sally with Jackie, and rely on Jackie for comfort. In the early stages of therapy, Allison focused mostly on Katie's relationships with both Allison and Jackie. She gradually focused more on Katie's past relationships with Mike and Sally, thinking that she would be more able to reexperience those past relationships more fully, within the context of quite different new relationships.

Allison only employs psychodrama while she is being very receptive to Katie's emotional response to the activity. She wants to insure that Katie is able to integrate the intense sensory/affective/reflective experience, rather than being overwhelmed with anxiety and shame that might lead to dissociating. Taking her cues from Katie, she determines if "Sally" should be verbally abusive of Katie or Jackie, if she should acknowledge the past abuse and neglect or deny it, and if she should threaten to take Katie from Jackie.

Allison indicated to Steven that she would have at least one more psychodrama involving Sally, in which she would give Katie an opportunity to experience sadness over Sally's failure to nurture her and her eventual abandonment of her. In such a session, "Sally" would acknowledge her own failings, express sorrow for not having been a better mother for her, make it clear that Katie did not deserve the inappropriate care that she received, and give her blessing for Katie's relationship with Jackie and her future progress. She would have made it clear that she did not have the ability to raise Katie in the way that she needed to be raised and she would have encouraged Katie to learn to love her new mother.

Frequently professionals question the wisdom of facilitating attachment security between a child and her foster parent when she will be moving into an adoptive home sometime in the future. But there really is no better option. With children with problems secondary to trauma and attachment insecurity or disorganization, it is only through beginning to relate easily with one's caregivers that they are able to begin to form an integrated, valued sense of self. It is only through participating in countless intersubjective experiences with Jackie that Katie can ever begin to understand that relating to a parent is a source of pleasure. Finally, it is within the safety of these experiences with Jackie that Katie will someday be able to integrate and learn from experiences that now elicit guilt and not shame, and experience repair in her relationship with Jackie fairly quickly.

If Katie is able to form a secure attachment with Jackie, and to a lesser extent with Allison, she will not forget how. When it is time to leave, she will grieve, but she will be able to begin to form a similar attachment with her adoptive parents. She can transfer the attachment because Jackie would have become a part of herself. Katie's sense of self would include a sense of worth and she would be able to enjoy reciprocal relationships with others. Katie would have discovered empathy and trust and she would anticipate that she might be "lovable" and "delightful" to caring adoptive parents.

When infants and toddlers are engaged in intersubjective experiences with their parents, they are able to experience and integrate the positive feelings of interest/excitement and joy/enjoyment. They are not able to generate and maintain these pleasurable inner states alone. They **need to be having** these intersubjective experiences in order **to be experiencing** the inner states of interest and joy. (This is made very clear in Allan Schore's (1994) very comprehensive work, *Affect Regulation and the Origin of the Self*.) Katie was beginning to experience interest and joy, while engaged with Jackie during "mom-time" or during other brief interactions during the day. But she could not maintain those pleasurable states alone! She has not yet internalized Jackie, just as an infant or toddler has not yet internalized her parents. She needs these intersubjective experiences before she is able to attain subjective pleasurable feeling states. When Jackie does not engage her with joint affect, attention and intentions, the inner pleasure evaporates. This truth is crucial in our attempts to initiate attachment security in these lonely and full-of-shame children. Katie will not be able to maintain a pleasurable inner state outside of Jackie's psychological and physical presence. Through experiencing this intersubjective presence and its associated inner state over and over again, eventually we can hope that she will be able to internalize Jackie's presence, and be able to maintain the state while alone. She then will have an integrated and coherent sense of a developing **self**, just as do so many three-year-old children.

# 15

## Maine District Court

When Dr. Allison Kaplan arrived at the Augusta District Court in the afternoon of March 18, 1995, she was dressed much more formally than she did for her treatment days. Sitting closely and comfortably with children required a much more casual look than she would need if she were going to convince a judge to take her professional opinion seriously.

Allison greeted Steven Fields in the hallway and he escorted her to a meeting room where she met Robert Craven, Esq., the Assistant Attorney General who presented the Children's Services cases before the court in Augusta. She shook Robert's hand and sat to discuss his line of questioning and what she might anticipate from the questioning of Rachel Nutting, the attorney for Sally Thomas. Robert assured Allison that Judge Paul Caldwell was a reasonable man who truly tried to determine what was best for the child within the limits of the law.

Robert Craven was arguing before the court that it was in the best interests of Katie Harrison to have the rights of her parents, Sally Thomas and Mike Harrison, terminated, so that she could be provided with another permanent home. To do so successfully, Robert needed to convince the court that Mr. Harrison and Ms. Thomas either were not motivated or did not have the ability to provide adequate care for Katie in a time period that would meet her needs. He wanted Allison to tell the court her professional opinion as to what Katie's needs were. Allison would need to address whether foster care or adoption would best meet her needs. She also would have to address whether it would be damaging for Katie to wait another few years in foster care if that amount of time were necessary before one or both of her parents could begin caring for her. Allison was the fourth witness for the Department of Human Services. That morning Steven had given the court an overview of Katie's life

since she entered protective custody and he had summarized the services provided to Sally Thomas and Mike Harrison. After Steven, Peter Jacobs, Ph.D.,
testified as to his findings when he provided psychological evaluations of
both Mike Harrison and Sally Thomas. He had testified that neither parent
had acknowledged the seriousness of the abuse of Katie. Nor had they accepted responsibility for it or demonstrated remorse. Mike had expressed
much hostility toward the Dept. of Human Services for interfering with his
rights to raise his child. Sally was less angry and she expressed a desire to do
whatever she needed to do to reunite with Katie. However, she minimized her
role in Katie's abuse and she did not see how she had failed to protect Katie
from Mike's abuse. Dr. Jacobs had evaluated Sally in January 1993, and again
in October 1994. He did not observe any significant differences in her degree
of accepting responsibility for her actions and in her understanding of Katie's
needs from the first to the second evaluation. This lack of change was evident
in spite of the fact that she had attended two parenting courses and had participated in both individual and group counseling. Her participation in counseling was sporadic. She would attend more regularly only prior to a court
hearing. Because of the missed appointments, her first two counselors refused
to continue to provide treatment. Her third counselor had indicated that Sally
seemed to love Katie but had a hard time committing to reunification because
of her relationship with Mike. Mike had completely refused any treatment.
When it became evident that Sally could not expect to have her daughter returned as long as she remained with Mike, she separated from him, but continued to see him regularly. Dr. Jacobs did not believe that the court could re-
alistically expect Sally to be able to raise Katie safely unless she began to
fully accept responsibility for her failings with her, participated in therapy in
a productive manner, and, after having shown significant progress, attended
joint sessions with Katie in which she could win back her trust. He thought
that entire sequence would take a minimum of two additional years, given her
lack of progress over the past two and one-half years. Attorney Nutting,
Sally's attorney, made it clear that Dr. Jacobs had not seen Sally in the past
five months and did not know if she had made significant progress since his
last evaluation. She also stressed that Sally was ready to visit with Katie but
was not being allowed to by DHS. Finally, she indicated that Sally had made
it clear that she would separate from Mike if necessary in order to win custody of her daughter. Attorney Nutting suggested to Dr. Jacobs that such willingness to even leave the man she loved for her daughter did prove her commitment to Katie.

   After Dr. Jacobs, Marjorie Taylor, Sally's current counselor, indicated that
she had only seen her client for four months and that she was still building a
therapeutic relationship with her. Sally attended most of the sessions but had

two appointments that she had forgotten. Ms. Taylor indicated that Sally had not accepted responsibility for hurting Katie and had only expressed sorrow for what Mike had done to her. Ms. Taylor thought that Sally might be able to more fully acknowledge her own responsibilities for Katie's experiences of abuse and neglect once she developed a higher degree of trust for Ms. Taylor. She agreed with Dr. Jacobs that the process would take at least two years and she was unsure about the likelihood of success. She was willing to continue to work with Sally to try to achieve that goal.

When Allison took the stand, she had her usual anxiety and doubts. Had she prepared as much as she needed to do? Would she be able to present her opinion of Katie's needs in a way that was thorough and believable? She worried that if she made a mistake in her efforts to make Katie's psychological needs very clear, then the court might come to a decision that she feared would truly hurt her. Making a mistake in court could be as damaging to Katie as making a mistake in therapy.

"Dr. Kaplan," Attorney Craven stated after first establishing her professional credentials and involvement with Katie, "would you tell the court your diagnosis of Katie?"

"Katie demonstrates a diagnosis of Posttraumatic Stress Disorder as well as Oppositional-Defiant Disorder. These are made more severe because she also manifests behavior that is consistent with a classification of attachment disorganization. This term is not a diagnosis but rather a research classification that is considered to be a risk factor for the development of psychopathology. Her behaviors which reflect her diagnoses and this classification include very vigilant and, at best, highly ambivalent relationships with her primary caregivers. She resists comforting, affection and experiences of mutual enjoyment. She also is extremely oppositional to her caregivers and she has consistently shown indifference to whether or not she is staying in a particular home. Her main goals in life are to be in control of anyone around her and have people give her things and do things for her. She has little awareness of parental love, and most often either resists it or is indifferent to it. These behaviors may also be considered to reflect a diagnosis of Reactive Attachment Disorder. However, that diagnosis still lacks a sufficient degree of professional consensus to make me comfortable using it."

"Dr. Kaplan, what is the cause of Posttraumatic Stress Disorder (PTSD), Oppositional-Defiant Disorder and attachment disorganization?" Mr. Craven asked.

"At this time the consensus is that PTSD is primarily caused by trauma which is unable to be resolved. When it is combined with behavioral features associated with attachment disorganization there is every reason to believe that the trauma was interpersonal and intrafamilial. Such trauma is likely to

include the 'trauma of absence,' which would be considered to represent neglect. A related cause would be multiple caregivers, which would cause the
child to lack predictable, safe care. After countless experiences of neglect
and/or substitute caregivers, the child turns to herself for what she believes
will keep her safe. Katie's behavioral patterns suggest that she experienced
considerable neglect of her emotional and social needs prior to her ever experiencing the abuse that let to protective custody. Because of that neglect,
she lost trust in her caregivers and no longer anticipates or strives to love and
be loved. I believe that the second diagnosis of Oppositional-Defiant Disorder is simply a summary of her symptoms that are secondary to the life that I
just described."

"What treatment does Katie need in order to be able to successfully recover
from her disorder?" Mr. Craven asked.

"Treatment needs to be very intensive and comprehensive. By that I mean
that treatment has to engage her in a deeply emotional way, prevent her from
using her pervasive need to control to avoid the issues, and then teach her, at
the most basic, preverbal level, that learning to trust and love her caregiver is
both safe and good for her, and also deeply enjoyable. Because of those goals,
Katie's foster mother, Jackie Keller, is an active participant in therapy. Mrs.
Keller also has special training and skills as Katie's parent to raise her at
home in ways that facilitate her ability to form a secure attachment with Mrs.
Keller. Providing Katie with a knowledgeable and committed parent is more
important than the therapeutic session itself," Allison said carefully.

"What does Katie need now, Dr. Kaplan?"

"In my judgment," Allison said in a deliberate manner, "Katie needs to be
able to live in a permanent home, where her developing ability to develop attachment security can be fully responded to with parents who are deeply committed to raising her into adulthood. I am referring to an adoptive home. She
is almost eight years of age. I believe that she needs to be placed in that permanent home soon so that she will have the opportunity to form a secure attachment with her parents while she is still fairly young. If we wait until she
is 11 or 12 we are likely to be greatly limiting our ability to provide her with
appropriate permanent caregivers as well as her ability to take advantage of
good parents."

"Given the problems that she has, Dr. Kaplan, will she be able to be provided with such 'good parents' who could meet her needs?" Attorney Craven
asked.

"She has made some progress and I am confident that over the next six to
twelve months we will see significantly more. If the court were to determine
that she were free to be adopted, it would take that amount of time before that
home could be found. She is still seven years of age. I believe that we have

begun working with her when she was young enough to benefit. I do believe that she will be able to function well in a good adoptive home."

"Dr. Kaplan, you have read the reports on Katie's parents from Dr. Jacobs and Ms. Taylor, among others. Why do you not think that it would be in Katie's interests to continue to work to reunify her with one or both of her parents?" Mr. Craven asked.

"Katie has already been in care for over two and one-half years. I believe that was ample time for one of her parents to have demonstrated full awareness of what was done to her, acknowledged responsibility and made significant progress in counseling to now be able to provide her with a good level of care. Based on what I have read, that has not occurred. I do not believe that it is in Katie's best interest to wait another two or more years to see if her mother or father will eventually be committed and able to adequately parent her in a way that meets her needs. Given the damage done to Katie, it will take an exceptional parent to raise her, not a poor one, or even a mediocre one. I have not read anything that gives me confidence that either her mother or her father will have the ability to provide her with the level of parenting that she will require. Katie's opposition to being parented is so intense that if she is placed in a marginal home, the placement is certain to fail and her disorder will, in all likelihood, be permanent."

"Thank you, Dr. Kaplan," Mr. Craven stated.

"Your witness, Ms. Nutting," Judge Caldwell said.

"Dr. Kaplan," Attorney Nutting began forcefully, "how can you say that Sally Thomas cannot provide Katie with the parenting that she needs when you have never met Ms. Thomas?"

"I based my opinion on my knowledge of Katie and my review of the reports of other professionals who have been involved with Ms. Thomas. If those reports are in error, then I certainly would reconsider my recommendation," Allison replied.

"But Ms. Thomas is participating in counseling and she did attend the parenting courses, Dr. Kaplan. Who's to say that if we give her another year or two that she could not adequately raise her daughter?" Ms. Nutting continued.

"I certainly am not saying that it is impossible," Allison said. "I am simply saying that after two and one-half years, I would have much greater confidence if we could see significantly more progress by now than appears to be present. I am also saying that we are placing Katie at great risk of never being able to have permanent, loving, and capable parents if we wait another two or three years for her parents to be able to raise her and it then does not happen. Overall, she will then have waited five years without a permanent home. Such a situation is damaging for any child and especially for a child who already has significant difficulty being able to trust the adults in her life.

Before taking such a risk, I am recommending that the Court see greater evidence that Katie's parents do have the motivation and ability to be her parents."

"Dr. Kaplan," Attorney Nutting began, seemingly changing her tactic, "if your impressions about Katie are right, it seems to me that we should leave Katie where she is now in foster care and allow her parents to visit her. If she has these disorders, I don't see how moving her again to an adoptive home would be beneficial to her."

"I agree that moving Katie to an adoptive home will be hard for her after she learns to form a secure attachment with her foster mother," Allison said slowly. "She most certainly will grieve the loss of her foster mother. But that grief will be temporary and the advantages of living in a permanent home far outweigh the temporary disadvantages of grieving the loss of her foster mother. It would have been more advantageous for her to develop her first secure attachment with her permanent parents. But that was and is impossible, given the legal situation and her level of needs. We could not afford to wait until the court decided on permanency before encouraging her ability to trust her caregivers. If we waited that long, Katie might never learn, both because of her increasing age, but also because of difficulty that we would have finding an adoptive family who would and could make a commitment to a child with such significant problems."

"Dr. Kaplan, if you are worried about finding good parents who are willing to commit to Katie, don't you think that you should look at Ms. Thomas. This *is* Katie's mother and she *has* been working to get her back, even though you don't feel that she has worked hard enough. Why not consider Ms. Thomas, Dr. Kaplan?"

"I wish I could, Attorney Nutting," Allison replied. "I would have loved to have read that Ms. Thomas truly understands and regrets the gravity of what she and Mr. Harrison have done to Katie. If I had confidence that she could soon raise her, I would love to be able to work hard with Katie to help her to begin to trust Ms. Thomas. However, if the Court does decide to try to have Katie returned to Ms. Thomas soon, I would be terrified of the effects on Katie. I have not read anything about Ms. Thomas that would indicate that she could provide Katie with what she needs from her."

"Not now, Dr. Kaplan," Ms. Nutting said, "but in another year or two she might be able to do so."

"I have read nothing that builds my confidence in that possibility," Allison said. "And because of that, I strongly urge the court not to make Katie wait any longer."

"That's all, Dr. Kaplan." Ms. Nutting said.

There was another five hours of testimony before the Court deliberated on the petition to terminate the parental rights of Sally Thomas and Mike Harrison. On April 9, 1995, Judge Caldwell issued an order that terminated all of their parental rights to their daughter, Katie.

## COMMENTARY

The devastating effects of pervasive emotional neglect and the lack of continuous caregiving are only slowly entering into court hearings and influencing the subsequent decisions that regarding the lives of these children. Sexual and severe physical abuse receive a much more consistent and adequate response by the legal system. Unresolved trauma, attachment disorganization, and reactive attachment disorder are the most severe consequences of abuse, profound neglect, and multiple placements on the development of children. The inability of a child to trust even the best parents immeasurably damages the self and the capacity to experience nurturance and a reciprocal relationship. Such a child, without significant, successful interventions, is at significant risk to never find a secure place in our society.

The legal and the social services systems are still too often inadequately aware of the need to provide a child with a timely decision so that he is able to move into a permanent home quickly enough to resume his developmental progress. Many children wait for years without any resolution of their temporary status in foster care. Often the system judges that their parents who were responsible for their entering foster care are not responsible enough to commit to reuniting with their child as soon as possible. Often parents have frequent delays and then make only half-hearted attempts to resolve their significant problems. The legal system must come to terms with the significant damage that is being done to children while they wait, year after year, often moving from one foster home to the next, to the next.

# 16

## The Coming of Spring

In late March, 1995, Katie was functioning the way many people in Maine do when they are ready for spring and it's still weeks away. She was irritable, testy, and engaging in considerable self-pity. The week or so of fairly agreeable functioning earlier in the month had long since passed. Whereas Mainers "muddle through," knowing that they will welcome each blade of grass when it finally appears toward the end of April, Katie had no such confidence in her future. It was as if she now sensed that engaging Jackie in ways that were mutually enjoyable, might, in fact, be in her best interest. However, she had her own plans as to accomplishing that goal that were not acceptable to her foster mother. She seemed to think that they would negotiate over what was appropriate or not in the family. She would "give a little" if Jackie would "give a little." In her mind, family life was a democracy with her vote having equal weight with Jackie's. When Jackie refused to cooperate on her terms, Katie decided to "get even." She would make Jackie's life more miserable as punishment for not being "fair." She would be more defiant, sneaky, grouchy, and, in general, not much fun to be around. In her mind, Jackie deserved such treatment.

Jackie probably should have seen this response coming after noticing that Katie's periods of cooperation and seemingly genuine contentment had become evident. The stress of integrating such experiences into her self-concept and her working model of relationships would be great. Katie was not likely to be able to accept these new features of her self and her life without considerable turmoil. But Jackie did not see it coming and she did not recognize it for five to ten days. As usual, she became aware of it only after noticing her own increased tension and irritability. She also noticed that she was disappointed in some of Katie's behaviors. She had begun to expect more from her

229

and Katie's continuing opposition had left her frustrated. She also noticed that she was blaming Katie for her own annoyances. "If only Katie would . . . !" were frequent thoughts that left her discontented.

She was becoming like Katie! This realization hit her toward the end of March when Katie missed the school bus. She was immediately upset and felt trapped. She did not want to be "stuck" with Katie all day and at the same time she did not feel like driving her to school. She felt like making her walk the six miles to school, and felt annoyed that was not an option. As she fussed about the situation, she glanced at Katie and noticed that she was sitting at the table as pleased as she could be. She had Jackie where she wanted her. Jackie was annoyed and upset and Katie had made her that way! Jackie left the room and paced around the living room, staring out the windows and talking to herself about her plight. The mud in the driveway seemed to represent her recent state of mind.

"Well, Katie, you caught me again, you little turkey!" she said to herself. "You are good at getting me to feel as miserable as you do. When you are able to 'get' me, you probably even feel a little better for a few minutes. You gave your gloom to me! Well, kiddo, the fight is not over. I figured it out, so whatever gloom you have is not sticking to me!"

Jackie was proud of herself that she now understood what was happening. How did Katie "catch" her again? Jackie paused for a moment and found herself reflecting on her recent discussions with Allison and her mother. Yes, it was similar! Disappointed! In some ways, she was disappointed in Katie in a manner similar to how she often felt that her mother was disappointed in her. When she had done something wrong, she thought that her mother had seen her as being selfish! Yes! And that's what she was now thinking when responding to Katie. And that was also how Katie was responding to her!

Katie thought that Jackie was being selfish, just as it seemed that her mother used to think about her. Wow! How easy it was to get into those old patterns of perceptions and responses. How hard to just stay in the present and to respond only to the meaning of the present! She would just begin again. Her recent work with Ruth at Allison's office had made this task much easier.

Jackie came back to the kitchen and cheerfully said to Katie, "Sweetie, I'm sad that you missed your bus. I know how much you want to go to school. Don't worry! I'll drive you there. But I am going to have to set aside some of my chores to take the time to get you there. So, of course, you can do them when you get home! That should work out fine for me." Jackie got her coat and keys and they headed for the car. Katie grumbled and said that she was not doing any of Jackie's chores. Jackie ignored her complaints and commented that it was too bad one could not move from winter to spring without going through so much mud. "Oh well, I guess it helps to appreciate spring even more when it finally comes. And it will come!" Jackie said in harmony with her returning optimism.

With Jackie again centered on preserving her own emotional balance and also accepting Katie's anger, resistance, and regression, life in the Keller home returned to normal. Of course, when one is living with a child similar to Katie, it is obvious to all how relative the word "normal" is. At least one could say that Katie was not able to distribute her distress and keep the home in an uproar. Also, Jackie began to notice that the moments of genuine enjoyment and cooperation that Katie had been showing over the past three months were again returning. By being able to protect her own inner life and the emotional atmosphere of the family, Jackie was able to make it easier for Katie to again inch closer to a newer way of living. Much of the pain of her existence was remaining within Katie, where it now needed to be if Jackie were to be able to help her to reduce it. Only in that way would Katie be motivated to find a way of living with others that would truly change her life.

**Jackie's Journal:**

April 7, 1995: Katie got a phone call from a girl in her class named Sandy. And the kid has no major problems! Her mother wants Katie to come over and play tomorrow afternoon. I suggest that she come here instead. Sandy is coming from 1:00 to 3:00. Katie off the wall. She sits and stays near me. Can't calm down. I suggest that she sit with blindfold on, as Gabe used to do once he had made some progress. She agrees and she immediately is calmer. This would not have worked unless she felt some trust in her surroundings. I sing and she joins in. Dinner OK and she enjoys bedtime game with dolls. Thanks me for letting Sandy come over. I suggest that she's simply ready for time with friend now.

April 8, 1995: Some success with Katie's first friend-visit. She was so anxious, she tried so hard to "be good" with her friend in order to be liked. She was able to share and let Sandy decide what they would do part of the time. Katie entered her personal space a lot and she chattered a lot. Sandy was a little frustrated. No aggression—verbal or physical. Later in day has to be sent from table—first time in couple of weeks. Hard to calm her at bedtime but not oppositional.

April 9, 1995: After church today, Katie asked many questions about Easter. She seemed to have real emotional response to fact that Jesus would die for us, so we can live. Also troubled by Judas being so "mean." Sad for Mary. With Katie, such empathy for others is rarely so strong. Mark took Katie for walk in woods. Saw fox family with babies. Initially excited then scared when mother fox saw them. Wanted to hold Mark's hand. Comes home with her riding on his shoulders. And she told me all about it! Seemed peaceful at bedtime.

April 10, 1995: Hard morning getting ready for school. Angry about clothing allowed to wear. Angry about breakfast. Empathy rejected. Comes home sad! Sandy did not play with her at recess. One of few times she showed that it mattered and was not mad about it. Accepts comforting. Able to help Diane clean up porch with good mood and following directions. Before bedtime sings lullabies to dolls, the same ones that I sing to her. Then asks me to sing same to dolls—and then to her.

April 11, 1995: Happy over playing with Sandy again. Possibility of friendship new experience. Healthy anxiety about it. Insecure. Asks for Children's Bible to read about Easter. Reads for more than hour. Less chatter, more conversation. Bedtime singing—asks Diane to come in and share her time with me. First time.

April 12, 1995: After school very angry, no clue as to why. Refuses to stay in kitchen, stays by swing set. Finally comes in at dinner time and angry that she has to first do 10 minutes of homework before eating. Eats cold meal. Misses TV show—doesn't explode, seems sad. Quiet during activities before bedtime. Accepts empathy and comforting.

April 15, 1995: Anticipating Easter services, excited and anxious. Has new dress. My mom and brother and his family coming for dinner. Many questions about Easter traditions. Bedtime, actually worried that she "won't be able to handle" excitement of day. Realistic fear—first time expressed. Something deep—and lovely—emerging.

April 16, 1995: Easter very special to Katie. Very alert, polite, controlled. Not want to get dress dirty. Stays very close to me at Church. Follows directions well before and after dinner. My brother sees her as much improved over how she was in January. Wants quiet talk at bedtime, no games. Discusses the summer. She does not want to go to school—ever. Wants to stay home "all the time."

April 17, 1995: Again, hard time Monday morning. Shows distress with anger at me. Rejects empathy. I surprise her by picking her up after school and taking her to playground in Waterville, with juice and cookies. She's perplexed, since she had some chores to do after school for her behavior in a.m. When she gets home, they've been done. I can see her wondering about it for some time. I get extra strong hugs at bedtime.

April 18, 1995: Therapy seemed to have an impact today. Allison has been working on differences between me and Sally for months. In her grown up voice she told Allison that Sally and I are different, as if Allison didn't know that. On the way home, she tells me that she was telling Allison the truth. Of course, when I sent her from the table for screaming over having to wait, she hated me. At bedtime she told me that she lied; she does not hate me, she was just mad at me. I tell her that I believe her.

April 19, 1995: I took Katie to store with me for a few groceries. She stole some candy that I discovered when we got in car. Back in to return it and apologize. She does as directed and seems more sad than angry afterwards. Accepts no dessert after dinner. She seemed to be giving herself a consequence for the stealing. We blow bubbles outside after dinner. Summer is coming! Bedtime goes well.

On Saturday, April 29, 1995, Jackie kept Katie busy with various small chores and activities. She had extra time that afternoon and decided to take her for a walk into the woods to search for some signs of spring. That morning they had counted 14 robins in the yard. By now, Katie was quite willing to accept what Jackie told her to do. Jackie did not think that she would continue to be so cooperative if she were to allow her more freedom. She knew that Katie had come to rely on the well-defined and structured external routine provided by Jackie. Katie could not maintain her friendly and co-operative behavior without her structure. A walk in the woods would be a variation but would still provide Katie with Jackie's decision-making.

They set out on the old trail behind the shed. It led over a rise, through a cove of white and yellow birch trees and down by a small pond that they always avoided in the summer when the mosquitoes were out. They began their search for early spring flowers, pushing through some old leaves near the shelter of trees on the south side of a small hill. Katie actually seemed interested in what Jackie was teaching her. They moved the leaves gently, alert to what lay among them. They found a small, fragile, yellow flower that Jackie identified for her. It was a trout lily, one of Jackie's favorites. Shortly after that, they found some deer tracks and a porcupine nest. Jackie was enjoying one of her favorite places to be and Katie seemed to share her sense of wonder and peace as they slowly made their way through the birch glen.

Eventually they stopped at another likely spot to search for flowers. Katie took a more active role this time. She seemed to want to find those magical yellow flowers that Jackie liked so well. In her excitement, she bent over and roughly pushed some leaves aside. When she found nothing she became somewhat agitated and began kicking more leaves. Jackie saw her and told her to be gentler or she would hurt whatever flower she might find. Katie seemed disappointed but complied and knelt down and began her search again. After a time she saw a flash of yellow and with glee, she pulled it up and carried it to Jackie.

"Look, Mom, a trout lily!" Katie shouted.

Jackie looked up to see Katie bringing the flower to her.

"Oh, Katie, those aren't for picking! Just for looking at and enjoying!" Jackie said.

Katie heard her disappointment and reacted as if she had been hit. Jackie saw her response and tried to reduce the impact of her words. "Thanks, sweetie, for showing me what you found. I know that you thought that I'd be happy that you picked it for me to see. Thanks, honey."

Katie did not respond to what she said. She threw down the flower and turned her back to Jackie.

"Honey, I should have told you not to pick them. You thought that I'd be glad and you didn't know that I just like to look at them." Jackie tried again to recapture their mood.

Katie walked a few feet further away and then began kicking the leaves. "I don't care!" She yelled. "I don't care! I don't care!"

Jackie got up and approached her. Katie ran down the trail. She was headed toward the house so Jackie did not worry so much. "Katie, stop and wait for me. I'm not angry with you. I want you to wait for me!" For Jackie, this was one of those sudden incidents when she had to intuitively decide how to respond. Should she chase her or continue to walk and call to her to stop. Or should she not let Katie upset her and simply continue her own exploration of the woods. She decided to casually walk back home, looking at her surroundings as she went. She saw Katie dart over the rise and she assumed that she would see her at home.

As she approached the edge of the woods, she paused for a moment to glance around. She was pleased that she did since she caught a glimpse of Katie hiding behind a tree about 20 feet from the trail.

"Katie, come on out so we can walk home together," Jackie said easily.

When Katie did not respond, she turned toward home, knowing that Katie would follow on her own terms. Katie was somewhat frightened of the woods, so Jackie had confidence that she would not stay there long alone.

As she approached the back of the shed, she heard Katie running up behind her. She smiled and turned to see Katie hurl a stone at her. She instinctively raised her arm and the stone glanced off the side of her wrist and hit her cheek. As she yelled, "Katie!" she turned down and away in a defensive position. She felt another stone hit her leg and a third flew past her shoulder. She looked at Katie again and saw that she had no more stones to throw. She took three quick steps toward her and grabbed her arms.

"Katie, I will not allow you to hurt me! I am angry at what you did! You could have hurt me badly! In our family we do not hurt each other!"

"I don't care! I hate you! I hate you!" Katie screamed.

Jackie was startled at the rage that she saw in Katie's eyes and face. She could feel the hatred. "Sweetie, I don't hate you for hitting me with the stones. But I am angry and I am not going to let you do it."

"Let me go! You do so hate me! You hate me!" Katie screamed again and tears came down her face.

"I love you, Katie. I love you!" Jackie replied and pulled her to her.

Katie screamed again and struggled to get away. She pulled backwards and down and Jackie lost her balance and they fell to the ground. Katie continued to scream and yell, "Let me go! Let me go! Let me go!"

Katie tried to kick and hit Jackie but her arms were pinned to her sides and her legs were too close to Jackie to be effective. She then tried to butt her with her head and scratch her arms. Jackie held tight and the two of them were now lying in the wet earth. Jackie was glad that there were no rocks under them or near Katie's hands.

"You're safe, sweetie. I'm mad at your hitting me with the stones but I do love you. I'll hold you as long as you need me to," Jackie said calmly.

"You hate me!" Katie began saying again. There was less intensity to her voice now and her movements had less force.

"No, Katie, I don't hate you. I was sad that you pulled up the flower, but I know that you did it for me. I simply had not told you that the flowers were for looking at. I don't hate you at all and I can understand why you were upset that I wasn't happy when you brought me the flower," Jackie spoke quietly and Katie listened.

Jackie felt her begin to relax. She raised her arm and began wiping Katie's tears from her face. "Oh sweetie, you got angry. You're learning to be close with me and you did something that you thought that I would like, but I didn't. You hit me with a stone, but I'm OK. We'll deal with the stone throwing later."

Katie now looked at Jackie and saw some blood on her cheek where the stone hit her. "You're bleeding!" Katie screamed in terror. "You're bleeding! I hurt you!"

"It's only a small cut, sweetie. I'm OK," Jackie said and smiled.

Katie stared at the cut. "No! Don't hold me. Please! I'm bad! Don't love me! Don't love me!" Katie seemed to be terrified.

"Oh, Katie, I'm so sorry that you think that you're bad! So sorry! I do love you and I'm going to keep loving you!"

"No, don't love me!" Katie remained in distress.

"Katie, Katie, Katie, maybe you hate yourself now but I don't," Jackie said tearfully. "I love you and I hope that someday you will learn to love you, too." Jackie began to slowly rock back and forth in the mud and grass. Katie began crying harder and she leaned further into Jackie. She buried her face in Jackie's neck and her sobs shook them both. They both continued to cry.

Katie pulled herself back to look into Jackie's eyes. She stared for a second and then said from some land of despair, "It's too hard. It's too hard to learn to love. I can't do it. It's too hard."

Jackie stared at this child who was raised on fear and loneliness and shame. She stared at her and realized that Katie was teaching her something that she must never forget. She could never know the depths of pain that this young child lived with. She would never know how hard it was—and how hard it still is. Jackie's tears and the pain in her throat made it hard to talk. She pulled her close again and whispered in her ear.

"I know it's hard, Katie. I know it's hard. I want you to keep trying. I want you to learn about love. It's worth it. I want you to know that!" Jackie said.

They rested for a while. Jackie ran her hands through Katie's hair and gently smiled into her eyes. When they began to feel cold, they helped each other up and walked home with Jackie's arm around Katie.

"What happened to you two?" Diane said in surprise as they walked through the kitchen door. "Did you fall into the pond?"

"What makes you say that?" Jackie said with some surprise. "We simply went for a quiet walk in the woods."

"Yeah," Katie smiled and looked at Jackie. "We just looked at the trees and flowers." They both laughed.

"Why don't you take a shower first, Katie," Jackie said, "I think you got a little wetter than I did."

Katie walked off toward her bedroom, more lightly than usual.

The next day, Sunday, after church, Katie and Jackie finished their walk in the woods. Jackie was able to show Katie her second favorite early spring flower—a hepatica.

At therapy, the following week Allison wanted to help Katie to integrate the important experience that she had with Jackie on Saturday. She was careful not to simply talk about it rationally since Katie would most likely use the words to minimize the emotional impact the experience had on her. If Allison was to help Katie benefit further from the experience she would have to facilitate Katie's ability to have the experience again—feelings and all—though without the same level of intensity as she had while alone with Jackie.

After establishing a positive and rich emotional atmosphere, and exploring various lesser events and ideas, Allison turned Katie's attention to Saturday.

"I hear that you and Jackie spent some time rolling around in the mud over the weekend," Allison said casually.

For a moment, Katie wasn't sure what she meant. When she realized what Allison was referring to, she seemed confused. It seemed that she did not know what she felt. She wanted to laugh and joke about it and also avoid the topic and what it might elicit. She cautiously went along with Allison's light mood. "We were covered with mud and it got real cold. We had to go in and I took a shower first."

"I was surprised that you two didn't wait until the summer when it would be warmer to roll in the mud. That's what pigs do." Allison smiled.

"We didn't want to get too hot, Allison," Jackie said. "And we wanted to see if spring mud would stick to our hair."

"Did it?" Allison asked.

"Yeah!" They both responded.

"And your walk started out so quietly and calm!" Allison said, "Who would have guessed how it would end up!"

Allison waited a moment. Katie would not be volunteering anything. Allison then asked Jackie to put her arms around her. She hoped to recreate their experience in the session.

Allison continued, sitting in a chair close to them, "It sounds like you both had a lot of feelings on that walk. It seemed to be very hard for you both, and very special too."

"It was, Allison," Jackie said.

"Katie, I can tell that you're feeling kinda upset that I'm talking about this. Tell your mom what you're feeling now."

"I don't want to talk about it." Katie said quietly.

"I'll bet you don't, Katie," Allison said quietly too, "now look at your mom and say it again."

"I don't want to talk about it." Katie said.

Allison asked Jackie to talk with Katie about the incident.

"I can tell that you really don't want to talk about it . . . and feel those feelings again. . . . You can just listen then. . . . That was so hard . . . so hard . . . for you."

Jackie continued, "You were so confused when you gave the flower to me and I was disappointed that you had picked it!" Jackie began to speak more loudly, "You thought, 'She doesn't want it! She's mad at me for picking it! . . . I can't do anything right! . . . I'm no good! I can never do anything right! . . . She hates me! . . . Well, I hate her too!' All those thoughts must have gone through your mind, Katie. And you felt so upset! You were so mixed up! And so mad! . . . And so sad that I wasn't happy with your flower! You hated yourself and you hated me!"

Jackie watched Katie as she spoke. Katie was now tense and she seemed disturbed. She did not want to have those feelings again. "Don't talk about it!" Katie screamed.

"You want me to shut up!" Jackie said back with a similar voice tone, "You don't want to feel as upset as you felt the other day. Tell me to shut up, Katie."

"Shut up!"

"Oh, Katie," Jackie said much more softly, "I wish I didn't have to talk about what happened again. But it was so confusing to you . . . and so important . . . that I think we have to talk about it again." Jackie gave Katie a quick hug but she did not respond.

"Katie, tell your mom, how hard it was for you," Allison said. "Say, 'Mom, it was very hard for me.'"

"Mom, it was very hard for me!" Katie said, looking at Jackie.

"I know it was, Katie," Jackie replied.

"Now say, 'Mom, I was very mad at you when you didn't like the flower!'"

"I was very mad at you when you didn't like the flower."

"I thought that I'd never please you!" Allison said.

"I thought that I'd never please you!"

"I thought that you were mean!"

"I thought that you were mean!"

"I thought that you didn't love me!"

"I thought that you didn't love me!"

"That made me really mad at you!"

"That made me really mad at you!"

"Now Katie, look at your mom and say, 'I'm mad at you for not liking my flower!'"

"I'm mad at you for not liking my flower!"

"Say, 'I'm mad at you for not liking me!'"

"I'm mad at you for not liking me!"

Katie began to cry. She tried to bury her head in Jackie's side. Jackie gently took her face and turned it until she was looking at her again.

"Katie, look at your mom and say it again, 'I'm mad at you for not liking me!'"

Katie continued to cry. She moaned as she said, "I'm mad at you for not liking me!"

"Now, Katie, tell your mom, 'I'm scared that you really don't love me!'"

"I'm scared that you really don't love me!"

"I'm scared that I'll never be good!"

"I'm scared that I'll never be good!"

"I think I'll always be bad!"

"I think I'll always be bad!"

"I can't believe that you really love me!"

Katie did not respond. Allison was about to repeat the directive when she could tell that Katie was struggling to speak, but was having trouble as she shook with tears and gasped for breath. Finally, she said, in desperation and despair, "I don't think . . . you . . . love . . . me." She burst into tears. Jackie rocked her and hummed quietly as Katie cried.

After a time, Katie became quieter and she and Jackie looked into each other's eyes. Jackie wiped her tears and smoothed out her hair. Jackie leaned over and whispered, "We can do this without mud, too." Katie smiled and they embraced again.

"You two really know how to hug," Allison said as she smiled. "I can see now how hard it must have been for you both the other day."

After further silence, Allison quietly added, "Katie, when you both left the woods, you threw some rocks and hit your mom twice. Tell her that you *really* thought she hated you after you did that."

Katie complied and looked at Jackie and expressed her fear that Jackie certainly hated her when she hit her with the rocks. She spoke quietly and with eye contact while still remaining relaxed in Jackie's arms.

"I thought you did, sweetie. I thought that when you hit me with those rocks you probably thought that I could never love you again because of what you did. I grabbed you then, to keep us safe, but also to try to get through to you that you were very upset and I still loved you."

Katie smiled at Jackie and squeezed her arm. She seemed so peaceful.

"Katie, tell Jackie that you're starting to figure it out but that this love stuff is hard!" Allison said.

"I'm figuring it out, but this love stuff is hard."

"What are you figuring out, Katie?" Jackie asked quietly.

Katie paused and stared at Jackie. She then looked away and looked back. Jackie and Allison were waiting and it seemed like they would wait forever.

"I'm figuring out that you love me," Katie finally said.

"I'm glad!" Jackie said, smiled, and hugged her again.

"OK, you two," Allison said. "Let's get back to work and save that loving stuff for the rest of the week."

"I'm going to love this kid in therapy, too, Allison." Jackie said and they laughed.

"OK, if you have to," Allison said, "but I still need to find out what kind of consequence Katie got for hitting you with the rocks."

"Should I tell her or do you want to?" Jackie asked Katie.

Katie wanted to smile but seemed to be a little embarrassed. Finally she said, "I had to clean all the mud out of our clothes with a brush in the sink. And then wash them in the washing machine." Katie then smiled.

"She also had to help me to put a band aid on my cheek," Jackie added and they both smiled again.

"Well, folks, I guess we can stop for the day. Don't get lost in the woods!"

During May 1995, Katie continued to explore her relationship with Jackie as if it were a completely new experience. And it was. She began to notice Jackie as a separate person. Jackie would find Katie staring at her frequently throughout the day. Katie would look away when Jackie smiled. When Jackie asked her to get something, Katie would comply immediately. Katie seemed to want to please her with a compulsion that almost rivaled her earlier efforts to defy her.

Katie also seemed to be trying to understand Jackie's motives for doing things. It seemed that whereas Katie had always assumed that Jackie did things to her because she was mean, didn't like her, or just didn't care about what she wanted, now Katie seemed to be trying to work out if there were other reasons. Maybe Jackie was just trying to teach her something. Maybe Jackie just needed to get something done. Maybe she needed help. Maybe she enjoyed helping her. Katie was noticing—watching Jackie carefully—and learning who her mother was.

Katie's rage at her life did not simply disappear. She still exploded but she did so less frequently and with less intensity. What was increasing was the rage that she directed toward herself. She began hitting herself in the face or banging her head against the wall. She did so when Jackie corrected her or did not allow her to do something. She seemed to want to limit her rage at Jackie and was willing to hit herself if necessary to do so.

"Well, Katie," Jackie said after school on May 16, when she noticed Katie smacking her face. This occurred right after she was told that she could not ride her bike. "You seem to be really hard on yourself. I'm sorry that you want to hit yourself when you get mad at me." Jackie walked away. If she tried to "save" Katie from her rage, she feared that these outbursts might simply increase. Katie would have found a way to frustrate Jackie that she'd be tempted to use. Jackie wanted her to see that she was the only one hurt by her behaviors. Jackie was sad for her but Katie was not hurting Jackie.

"Katie," Jackie said the next day when she noticed Katie's self-abusive behavior following a fairly minor frustration, "Why do you think you hit yourself so much when you get upset?"

Katie stared at her for a moment before responding, "I just feel the pain . . . and then . . . it goes away."

Jackie leaned over and hugged her. "You don't have to feel that kind of pain anymore, Katie."

"It's not bad. It doesn't last long. And I feel good when it stops," Katie said without any emotion. If anything, she was confused over Jackie's concern.

"But you really don't have to feel that pain at all, Katie. If you don't hit yourself, everything will still be the same. You don't have to punish yourself for me to forgive whatever you did."

"No!" Katie responded forcefully. "I have to hurt myself. It's the only way I can feel good again. But don't worry, Mom. It's OK. It doesn't hurt much and then I feel better."

"Oh, Katie," Jackie said as she continued hugging her. "I'm sad that you think and feel that, but I can understand. It's so hard for you to feel good about yourself. My love is helping but I guess it will take longer."

"No! You don't understand!" Katie yelled. "I have to do this!"

"I do know, Katie." Jackie said. "You think that you don't deserve any better."

Katie jumped up from her chair and as she did so, it fell over backwards. She looked at the fallen chair and then exploded. She ran to the back door and before Jackie could stop her, she was on the porch and with one swing of her arm, knocked over the flowerpot. Jackie did not hear it hit the ground because of Katie's scream. A moment after the geraniums splattered on the ground, Katie was there, kneeling among the pieces of clay, the potting soil, the roots, stems, and petals.

"No! No! No!" Katie screamed. "You made me do it! Why don't you let me hit myself? Why don't you?" Her hands were in the dirt as she seemed to be frantically trying to put it all back together again.

"I'm not stopping you, Katie!" Jackie said. "I simply want you to know that you don't have to do it anymore."

"I do! I do! You still don't understand!" Katie looked up at Jackie through her tears. "If I don't hurt myself. . . . If I don't . . . hurt . . . myself, I'll hurt . . . you . . . or your flowers!" Katie burst into tears. She cried harder than Jackie had ever seen her cry before. She held a red geranium to her face. Jackie knelt in front of her and pulled her into her arms.

"I don't want to hurt your flowers!" Katie continued to sob.

"I know, Katie. Katie, I know," Jackie said quietly as she gently rocked back and forth.

"Why do you want me to hurt your flowers?" Katie asked from within Jackie's arms.

"I don't, Katie, I don't," Jackie replied. "And I don't want you to hurt yourself either. My flowers are special to me but not as special as you are. That's what I want you to know someday. I also hope that you can discover that you don't have to hurt either me or you when you're mad. Your mad feelings do not have to be the boss of you, Katie. They don't have to be connected to hitting and hurting. Feeling mad is simply a feeling and can be a signal for you that something's bothering you. Try talking with me or Mark when you're feeling mad. Or finding ways to think about something else. Or write about it. Or growl in your room. You don't have to hurt me or you, sweetie, mad or not."

"I'm afraid I haven't learned yet how to do those things, Mom."

"Not all the way, Katie, but you're getting better at it and you're trying. Sure, you'll slip once in a while. I can deal with that and still love you. Our love is bigger than any old mad-mistake."

Jackie noticed that Katie began to relax in her arms. She breathed deeply a few times and actually shuddered and quivered. She rocked her gently.

After five minutes, Katie pulled back and held the flower up to Jackie. "Can we plant these again? Will they be OK?"

Jackie gently took the somewhat mangled geranium from Katie and said, "I think so, sweetie. Run to the back of the garage. On the bench you'll see more flowerpots like this one. Bring one back here."

Katie jumped up and ran into the garage. She immediately returned, with the dedication of someone carrying the Olympic Torch. She and Jackie then carefully repotted the flowers and returned them to their spot in the sun on the railing.

They stared at the geraniums, made redder by the bright sunshine.

In therapy, Allison noticed some changes too. Katie was managing their discussions of her poor choices at home without immediately entering her defensive, angry, and resistant attitude. She spoke of hitting Jackie without blaming Jackie for the incident. She actually seemed to show some remorse for what she had done and some willingness to accept the consequences. She showed some tentative signs of feeling proud when Jackie spoke about some situation that Katie had managed well. Maybe Katie's shame was beginning to weaken and break. Maybe it was losing its hold on Katie's mind, heart, and behavior.

During the session of June 5, 1995, Allison again explored some of Katie's past experiences. Katie was now much more receptive to speak about whatever memories she had. She was relaxing in Jackie's arms while Allison sat close to them on the couch.

"He hit me with his belt just because I turned off the TV that he was watching! He was always mean to me!" She spoke loudly about her father, Mike.

Allison held up a note pad with a picture of Mike that she had drawn.

"Tell him, Katie!" Allison said, "Tell him he shouldn't have hit you!"

"You shouldn't hit me, Mike! You were bad! You shouldn't hit me!"

Allison held the picture closer. "Tell him that you weren't bad, Katie. He did a bad thing to hit you with his belt!"

"I wasn't bad! You were bad! You shouldn't have hit me! You were bad!" Katie screamed at the picture.

"Tell him you were just a little girl. You needed love, not hitting with his belt!"

"I was little! Fathers are supposed to love their kids, not hurt them!" Katie yelled.

"Katie, tell him he shouldn't have hurt you for other things, too!" Allison leaned over Katie and spoke close to her ear.

"You shouldn't hurt me! Why did you hurt me? I was just crying!" Katie screamed.

Allison leaned closer, "Say it again, Katie, 'I was just crying!'"

"I was just crying!" Katie screamed and then took her eyes away from the drawing. She suddenly pushed up with her arms, trying to break out of Jackie's arms. Her eyes were unfocused. She screamed, "Let me go, I can't breathe! I can't breathe! Please, let me go! You're not letting me breathe!"

Jackie held her tighter as she struggled, looking to Allison for guidance.

"Oh, Katie, this is hard for you. You're really scared now. But you can breathe, you can breathe."

"No, I can't breathe, please let me go!" Katie screamed.

"Katie, you're safe, this is so hard. . . . Oh, Katie, I'll never hurt you . . . you're safe, you can breathe," Jackie said quietly as she stroked Katie's hair and shoulders. She did not touch her face now, fearing that Katie would interpret it as covering her mouth.

"No! No! Stop! I can't breathe!" Katie screamed.

"You're safe Katie. This is so hard. You're so scared. You're feeling Mike hurt you now . . . like you felt it years ago. Jackie's not Mike. She's your foster mom. You're safe. She'll never hurt you," Allison said quietly.

"AIIIEEEEEE! AIIEEEEEE!" Katie screamed and shook and screamed again. Jackie continued to hold her, keeping her safe while she struggled and kicked out and shook her head. "AIEEEEEE! AIEEEEE!" Over and over.

For what seemed like hours Katie screamed. Her screams gradually became loud cries of despair. Jackie still held her, but did not pull her closer for fear that Katie's conviction that she could not breathe would return.

Katie then squeezed Jackie tightly and cried even more intensely. Jackie embraced her and rocked slowly. "Katie, Katie, you're safe. You're with mom. You're safe. Mike will never hurt you again."

Katie burrowed further and continued to cry. Jackie looked to Allison for confirmation that she was doing what Katie needed. Allison nodded.

"Katie let herself remember more about her abuse from Mike than she probably ever did before," Allison said quietly to Jackie. "Katie seemed to remember Mike hurting her for crying. . . . Katie felt herself being hurt. . . . I think that Mike might have choked her when she cried. Or he might have smothered her with a pillow. Or something like that. He terrorized her for crying. . . . He terrified a little girl for crying . . . for crying."

Allison waited quietly at her desk for 15 minutes while Katie and Jackie gradually pulled apart a bit, smiled, and Jackie ran her hand gently over her face and through her hair. They began to talk quietly and even began to laugh. They looked at Allison.

"When you draw a picture, you really make it seem real don't you!" Jackie said and they all laughed.

Allison sat next to them on the couch. She put her arms around them both. After a moment she said to Katie, "Sweetie, I wish that you didn't have to go through so much hurt in order to be well. In order to learn about love from Jackie. I really do. I'm sad that this is so hard for you. You really thought that Jackie was not letting you breathe! How scary that must have been! You thought that she was hurting you!"

Katie simply stared at Allison, who continued, "I really think that learning to love good parents is worth all of this pain. But I'm not you, sweetie, I can't imagine how hard it must be for you."

Allison noticed the tears rolling down her own cheeks as she rested her hand on Katie's. Katie lifted her hand and squeezed Allison's. Then she reached for a tissue and—so very carefully—wiped Allison's tears. Then she closed her eyes and snuggled closer to Jackie. Katie, Jackie, and Allison rested.


## COMMENTARY

When Katie began to show signs of making progress, Jackie was understandably pleased. However, Jackie went beyond simply feeling satisfied over her gains and she began to expect that the progress would continue uninterrupted. When Katie began to demonstrate more dysregulation, Jackie then began to feel annoyed with her and to resent her problems, which, a few months earlier, would have left her quite satisfied.

Jackie had drifted into imposing a standard of improved behavior on Katie and then resenting her when she did not meet those standards. She began to act as though Katie's behavior suggested either that she was a poor mother or that Katie was not trying hard enough. Without being aware of it, Jackie was no longer accepting Katie as she was. Katie immediately sensed this, experienced it as rejection, and also knew that it gave her an opportunity to gain control over Jackie's emotional life. Only through becoming aware of her beginning to lose the acceptance quality of her therapeutic attitude would Jackie be able to regain control over her own emotional well-being as well as the overall atmosphere of the family. What helped Jackie to gain this awareness was her increased awareness about her past relationship with her mother. When she was able to perceive old mother-daughter patterns affecting her current interactions with Katie, she was able to reduce the impact of those patterns.

The five qualities of The Attitude are very interwoven. When Jackie began to have difficulty *accepting* Katie's behavior she also had less *empathy* for the difficulties that she had to face if she were to learn to attach. She most certainly had less *curiosity* about the choices that Katie would make and the reasons for making them. She was less *playful* in her own response, since she focused on having Katie act a certain way. Finally, her *love* for Katie, although it may have remained strong in being committed to her, lost some of its affective tone of enjoying her. Once she reestablished her overall attitude, Jackie was able to again find it much easier to attune with her affective life and to assist Katie through her shame experiences.

When Katie was beginning to want to please Jackie, she was taking an important step in forming attachment security with her. At the same time, Katie was trying to understand Jackie's inner life. She began to study Jackie's motives and interests and wishes. For the first time since she was a toddler she was being motivated by wanting to be liked by her parent as well as "to be like" her parent rather than finding a way to manipulate her. These efforts reflected the new meaning of having a relationship with a parent as well as her new realization that she had enough worth to be able to bring pleasure to an important person in her life. For these reasons, it was very important for Katie that she be successful in her early efforts to please. When she picked the flower for her and discovered that Jackie was displeased and misattuned with her affect and intention, Katie experienced the act as a rejection of her. She had failed in this new endeavor! The shame that she felt was intense and she immediately fell into rage at Jackie.

When children like Katie begin to want to genuinely please their parent, they are certain to fail periodically. While Jackie might have been more sensitive to how important it was for Katie to give her the flower, we cannot expect her to be constantly vigilant about not responding with attunement to her efforts. While being aware of the importance of these efforts in Katie's overall progress, Jackie still needs to give her a realistic response to the impact of her behaviors on her. If Katie was not successful in her efforts to please, Jackie again needed to turn to The Attitude to help her through the shame that her failure elicited. If Jackie can do that consistently, eventually Katie will be able to integrate the disappointment that she feels when her efforts to please are unsuccessful and gradually learn what will actually bring pleasure to Jackie.

Often when the child without attachment security is beginning to want to please her parent and to seek experiences of mutual enjoyment with her, she discovers that she does not know what to do with her periods of anger toward her. Katie was beginning to try to avoid having angry outbursts toward Jackie, yet she was still often subject to misperceiving Jackie's motives and behaviors toward her. At times, she felt that Jackie did not want to be with her enough or that Jackie was being unfair. What was she to do with her anger toward Jackie when she did not want to become angry with her? Katie's solution, as is often the case, was to turn the anger toward herself. Many children with Katie's history engage in self-abusive behaviors. Others show little of such behaviors until they are beginning to form an attachment. Katie would rather hurt herself than risk hurting Jackie or their developing relationship. Also, she was actually feeling anger toward herself, thinking that her anger toward Jackie simply reflected the "bad self" that she still needed to control. She was making more progress realizing that Jackie was not "mean" than she was realizing that she was not "bad."

When Jackie tried to discourage her from hurting herself, Katie felt trapped. By following her solution to managing her anger, she was displeasing Jackie. Yet one of her motives for doing it was to please Jackie, since by hurting herself she was not hurting her! Also, Katie knew that the pain that she felt when she hurt herself was minor compared to the pain that she would feel if she lost what was beginning to be the most important relationship in her life. Why couldn't Jackie understand that?

Both Katie's efforts to please Jackie as well as her efforts to manage her anger by directing it at herself represented significant progress in her psychological development. Her intrinsic motivation now included her emerging relationship with her mother. Rather than simply being driven by efforts to manipulate and control, she was integrating this relationship into her sense of what was in her best interests. Her solutions might not yet be the healthiest, but they were qualitatively different from, and better than, the self-destructive motives that emerge from being alone, reenacting trauma and manifesting attachment disorganization. I have suggested to a number of parents when their child was at this stage of his progress that they we had successfully helped him to become neurotic! Compared to where he had come from, he now was at a stage in his development that would be much easier for him and us to work with.

When Jackie was holding her and exploring her relationship with Mike, Katie experienced an intense reenactment of the experience of Mike's terrifying her—and possibly smothering her—when she cried. Although such experiences do not occur frequently, they do happen when working with abused children in this emotionally intense and directive manner. I have never found such an experience to be traumatic to the children with whom I work. Rather, the experiences have served to assist the child in resolving the trauma. In the same way, I have never found a child to remember more than she was able to integrate. Finally, I believe that the high degree of emotional and physical nurturing and support that this treatment offers provides the child with the degree of psychological safety that she needs to allow herself to recall and then resolve the trauma. Such reenactments tend to occur only after the beginning stages of treatment and following some progress in facilitating the attachment.

If the child does re-experience the trauma in the acute manner suggested by Katie, the therapist needs to maintain her accepting and empathic attitude, communicating how hard the experience is for the child. The therapist also calmly communicates that the child is not being abused now and the child is safely with the therapist and parent. The therapist also clearly defines the incident that the child is reexperiencing as having been abusive, and elaborates, if possible, on the physical, sexual, and/or psychological ways that the child experienced the abuse. The therapist also speaks about how the child may have interpreted the meaning of the abuse at the time (i.e., I was bad), and provides a new interpretation for the child to integrate (i.e., he acted badly).

# 17

## Summer Again

On June 9, 1995, for the first time, Katie completed one year of living in the same foster home. Jackie wanted to acknowledge the anniversary, but as usual, thought it best not to make it into too big a deal.

That morning she made Katie's favorite breakfast—sausage and pancakes—and presented it to her when she sat at the table. "Here you are, kiddo. This is the anniversary of your moving here one year ago today," Jackie said. "You get to pick dessert for dinner and I get to give you an extra hug." She reached over and hugged her. Katie noticed the breakfast more than the hug.

"What does it mean?" Katie asked. "What does having an anniversary mean?" She had eaten most of her meal before she demonstrated that she had been thinking about what Jackie had told her.

"It means that you have lived with us for one whole year. Twelve whole months. Three-hundred and sixty-five days," Jackie replied.

Katie thought about it some more. "Do you mean that every day will be the second time that I lived with you on that day?"

"That's the idea, sweetie," Jackie replied. "So on July fourth, fireworks day, it will be the second time you'll be with us on fireworks day. It's the same for your birthday in August and my birthday in September. Each time will be the second time."

"Can I have a big party on my birthday?" Katie asked. "Can Sandy and Emily and Elise and Erica come?"

"Your birthday is still quite a ways off, sweetie. If you can handle a big birthday then, you will have a big birthday," Jackie replied. "I'll let you know five or ten days before your birthday if I think that you can handle it."

"I'm different now, Mom. Can't you tell?"

Jackie put down her fork and looked at Katie. What was she getting at? Did she mean that she was bigger, or smarter, or simply older? "How do you think you're different, sweetie?"

Katie sat for a moment. "I'm not bad anymore."

"Oh, sweetie! Wow! You don't think that you're bad anymore. That's great. You're starting to see yourself the way I see you. Wow!" Jackie said. " And you are learning how to make good choices a lot better, too."

"I used to always feel I was bad." Katie said slowly. "I just didn't know I felt bad. Now, I don't *feel* bad anymore."

"Oh, Katie," Jackie said as she reached over to put her hand on her arm, "I'm so glad for you. It must have been so hard always feeling that you were bad."

Katie smiled at Jackie without looking away.

"Why do you think you've changed?" Jackie asked.

"You and Allison taught me that I am a good girl," Katie calmly said.

"How do you think we did that?" Jackie's amazement continued.

"I don't know," Katie quietly said. "But I think 'cause you love me."

"I think you're right, honey. And I do . . . I do love you."

"I know, Mom."

Jackie got up and embraced Katie. "I don't think I'll cry now, sweetie, because you might start crying too, and you have to get off for school in five minutes. I am happy for you about all this stuff you are figuring out. And I am going to miss you while you're at school today."

"It's OK, Mom," Katie said. "I'll be back this afternoon. And I only have two more school days before summer."

Jackie smiled. They finished their breakfast. Katie hugged her mom and got on the school bus.

Jackie needed to talk with someone. Although Allison had always cautioned her not to get too excited about anything until it had been around for a while, Jackie decided that this would be an exception. Allison would see that Katie had just confirmed that something special had been happening for a while now. Jackie called Allison and shared the good news. Allison agreed that something special had been happening.

**Jackie's Journal:**

June 15, 1995: First day of summer vacation. Katie seems happy and relaxed. Really think that she wants to be home now much more than ever. She was happily working in the garden with me, tying up the peas, both of us feeling kinda hot. She says, "The sun never shined in Augusta." I didn't know what she meant. She said, "When I lived in Augusta, with Sally and Mike, the sun never shined there." I told her that I understood how it must have felt that way to her. She replied, "No, Mom. It *really* never shined there." I said that I was glad that the sun shined in Vassalboro and she agreed. Nothing else to say.

June 17, 1995: I told Katie that tomorrow was Father's Day. She spent most of the afternoon working in her room. She drew six pictures of things that Mark had done with her like swinging her in a "hammock" blanket, taking her to see the foxes in the woods, and fixing her bed lamp that she had broken in anger the month before. At the top of each she wrote, "My dad does." On the seventh page she wrote, "That's why I love my dad." I helped her to make them into a book after promising that I would not tell.

June 18, 1995: Father's Day was a success for Katie. Mark was surprised and touched. He looked to me for the OK to get excited about it. I said fine. He grabbed her and spun her around before sitting her on top of the fridge. He told her that he would be doing a lot of different things with her so that she would have even more pictures to draw for him on his birthday. He does seem to be more important to her.

June 22, 1995: First tantrum since school got out. Upset that she could not go swimming with Diane. Blamed me although I had nothing to do with it. Stomped around the kitchen and porch. I suggested that she stomp around the garage three times and she did. To give her a rest I "let" her weed the garden with me. She said that I was tricking her but she only smiled and then helped. On the way back to the house I squirted her with the hose to keep the dirt from getting into the kitchen. When I had to return to the garden to get the pail that I had forgotten, she was waiting for me with the hose and she cleaned off my dirt.

June 25, 1995: Her school friend, Emily, visited this afternoon. They were in and out 40 times. Katie actually reminded me of Diane when she was her age. Once she screamed at Emily for getting her doll dirty but she recovered fast and apologized before bringing her favorite dolls back inside. I might try having her visit Emily at her house next. She calmed down easily after Emily left. She seemed relieved that she was gone and she didn't have to control her behaviors so much. Quiet and close bedtime.

June 28, 1995: Trip to K-Mart. Katie sees a mother scream at her little boy and roughly pull a toy out of his hand and drag him, screaming, down the aisle. She became upset at how the boy was being treated. She said that the mother must have problems because she was mean to him and did not know how to tell her son to put the toy back. She asked if the boy would need a home like hers to be safe and to learn how parents can love their kids. She seemed disappointed when I told her that kids really had to be hurt bad, like she was, before Child Protective Services would remove a child from his home. She was confused about how someone could decide what was bad enough.

During Katie's therapy session on July 2, 1995, Allison decided to show Katie some pictures of Sally and Mike that Steven had managed to get from them. He had visited them to request information and pictures for Katie's Life Book that he would use in preparing her for adoption. This book would contain her history from birth to adoption and be something that she would have throughout her life to refer to when she looked back on her difficult first years. Allison had separate pictures of Sally, Mike, and Katie. A number of pictures of Katie showed her as an infant, with a few others showing her when she was older. There was one picture of Katie being held by Sally and another of Katie and both of her parents posing for a photo.

"Well, Katie kiddo," Allison said, "your mom tells me that during the last couple of weeks you've seemed to be fairly happy and making some pretty good choices. Is that how you see it?"

"Yeah," Katie replied. Then she added, "I'm having fun this summer."

"That's pretty neat. And you did well even though you didn't see me last week because of my vacation. I wonder what that means!"

"It means that I don't have to see you anymore!" Katie smiled.

"Not so fast, kiddo," Allison replied. "You think that you can get rid of me that easy? No way. I want to be able to pick on you till you're 50 years old!"

"No you won't. I'm learning how to be a regular kid in Mom's home and you said that was what you were seeing me for," Katie smiled.

"Well, listen to you!" Allison said. "And Jackie also said that you are. Now what does that mean?"

"I don't think I'm bad anymore," Katie said simply.

"Gee, I'm happy for you that you figured out that you are a good kid," Allison said. "You've really been working at this, I can tell."

"Yes, and Mom says that I can handle a stream of fun now," Katie said proudly.

Allison looked at Jackie curiously.

"Remember, Allison, a long time ago we were telling Katie that she could only handle a trickle of fun at a time, so we were careful not to give her too much. Well, lately I've decided that she can handle a stream of fun so she's getting more than she used to. And just in time for the summer, too!"

"Soon I'll be able to handle gobs of fun!" Katie said.

"Gobs! Listen to you! You sure got plans for yourself, girl," Allison said.

"Well, it's a stream for now," Jackie smiled.

"OK, fun girl," Allison said. "So you don't think anymore that you're bad, and you're making good choices, having fun and loving your mom easier. You have had a busy year."

Katie looked at Jackie and smiled. Jackie winked.

"Your mom tells me that you made a really neat present for your dad for Father's Day," Allison said. "We never talk about your dad much. Sounds like things are going well with him, too."

"I made pictures of things that he did with me," Katie said rapidly. "And he said he was going to do a lot more with me so I would make him more pictures for his birthday."

"What a great plan that is, sweetie," Allison said. "He sounds like a pretty special dad to me."

"He is," Katie smiled at Jackie again. Jackie winked.

"What a difference between Jackie and Mark, your mom and dad now, and Sally and Mike, your first mom and dad," Allison said.

"Sally and Mike said I was bad, and Jackie and Mark say I'm good," Katie said. "And Jackie and Mark love me. Sally and Mike were mean!"

"Those are big, big, differences, Katie," Allison said. "I felt sad for you when it was hard for you to see how different Jackie and Mark are from your birth parents. You used to get so mad at Jackie when she would not let you do something or when she had you sit for a while and stay near her."

"I thought that she was being mean, too!" Katie said. "I didn't know she was giving me . . . consekences."

"Yeah, you thought that she was being bad to you and that you must be bad too!" Allison said. "I wonder how you figured out that you both were not bad."

"Mom kept loving me when I was mean to her," Katie said. She seemed to be able to go right to the central truth. "And I don't have a wall around my heart anymore."

"You know, Katie, I think that you're right," Allison said.

"I am," Katie said.

Allison and Jackie looked at each other and smiled. Katie smiled, too, then she winked at Jackie. They all laughed.

"Well, Katie," Allison said, "we still got some work to do."

Katie looked disappointed and then calmly looked at Allison.

"Steven gave me some pictures of you when you lived with Sally and Mike and other pictures of your birth parents," Allison said. "I'd like to look at them with you now, and see what you think. Jackie, would you sit real close to Katie on the couch while she looks at these photos?"

"Sure, Allison," Jackie said.

Allison gave Katie a picture of her when she was about three months old, lying on her back on a blanket on the floor.

"That's me?"

"Sure is, sweetie."

"Oh, Katie, what a cute baby you were," Jackie exclaimed. "What large, lovely eyes. And your hair was so light."

Katie stared at her picture. Jackie and Allison waited for her. Finally, Katie looked at Jackie.

"I wish I could have cared for you when you were three months old," Jackie said.

"What would you have done?" Katie asked.

Jackie pulled Katie toward her in her arms. She began to sway slowly and then she said quietly, "I would have looked into your eyes and seen how wonderful you were. I would have rocked you like this, and looked at your tiny fingers like this. Then I would have squeezed you gently like this and quietly sung you a lullaby. And I would feed you and hold you carefully. And I would do it for hours every day and you would know that you were good and special to me and that I loved you."

Jackie continued to stare at her until Katie reached up and hugged her tightly.

"I wish you had been my mom when I was born," Katie said. "I wish I had been inside of you like Diane and Matthew were."

"That would have been wonderful to me, too, Katie," Jackie said.

They smiled and winked and laughed again. Then Jackie sat her back up next to her and Allison showed her some more pictures.

When Allison gave Katie the picture of her at about 18 months with both Mike and Sally, Katie became quiet and tense. She stared at the photo, looking at each person intently.

"Pretend Sally and Mike are here, Katie, just like they are in the photo," Allison said, "Say whatever you would like to say to them."

Immediately Katie began to talk to the photo, "Why were you mean to me? Why didn't you take good care of me? You were bad the way you treated me. Parents aren't supposed to treat their kids that way! You made me think that I was bad! You hurt me a lot. Why didn't you take good care of me?"

Katie stopped and stared at the picture some more.

"Tell them that they'll never hurt you again, Katie," Allison said.

"You'll never hurt me again. Jackie is my mom and she keeps me safe. She loves me and shows me I'm good," Katie said. "I'm good and you won't be mean to me anymore."

Allison took the photo and then gave Katie one of Sally alone. "What would you like to say just to Sally, Katie?"

"Why didn't you take care of me? Why did you let Mike hurt me?" Katie looked at the photo quietly. "Sometimes I still miss you and wish that you had taken good care of me. Sometimes I wish that you loved me the way Jackie loves me."

"It is sad, Katie," Jackie said, "that Sally didn't do a better job of caring for you and loving you. I know that sometimes you miss her and love her, too, besides being mad at her. Sometimes, I'll bet Sally did hold and rock you and show you that you were special to her. It's just that she couldn't do it as often as you needed. As often as any baby would need. I can see why you sometimes wish that she had cared for you better so that she could still be your mom and be a very good mom to you."

After a few moments, Allison showed Katie a picture of Mike. "What would you like to say to Mike, Katie?"

"I don't miss you! You were very bad and mean to me. You never held me and you never loved me. Sally did but you didn't! I don't miss you at all!" Katie was strong and certain in her words. She felt only rage toward Mike at that time, and possibly for a very long time to come.

After placing the photos on her desk, Allison told Katie that Steven would be making a photo album for her with those photos and many more from her life in foster care, including her first three homes.

"I don't want pictures of my other homes," Katie said.

"Why is that, Katie?" Allison asked.

"Because I wasn't happy in those homes. I don't remember them or think about them," Katie replied.

"What do you remember about those first foster homes?" Allison asked.

Katie thought for a moment. "I remember that they didn't know how to care for me. They got mad at me a lot. They didn't take care of me the way Mom does."

"How is your mom different from the way Ruth and Susan were?" Allison asked.

"Mom didn't hate me back when I hated her," Katie said, "I don't know if the other moms hated me, but I felt that they didn't like me so I didn't like them even more!"

"It sounds like you still felt that you were bad when you lived with the other moms and they didn't know how to teach you that you're good," Allison said.

"Yeah," Katie said. She was beginning to lose interest. Allison decided that this girl, not yet eight years old, had worked enough. She told Katie that she had earned a short session so that she could now get back home and turn on that stream of fun again. Katie agreed and Jackie winked at her.

When Jackie and Katie left, Steven remained for a few minutes to speak with Allison.

"What has been happening?" He asked. "This is not the same kid that I knew six months ago or even three months ago."

"I think you're right," Allison replied. "Katie is a different kid."

"Why? What did the trick?"

"Not one incident. Jackie and I have been working with her for 13 months. What happened during the first week and the first session was as important as

what happened last week. She finally was able to notice what Jackie was offering her and to begin to integrate that into a coherent self that does not have
pockets of self-hatred, rage, isolation, despair, and fear. With Jackie, she has
begun to feel safe and so she has been able to depend on her, trust her, be
comforted by her, and have fun with her. Jackie was seeing—discovering really—wonderful things about that girl that she never knew were there. Sally
had not seen them often enough. Now Katie is beginning to see them, too."

"How come so suddenly?"

"It's been happening for quite a while," Allison said. "We noticed moments
of self-reflection, acceptance of authority, and an ability to have fun and experience genuine affection back in January. An internal process of self-integration
and self-acceptance has been occurring that mirrors an external process of coming to know, trust, and form attachment security with Jackie. What we are now
seeing can let us assume that she is integrating Jackie's experience of her into
her experience of herself, something that she had never done this way before
with anyone, including Sally."

"Is this likely to be permanent?"

"I believe so," Allison replied. "Certainly under conditions of stress in the
future she may well become dysregulated a bit. When that happens Jackie
will simply be 'present' for her again, focus again on maintaining The Attitude, and then reduce the choices that Katie has that she can't manage. As
soon as she's ready, Jackie will present her with her 'gobs' of fun and love
again.

"But the basic psychological realities for Katie have changed in ways that
I am convinced will be lasting," Allison said. "She now knows what love is
all about. I can't imagine that she'll turn her back on it again like she did
when she was an infant. She also knows, I mean *really* knows, that she's a
good kid, a great kid. She may have doubts about that from time to time, but
she has started to realize that truth, *in her gut*, and she's not likely to forget
it."

"Some kids struggle with this for a longer time than Katie has. For that,
we're fortunate. Some kids never get it to the degree that Katie seems to be
getting it. Her whole world is opening up, with new awareness that she never
had before. Empathy, remorse, deep laughter, friendships, excitement that is
truly enjoyed, being curious, discovering her talents. These were all just
words before for Katie that had no relevance to her real life. Now they do.
Wait until you see her a year from now!"

"But before we talk about a year from now, we need to discuss adoption,"
Allison said. "I imagine DHS will be starting to work with her on adoption
soon. I'm certain that she'll have a hard time so we'll get a chance to see how
much she has integrated the gains that she has made."

"I'm glad you brought that up," Steven said. "I managed to get Kathy to give me permission to remain Katie's caseworker through the adoption process. I'll have a different supervisor for her now who can show me how to prepare her for adoption. Actually, I'm planning to call Jackie and you soon and set up a meeting where we can come to a decision about how best to talk with Katie about being adopted and moving."

On July 6, 1995, Steven called Jackie to say that he and Janis, his supervisor for the adoption work, would like to meet with Jackie and Allison to talk about making plans for Katie's adoption. He said that they needed to discuss how the adoption process would go, who would tell Katie about it first, and how long the process was likely to take. He finally said that she should give thought to the type of parents who would be most suitable for Katie. He said that Allison was free on Monday, July 10, and Jackie agreed to meet then.

That evening, Jackie and Mark talked about the phone call and what that would mean for Katie and them. Jackie was feeling protective of her child who had now lived with her for over a year. She knew that she had made some real gains, but shouldn't she have more time to really stabilize the progress that she had made? Was Katie ready for the ordeal that the announcement of her move would cause? Was her attachment to Jackie strong enough to withstand the knowledge that someone else would be her mother? Would she let Jackie comfort her? Periodically she and Allison had mentioned to Katie that she would be staying with Jackie only temporarily. A foster home was a "helping-kids home" until the child was able to go to a "growing-up home." Katie never responded much to that information. It probably did not mean that much since Jackie had not been very special to Katie yet. It would now.

"Mark, I just don't know. I knew with Gabe. There was something about him that was more open and trusting. Maybe it's simply that we had more time with him and we were certain that he was going to make it before we started working on moving on."

"I see what you mean," Mark replied. "Katie still has a lot of work to do; more than he did. I don't want her to lose all the gains that she made, either."

"I'm worried that she doesn't love me enough yet to be able to grieve my loss. If she doesn't do that, I'm afraid that she'll never be able to form a secure attachment to someone else. Still, I know that she's almost eight and we can't expect her to wait another year before being able to meet her adoptive parents," Jackie said.

"Why do we have to put her through it?" Mark asked. "Let's adopt her."

Jackie pulled back and stared at her husband.

"What? What did you say, Mark?"

"Let's adopt her," he replied.

"You want to adopt her?" Jackie asked. "You really do?"

"Allison and Steven and the others seem to be saying that adoption is best for her," Mark said. "You love her, I love her. As much as she can, she's learning to love us, and she sure needs us. So . . . nothing else really makes much sense."

"You never said anything about that before," Jackie said.

"It's only recently been talked about. And I didn't want to make you feel guilty, if you didn't want to adopt her. You do just about all the work with her. It's easy for me to say 'Let's adopt' when most of the follow up is your responsibility. So I haven't said anything, waiting till you brought it up."

"Why did you say something now, then, Mark?" Jackie asked, truly puzzled.

"I see the look on your face when the word "adoption" is spoken. I know you. You've been trembling in front of my eyes. I know you want her as much as you want the rest of us."

"You're not saying that we adopt her just for me, are you, Mark?" Jackie asked.

"I'm saying that we adopt her because she's already in our blood. Let's make it legal," Mark said. "Now, do you want to cry first, or hug me, or do them both at the same time?"

They did both at the same time.


On July 10, 1995, Steven and Janis Marshall, the adoption supervisor, met with Jackie and Allison to talk about adoption. Janis had instructed Steven in the general procedures that they would be following in preparing Katie. They met at Jackie's home to discuss how to proceed.

"I think that I should come to your home and tell her formally that I will be working with her on her Life Story. I'll explain what that is and why it is important before we start looking for the right home. I'll make sure that she knows that her thoughts and feelings about the right family are very important, so she'll be a big part of the process," Steven said without much enthusiasm.

"Before we go further, Steven," Jackie said quietly. "I'd like to say something."

They gave her their full attention because they could tell that Jackie was hesitant and at a loss for words, something that was rare for her.

"Mark and I have been talking about this a lot," She finally said. "We do not want her to move."

There was silence. Janis eventually managed to say, "But, she's already seven, Jackie. I don't think that we'd be able to consider long term foster care."

"I know," Jackie replied. Again, silence. Then she smiled.

"Jackie!" Allison yelled, with an intensity that Steven had never heard before. "You want to adopt Katie!"

"Yes, Allison. We do."

"Oh, Jackie!" Allison got up and came to Jackie and embraced her. Steven and Janis sat and stared. They felt a little uncertain. This was not what they had anticipated.

"I'm happy with your decision, Jackie," Steven finally said, "But a few months ago you said that you were not going to adopt her. What changed your mind?"

"I don't know, Steven," Jackie replied slowly. "I have some sense that Katie is different from Gabe. I knew that it would be hard for Gabe to leave us, but I also was sure that he would be able to become securely attached to his adoptive family and have a good life. Somewhere within me, I have doubts with Katie. I don't know if she could transfer what she is learning with me to another mother. I don't know if she would be able to understand why I did not choose to keep her after all we've been through together. I don't know if she would recover from the trauma of the move. I don't want to lose her now, Steven."

"I hear what you're saying, Jackie," Allison said quietly. "I know how much this kid has come to mean to you. I also know that she is making real gains now and that if she is told within the next few weeks that she'll be adopted sometime during the next year by another family, that she will be able to make the transition. It will be a trauma, yes, but she will be able to rely on us to resolve the trauma, grieve the loss, and become ready to develop a secure attachment to other parents. Because of you, Jackie, she is now resilient. She will be able to move on, and you can stay in her life in a secondary role. You don't have to feel trapped and think that you have to adopt her, Jackie."

"I don't feel trapped, Allison. Mark and I want to adopt her," Jackie said with increasing firmness in her voice. "If I were as sure as you that she will be healthy enough to move on to another home, I don't know what we would want to do. But I don't have your confidence. That's my reality. But we're not martyrs. We know that we don't *have* to adopt her. We want her. We choose her. We love her. She is part of our family now and we want her to remain in our family. If she continues with her progress we will celebrate her future. If her progress stops, we still want her. She's a part of me now in a way that I cannot express."

"We certainly will give priority to your application to adopt her," Janis said. "We can't give you the OK today, though, since there's a home study that we have to complete. This will include interviews with the whole family, including Katie.

"I know that, Janis," Jackie said. "Mark and I have discussed it. We have mentioned it to the three older kids and they are supportive. We certainly have said nothing to Katie. But I wanted you to know now, since I imagine that this will affect what you say to Katie and when you do it."

"Jackie," Allison said, seeming to have some difficulty speaking. "I know that you love her. But again, I want you to be sure about this. Preparing her for adoption by others is a valid choice. Do you really *want* to adopt her or do you feel you *have* to?"

"Allison," Jackie said, "in many ways I love you more than a sister. Without your knowledge and support I would never have been able to raise Katie. Or Gabe. I trust your judgment more than I can say." She paused; it was hard for her to speak.

"Now I am asking that you trust me," Jackie said with tears in her eyes. "My love for Katie has brought a knowledge of her that just does not fit into any category. She is part of me and I am part of her. *Wanting* to adopt her or *having* to adopt her is a false distinction. I trust your judgment that she can make it in another home. Trust mine that this is necessary for Katie, and for me. I do have a choice, but I don't have a choice. She can make it somewhere else but for some reason she must make it with me. I know that this is necessary and right. I am filled with joy and fear, with gratitude and humility. This must be the way it is."

Allison stared at this woman as she had often done over the past few years. Now she was understanding Jackie in a new way. She was understanding differently the work that she and Jackie had been doing. Jackie's love for Katie took her to a knowledge of Katie and of a relationship with her that left Allison observing from a distance. Of course, Allison would trust her judgment. How could she not do so?

"I have no doubts, Jackie. You know her and your family better than I ever will," Allison finally said, and they smiled when they noticed that they both had tears, just as happened so often in the past.

"Mark and I have one question for you," Jackie said to Allison. "It's about Gabe. When he discovers that we are adopting Katie, and did not adopt him, will that cause any problems for him in his adoptive home?"

"I don't think so because he is doing so well," Allison said. "He seems to have a very secure attachment with his new parents and I think that he will simply feel now that his moving from your home was best for him and he probably won't wonder why. If he were not doing well in his adoptive home, I might worry about the effects on him of Katie staying with you."

Steven thought about what he needed to say next. The meeting certainly had gone off in an unexpected direction. Finally, he smiled too and got out of his chair. "Can I have a hug, too?" he asked with some hesitation. He wasn't sure if this would remove him from being Katie's adoption worker. He'd worry about that later.

## COMMENTARY

Often when children who have not known attachment security have begun to make significant progress in forming a secure attachment with their new parents, they express the realization that they are "different now." Frequently one is amazed at the level of insight that they have into the changes that have occurred within themselves and with their relationships with their parents. On a number of occasions, the child has put his thoughts in writing and been able to eloquently express his new view of the world.

Katie is discovering what other children, raised with a secure attachment with their birth parents, take for granted. At the same time, she is discovering how to use words to communicate her inner life of thoughts and feelings. As she becomes aware of love, mutual enjoyment, being comforted, sharing joy, playful teasing, and quiet times of learning about the world together, she often spontaneously comments on this new reality. The words are obviously genuine. They indicate that the hardest work is now behind her. The varied, complex intersubjective experiences that she has had with Jackie have released a torrent of subjective experiences that had been beyond her ability to discover about herself, parents, and the world.

Jackie's decision to adopt Katie does not change the fact that many children can form a secure attachment with their foster parent and then successfully move to an adoptive home. These children definitely grieve the loss of their foster placement, but they show the ability to work through the stages of grief and become receptive to being adopted by another family. A future adoptive home is no reason to discourage the child from learning who he and his "parents" are in his foster home. Such delays waste years, and the difficulties with learning to engage in secure attachment patterns would be much greater when he is that much older. Also, many adoptive parents would not commit to bringing an unknown child into their home if they were aware of the significant problems associated with unresolved trauma and lack of attachment security.

While this story did not recount the point, Steven, Jackie, and Allison would have made it clear to Katie from the moment of her placement in Jackie's home that she was not there on a permanent basis. Jackie would have casually wondered about Katie moving someday, possibly while saving some things to show her birth or adoptive parents in the future. It is best to tell a foster child that it is a temporary home, and that eventually she will

either return to the birth parents or advance to an adoptive home. Even
when the foster parents think that they might choose to adopt their child
when she is free for adoption, they should still maintain that it is a temporary home. It is much easier for a child to be first told that it is temporary
and then later discover that it is permanent, than it is for a child to think that
it might be a permanent home and then be told that it is temporary.

# 18

## Fear and Joy

On July 14, 1995, Katie was weeding the garden with Jackie when Steven drove into the yard. This was the day that he would begin talking with Katie about adoption. Jackie was not sure how Katie would respond. Her sense of security and her expressions of attachment to Jackie and Mark seemed to be stronger every day. Would this discussion about her future set her back or would she take it in stride?

"There's Steven, sweetie." Jackie said. "Run over and say 'hi' and take him into the kitchen. I'll be in a minute. You can get out the lemonade and crackers. If he wants coffee, I'll take care of it when I get there."

Katie needed no encouragement to end weeding early. She greeted Steven as if he were her best friend from school. By the time Jackie entered the kitchen, Katie and Steven were both enjoying their drinks.

Somehow Katie had discovered that Steven had a little girl named Rebecca, who was now two and one-half years old. Steven showed her Rebecca's picture and Katie happily handed it to Jackie.

"Isn't she cute?" Katie said.

"She sure is!" Jackie said. "She reminds me of the pictures of you that we saw at Allison's office."

"I wasn't that cute," Katie said.

"Say that again, sweetie," Jackie smiled. "And I'll have to give you a 'mom circle' right in front of Steven."

"No!" Katie giggled. Eventually they finished their crackers and lemonade.

"Katie," Steven said, "I came here today to talk with you."

This was unusual. Steven's serious tone immediately brought Katie to her hypervigilant state and she stood up and moved toward Jackie. In the past, she would not have sought comfort from Jackie in the face of something that was frightening to her.

"I can hold you if you'd like, sweetie," Jackie said. She pulled the now tense child into her lap.

"Katie," Steven continued, "I told you a few months ago that the Judge said that you would not be going back to live with Sally and Mike. He said that they had not learned how to be better parents and that you should not have to wait anymore to find out if you would be living with them."

Katie stared at Steven, motionless, so he continued, "Now that we know that you'll not be living with Sally and Mike again, it's time to decide what home you'll be growing up in. Your adoptive home. This home has been your foster home—your 'helping kids' home—and now it is time for you to be in your 'growing up' home. You need to be able to just have a family like other kids and no longer be a foster kid who has to worry about moving all the time."

"I want to stay here. I want to stay with my mom, Jackie," Katie said in one breath.

"I know you do, Katie. This is a wonderful home—a great foster home. But right now I cannot promise that you can stay here. First, Jackie and Mark have to apply to adopt you. And they did! So now I will be coming back and ask them and you and your sister and brothers a lot of questions so that I get to know a real lot about your family. I have to be sure that this is the best place for you before I can promise you that you can be adopted by Jackie and Mark," Steven said with difficulty.

"I want to stay here! I don't want to go anywhere else!" Katie yelled. She looked frightened. She turned to Jackie. "Tell Steven, Mom. Tell him I can stay here." When Jackie hesitated she looked terrified.

"Sweetie, I know you do and I'm very happy that you want to stay with us. We want you to stay. Mark and I want to always be your parents," Jackie said quietly as she held her closer. "We love you so much and we have asked Steven if you can stay with us."

"Why can't you decide, Mom?" Katie asked in confusion.

"Because when you moved here, Katie, Steven asked us if we would be your foster family to help you. We were asked to be a 'helping-kids' home for you. Now you need to have a 'growing-up' home and that's different. Daddy and I will apply to adopt you and then Steven will have to get to know our family better like he said before deciding if we would make the best growing-up home for you."

"You are, Mom! You're the best home for me!" Katie needed to put an end to this fear. She needed a promise that she could stay forever.

"Katie," Steven said, "Jackie and Mark are a great home. I am really happy that they want to adopt you. They want to always be your parents. I think that they would be great parents for you. But I can't promise now that they will be adopting you. Jackie and Mark and I will work hard to make sure that this is the best family for you to grow up in."

"Tell me now!" Katie screamed.

"I can't, Katie," Steven said. "I will tell you as soon as possible."

"No!" Katie erupted. She pulled herself away from Jackie and ran from the room. Jackie heard her bedroom door slam shut.

Jackie looked at Steven. "She's scared to death. She so much needs to know for sure that she's staying with us. I know you can't make false promises, but please, do whatever interviews you need with us and the kids as soon as possible so you can decide soon. Please, Steven. Waiting for her will be torture. Every day will be an agony."

"I'll talk with Janis this afternoon," Steven replied. "I'll try to call you with a general idea of how long this will take."

"Thanks," Jackie said, "I know you'll work as fast as you can."

Steven soon left and Jackie went to find Katie. She knocked on her door. There was no response but she heard Katie crying. She opened the door. Katie had rolled herself up in a ball on her bed. She held her large stuffed rabbit in her arms. Tears streamed from her eyes onto the rabbit and the spread. She was gasping for air and staring into the corner.

Jackie quietly closed the door and walked to the bed. She lay down behind Katie, wrapped her arms around her, and pulled her against her chest. She whispered her name into her ear and then she was quiet. Her breathing soon matched Katie's. She felt her shivering in her arms. The tears continued, seemingly forever. Jackie's enveloping touch would have to reach her.

"Mom," Katie began to talk at the time that Jackie had thought she would never again hear her voice, only her ocean of tears, "why is it . . . never . . . easy? Why is it always so, so hard? Why, Mom? Why will . . . I . . . never be happy?"

"Oh, my Katie. I know how scary this must be for you. I know how much you want a promise that you can stay. I hope you can. I think that Steven will know that it's best for you to stay. Mark and I will answer all of his questions and he'll really get to know us. I think that he'll agree with us that this is where you need to stay."

Jackie was quiet again and she continued to rock slowly in the bed and to hold Katie tight. Then she whispered, "You and I will be scared together, sweetie. As long as we have to wait for Steven to decide, I'll be scared with you."

Katie turned around to face Jackie. She hugged her and squished the rabbit between them. Then she kissed Jackie's cheek. "OK, Mom. If one of us is scared, we'll hold each other's hand."

On July 17, Steven called to say that Janis and Kathy had recognized the need for a quick decision and had allowed him to work almost exclusively on their home study so that they could make their decision rapidly. Usually the adoption worker spent time with the child getting to know her, but since Steven already knew her quite well that time would be saved. After the home study was complete, they would review Jackie and Mark's application and make the decision. The Life Story could wait.

Since they already had a home study done when they got their foster care license, the actual study would not take as long as usual. What was usually a process that took months, might conclude in weeks. Jackie was relieved and told Steven of her gratitude. They arranged for Steven to begin his interviews with Jackie and Mark that Friday. They already had completed most of the application forms and had arranged for medical exams on July 24. If Jackie had her way, they would be setting a record for the shortest amount of time it took to obtain approval for adopting a child. Of course, Katie had lived with her for 13 months and she thought that should count for something.

On July 23, after church, Jackie told Katie to hang up her clothes and make her bed before she could go swimming at Weber Pond with Diane. Ten minutes later Diane and Katie climbed in the car wearing their suits and carrying their towels. Jackie was amazed how easily they got along now. During the winter, Diane often wondered about the wisdom of having this angry and sneaky girl living with them.

Jackie found Katie's shoes in the living room and she decided to put them away for her. She opened her bedroom door and saw Katie's church clothes on the floor and the bed unmade. She had gone off without doing her work! Katie hadn't done that in a couple of months. Jackie had plenty of time to consider how to respond.

When they returned from their swim two hours later, Jackie met them at the kitchen door. "Sit down, Katie, how was your swim?" Jackie began.

"Great, Mom, Diane says that soon I won't have to wear my life jacket."

"That's wonderful, sweetie," Jackie replied. "But I've been wondering why you went off without making your bed or hanging up your clothes?"

"I forgot, Mom." Katie said quickly.

"But I had just told you, Katie," Jackie said. "So my guess is that you really wanted to leave quickly and did not want to have to wait while you got your work done."

"I forgot!" Katie yelled.

"I know that this will be hard on you, sweetie, but so you work harder not to forget your chores," Jackie said, "the next time Diane goes swimming you won't be able to go."

"That's not fair!" Katie yelled. "I forgot. I'll make my bed now and pick up my clothes."

"Yes, Katie," Jackie said quietly. "I would like you to do that now. But you still can't go swimming the next time."

"You're mean!" Katie yelled.

She threw her wet towel on the floor and ran to her room. She threw open the door and began kicking her clothes. Jackie followed her closely and saw her rage.

"Katie, don't do that to your clothes," Jackie said.

Katie spun around and kicked Jackie. Then she screamed and ran toward the window. Jackie caught her before she hit the window with her fist. Jackie picked her up and carried her to her bed. She sat with her, holding her to her chest while she fought and screamed.

Katie struggled hard for over 10 minutes before finally beginning to lose her strength. It was another 10 minutes before she was quiet. Jackie spoke quietly to her as she struggled, accepting her anger, telling her that she was safe, allowing her to set her own pace. Katie initially screamed at her to stop talking. Gradually she became quiet and Jackie could not tell what she thought and felt.

Finally Katie said quietly, "You don't want me anymore. I hurt you again. I'll never stop hurting you so you don't want me!"

"Oh, Katie, how hard that must be for you if you think that. I do still want you. I'll never stop wanting you. You just got mad at me and hit me. I don't like being hit. You know that you don't hit me nearly as much as you used to. Do you think one little kick is going to get me to stop loving you? Oh, sweetie, my love doesn't work that way."

"Why, Mom?" Katie asked. "Why do you still love me?"

"Because, Katie," Jackie replied, "because you're my kid. That's all there is to it. Nothing you do, or say, or feel, or think, can stop me from loving you. I'm your mom, sweetie. And that's the way it is. I love all the parts of you—your happy parts, your angry parts, your sad parts, your fun parts—all your parts."

Katie sighed. She relaxed further in Jackie's arms. Jackie continued to sway slowly and hum to her. Five minutes later, Katie was sleeping! Tears came to Jackie's eyes. She was again amazed how often Katie could get her to cry. Now she cried simply because the kid fell asleep in her arms!

Jackie quietly laid Katie on her bed, covered her, and slowly crept out of the room. An hour later, when she checked on her, Katie was coloring at her desk. She had made her bed and picked up her clothes.

"What are you up to, kiddo?" Jackie asked.

"I'm drawing a picture of Diane and me swimming. She's holding my foot in her hand and she's going to throw me."

"Neat."

"What's for supper, Mom?"

"Chili and muffins with our garden salad, which you're going to help me pick."

"Neat."

Jackie left. If they were going to eat on time, she had to start the muffins.

## Jackie's Journal:

July 24, 1995: Today I talked with Katie about her birthday next week. I said that she could invite four friends for the afternoon. Diane and I would take them swimming, we'd come back for a dinner that she picked. Then we'd have cake and ice cream and open her presents. I told her that the family would have a party for her the next day. She was both ecstatic and terrified. She wanted reassurance that I really thought that she could handle that amount of excitement.

July 25, 1995: Katie called her friends. Sandy will be away on vacation. But Erica, Emily, and Elise will all be able to come! She couldn't believe it. She had to tell me what she likes about each one. According to her, they are the three greatest kids in all of Maine. No, the whole country. I suggested that we would then have the four greatest kids in the country that day. She asks me to go over the whole schedule with her. It seems that she might need to have every minute of the day programmed. Later, I had to go shopping and Katie stayed with Diane. They were up to something when I was gone. Lots of looks and giggles together over dinner.

July 27, 1995: Mark took Katie and Diane camping for two days. She was so torn! She would run around trying to help them pack and asking dozens of questions. Then she'd run back to me, finding a new reason each time for me to go with them. They would be camping up at Moosehead Lake and Katie reassured me that they would not set up the camp too close to the water. She and Diane are still doing a lot of whispering. When they finally left, Katie gave me an extra long hug, and then grabbed Diane's hand without looking back. She had made up her mind and she was going through with it, by golly!

July 29, 1995: At 2:00 p.m. I heard the car coming up the drive with Katie honking the horn. She hopped out of the car and almost knocked me over. Did she talk! I learned about every adventure they had. They saw a moose and a bear. They rented a small boat and had lunch on an island in the lake. Their hot dogs were delicious but their soda was warm. The first night Katie heard noises and she woke up Diane. That wasn't much help so they both woke up Mark. Their brave leader managed to poke a flashlight out of the tent and he discovered a skunk family going through the garbage that our three out-doorsmen had failed to put away properly. They did not sleep well that night.

July 30, 1995: After church and lunch Katie and Diane asked the rest of the family to come outside. Katie sat me and Mark down on the porch and she ran to the driveway. Her jump rope from last year's birthday appeared. As she and Diane called out a rhythm, Katie jumped. She missed the beat a couple of times at the beginning. She was so earnest. Then she had a long spell with no misses and she was bursting with excitement. She ran to the porch and hugged me and Mark. She insisted that I jump too. She chuckled when I missed a num-ber of times. Then she offered advice and was supportive, like Diane must have been with her. She clapped when I got it. She was proud of me.

August 1, 1995: Therapy tends to be fairly typical now. We discuss the week. Actually the discussions tend to become involved conversations of routine events. There's usually a lot of laughing and teasing. Allison always makes a fuss about what a neat and crazy family we have. When we discuss something that she has done wrong, Katie handles it with little or no stress. If she got any consequences she is quick to tell Allison what they were and how she man-aged them. Today Katie asked Allison directly if she would tell Steven that she was in the right home and should not have to move to another one. Alli-son indicated that she had already told Steven that, and in fact, had written a letter with that recommendation. Katie asked to see the letter. Allison showed it to her. Katie read the letter to me, with some help from Allison over the tricky words. The letter seemed to give Katie confidence. She left the session holding my hand like she now had everything under control.

August 4, 1995: The day finally arrived. Katie is eight. As is the custom in our home, I left her a small present on her pillow while she slept. She awoke to find a new outfit for her favorite doll. She was so surprised and pleased. Last year she got no such surprise! She quickly dressed up her doll to look nice for her friends when they came. Erica, Emily, and Elise, the 3Es Diane calls them, what a group! The four of them laughed and swam and talked and ran all afternoon. Thank goodness for Diane's youth to keep up with them. A few times during the day Katie would come running to me, give me a quick hug, and go running back to her friends. When I put her to bed she gave me the biggest hug, I could hardly breath. She whispered, "Thanks, Mom." as she fell asleep holding her doll.

It's been quite a year, actually 14 months.

On August 18, 1995, Steven stopped by to tell Katie the good news. He was going to tell Jackie at the same time but she would have none of that so he told her when he called to arrange for a time to meet with Katie. She did not tell Katie that he was coming until after lunch, about an hour before his arrival. Katie spent the hour cleaning the house. Jackie decided that Katie was becoming more like her every day!

When Steven arrived, Katie waited on him with milk and crackers. It was her idea and she even joked about it, saying that she did not spill one drop. Mark asked to be served, too. With a look of mild annoyance at a father who did not know when to tease and when not to, Katie managed to get him some milk and crackers, too.

After an eternity to her, Steven said, "Katie, as you know, I've been talking to your whole family and even some of your mom and dad's friends, about you and your home. Back at the office we all talked about your family and we've decided that . . . this is the best home for you. We want you to be adopted by Jackie and Mark."

Katie shrieked. She jumped up from her seat and hugged Jackie. She pulled back, looked at her, shrieked, and hugged her again. The minutes went by with Mark and Steven sitting in the silence. Finally, Katie pulled back and stared at Jackie.

"You're my mom forever and ever."

Then she hugged Mark and said, "I love you, Dad."

Katie turned and hugged Steven. Then she was off. They heard her run upstairs looking for Diane, Matthew, and John. She found two out of three and Jackie, Mark, and Steven heard them cheer. She ran downstairs calling for Whimsy. The old dog found some lost energy and they rolled around on the living room floor. Katie was back in the kitchen, with Whimsy following close behind. Out the door they ran with the adults following. Katie jumped and skipped, grabbed her bike and tore down the driveway. Whimsy barked and even seemed to skip himself as he ran beside her. By the road she slammed on her brakes, turned and sped back toward the house.

She left her bike by the car as she ran through the garden, swung around her swing set, and darted out into the field. She and Whimsy were rapidly losing their momentum as they headed back toward the house. But she was not done yet. She turned and made a line toward the swing under the maple tree. She pumped the swing a half a dozen times and cheered until finally leaping off without waiting for it to stop. She stood panting and searching for something that she may have forgotten. She suddenly spun around. She took three giant steps and then hugged the tree. Whimsy ran around it a few times and then sat beside her.

Jackie, Mark, and Steven stood on the porch motionless and in silence.

Finally, in awe, Jackie said, "She's claiming her home."

"She is!" Mark said. "She's now at home."

"And she's claiming herself, too."

"Yes."

"Our crazy, lovely, and wonderful daughter," Jackie said as she put her arm around Mark. "Katie Keller. Our daughter. She cries and laughs . . . and weeds the garden . . . and swims and jumps rope. You know, the basics.

"Oh, and yes, she hugs trees too."

She paused and smiled.

"In Vassalboro, Maine. Where the sun shines."

# 19

## General Principles of Parenting and Therapy

### PARENTING

For Jackie to parent Katie well she needed to maintain general principles that would guide her interactions with Katie and at the same time maintain her own family well-being. These principles—much more than specific techniques—guided Jackie. A child like Katie would find a way to make any technique ineffective within an hour. If Jackie could follow these principles, she would be more likely to think of a unique intervention that fit a given situation. She might never use that intervention again, since each situation was unique and also because Katie was likely to have developed a strategy to resist it.

The therapeutic *attitude* described throughout this work was central to Jackie's ability to adequately maintain an emotional tone in the interactions with Katie that would facilitate intersubjectivity. A playful, accepting, empathic, loving, and curious attitude was most able to meet the psychological needs of both Katie and the entire family. It enabled Jackie to protect her own healthy manner of relating and living so that she could share it with Katie.

Jackie was aware that she had to provide Katie with opportunities for countless intersubjective experiences. Katie needed to gradually accept and enjoy these experiences of joint affect, shared attention and interests, and complementary intentions if she were to learn a more positive and coherent way of experiencing herself and others. These experiences were characterized by eye contact, smiles, touching, voice prosody, gestures, and movement. They often occurred with humor, gentle teasing, empathy, and surprise. They consisted in songs, repetitive activities and movements, and various "pre-school" messy activities. They consisted in quiet comments and discussions, interest in the curls in Katie's hair, curiosity about the weather. They involved Jackie's manifesting a continuing process of discovery of who Katie was — underneath her symptoms. They occurred regardless of whether or not Katie was making good choices. They had to occur because they were the wings on which Katie flew in order to develop a core of affective pleasure, openness to self and other, and a core of trust in Jackie. They had to occur if Katie were to discover and actualize the person she was at birth.

Such intersubjective experiences occurred spontaneously and unexpectedly throughout the day. If Katie seemed to have difficulty accepting direct expressions of affection, she might be more receptive to moments of humor and relaxed "small talk." She would then feel close to Jackie without realizing it and without having to acknowledge that she wanted to be close. Jackie also might surprise Katie with a brief, fun-filled activity so that Katie would gradually begin to trust that when the unexpected happened in Jackie's home, it would be enjoyable and not traumatic. Katie would gradually begin to trust in a future that Jackie, not Katie, would be able to keep safe. Jackie would present those surprises to her because she was her mother and they were good for her. They would not occur because Katie had manipulated, threatened, screamed, or charmed Jackie into doing them. Since they were unexpected, it would be harder for Katie to sabotage them.

When Katie had intersubjective experiences at a predictable time, she resisted them initially until they gradually took on special meaning. Jackie decided to have a special time, which she called "mom time" every evening before bed. Katie would discover that "mom time" occurred every day regardless of her behavior. It would enable her to begin to relax and feel secure at the end of the day, no matter how angry she had been with Jackie throughout the day.

Since Katie had difficulty being aware of and expressing her inner life of thought and emotion, Jackie constantly would have brief conversations with her that involved the expression of thoughts, feelings, wishes, fantasies, plans, and memories. Jackie would initially do most of the talking, both about her own inner life and also about what she thought Katie might be experiencing. Jackie needed to be very patient, knowing that it would be months or longer before Katie was likely to make the conversations truly reciprocal. As Jackie responded — both verbally and nonverbally — to Katie's expressions of her inner life, Katie gradually began to notice her experience more clearly, to accept if more fully, and to discover ways of more actively expressing it herself.

Conversations that Jackie held with Katie also would involve explorations of the past and future. Since shame-based experiences dominated Katie's past, Jackie — by calmly mentioning those experiences — was communicating that she knew and accepted all aspects of Katie and her story. Jackie would also share aspects of her own past with Katie, in an effort to help Katie to feel more a part of the continuity of the Keller family. By discussing the future with Katie, Jackie would be communicating confidence in their future life together, inviting her into family rituals, and helping her to manage her anxiety about the unknown by familiarizing her with guideposts that she would meet along the way. At times, Jackie would wonder about the years ahead with Katie, expressing hopefulness about the person she would someday become.

Along with general intersubjective experiences, it is equally important for Jackie to provide Katie with those that were *shame-reducing*. Katie was certain to engage in many provocative, defiant, and aggressive behaviors that would function to disrupt the family and attempt to maintain control of its emotional tone. Such behaviors also were evidence to her of how bad and worthless she was. She invariably experienced discipline as a statement of her inherent evil, rather than being an effort to teach her how to live within the social realities of family life. Jackie needed to socialize Katie if she were to ever live in harmony with others. But she also needed to be mindful of Katie's shame.

Jackie's therapeutic attitude served as the best context in which Katie's experiences of shame could occur. When Jackie needed to discipline and structure Katie's behavior, shame would be a side effect. By remaining emotionally available to her immediately following the discipline, she would be limiting the experience to the actual behaviors and reducing its impact on her vulnerable sense of self. At these times, Jackie is first communicating empathy for Katie over her sense of shame. She is not trying to talk Katie out of the shame, but rather is being with her, and helping her to co-regulate the affect and co-create a deeper meaning to the behavior. In this manner, Katie is gradually able to tolerate and then accept her experiences of shame, reduce it, experience guilt about the behavior itself, and finally integrate it into her self-identity. At the same time, through providing empathy to her following the experience, Jackie is enabling Katie to gradually learn how to accept being comforted following distress. This **Interactive Repair** is a central feature of relationships characterized by attachment security.

Frequently discipline involves a parent being mildly annoyed with her child for her behaviors and then giving her a consequence. If the child objects, the parent might become even more annoyed and give a greater consequence. This practice of discipline would be completely ineffective with Katie. The annoyance would immediately increase her sense of shame and be experienced as rejection. For this reason, Jackie needs to consistently maintain the therapeutic attitude when she disciplines Katie. She is then able to accept and have empathy for Katie's defiance and resistance. She also can communicate a curiosity about Katie's subsequent responses and she can choose to be playful, rather than defensive, during the interaction.

Otto Weininger's lovely small parenting book, *Time-in Parenting* (2002), describes the need for parents to keep children closer to them—rather than isolating them—when their children need them the most. Another parenting book, by Alfie Kohn, *Unconditional Parenting* (2005), provides a general guide for parenting that is congruent with the PLACE model described here and, while written for all families, has special relevance for children with the severity of problems that Katie manifested. Caroline Archer has also written two books (1999a, 1999b) that are excellent guides in understanding and caring for children with histories and difficulties similar to Katie.

Jackie knew that she most likely would have to restrain Katie, if attachment security were going to develop between them. Jackie would restrain her when Katie was unable to control her own impulses and thus was a risk to the safety of herself or others through aggression or destructiveness. By restraining her, Jackie would be providing her with the control that she could not give to herself. However, she also would be communicating her acceptance and empathy for Katie's distress and she would be facilitating Katie's ability to establish an emotional bond with her at a time when she most needed it and was most likely to permit it. Some cognitive therapists suggest that when it is necessary to restrain a child, caregivers should restrain with neither affective expression nor eye contact, out of concern that attention will increase the behavior. I recommend giving eye contact and empathy with a nonjudgmental tone and have not found this to increase the frequency of the need for restraints. Katie's attachment tendencies would be likely to intensify during those periods of distress, and they would strengthen if Jackie were able to be emotionally receptive and available. In those circumstances, Jackie knew that one day Katie's emotion would be likely to move from screaming rage to gentle tears and also to giggling smiles.

Jackie also would hold Katie in a nurturing and affectionate way, bringing her close to her just as a mother holds her infant or toddler. Such holding is the best replication for the intersubjective experiences that Katie missed during her first year of life. Jackie began by approaching her with quick touches and brief hugs, using this physical contact as the bridge to longer periods of snuggling, rocking, and caressing (frequent activities during "mom-time").

While it was helpful for Jackie to be predictable in her attitude toward Katie, it was less beneficial for her to be predictable in her choices of consequences for her behaviors. Children like Katie often misbehave in order to feel that they have control over what consequences their parent will give them. They often seek consequences that will give them a reason to be angry and to believe that their parents are mean (negative attributions). Katie might choose to misbehave in a compulsive effort to make Jackie get angry with her and reject her. The sad reality is that often such children want to validate their sense of shame, to extinguish all reasons for hope, and to discover nothing of worth within themselves. For these reasons, Jackie needed to keep her off balance by choosing a variety of consequences for a given behavior.

Paradoxical responses are often helpful in preventing a child from gaining control over the consequences. For example, if Katie were to scream loudly in the kitchen while she was working, Jackie might have told her to scream more loudly and then time how long it lasts. Or she might have suggested that she practice screaming twice a day, at a given time and place. Jackie might also have taped the scream to play at therapy. Or she might have screamed along with her and asked the other children to judge who was the best screamer. Such paradoxical responses work in a great many situations with various behaviors, as long as Jackie is able to accept the behavior that she is telling Katie to do. Such paradoxical approaches should never be done with sarcasm or humiliation.

A final general parenting principle that Jackie used with Katie involved providing her with experiences that we typically provide for toddlers. These experiences served to acknowledge and accept that Katie's affective/cognitive development had features of dysregulation and impulsivity that more closely approximated those of a toddler than those of a seven-year-old. Jackie provided both *nurturing* experiences that facilitate affective attunement and *structuring* experiences that reduce shame and serve to facilitate socialization. Both nurture and structure also increase the child's sense of safety. *Nurturing* experiences included singing and playing toddler songs and games, washing, dressing and combing her hair, and quiet cuddling with books and music, and, when comfortable to both, giving her a bottle. They involved eye contact, smiles, movement, and touch. For ideas of such activities, see *Games Babies Play* (1993) by Vicki Lansky and also *Fun To Grow On* (1999) by Virginia Morin.

*Structuring* experiences involved providing her with a well-organized routine that alternated active and quiet activities. Within that routine, Jackie could be near her and supervise her closely just as she would if Katie were 18 months old. Finally, just as she would if Katie were a toddler, Jackie made most of her choices for her, even including what she would wear and eat. Such structuring experiences were as important in enabling Katie to take advantage of Jackie's affective/reflective presence as were the nurturing ones. Through providing Katie with the opportunity to rely on her physical presence and decision-making, Jackie was providing her with a very safe environment. Katie gradually felt very secure within that circle of physical and psychological proximity that Jackie maintained for her. Within that safety,

Katie was more able to reduce her own need to be in control and to rely on Jackie as being present, assuring safety, and being the source of interests, comfort, and enjoyment. She was accepting Jackie for who she was—namely, her mother.

Parents and therapists need to recognize that the caregivers' (and therapists') own attachment histories frequently emerge in response to the trauma-attachment problems manifested by their child. The child's intense affect (rage, fear, sadness, shame) is likely to arouse the parent's similar affective state. If the parent has not integrated and regulated the associated affect, the parent is likely to react with rage, anxiety, despair, or shame. Each encounter now risks intense negative affective cycles. Each reaction may trigger a more intense reaction. The child's anger may trigger anger from the parent or it may activate anxiety. Either way, the parent's intense affective state will make it difficult for her to remain focused on co-regulating her child's state. At that moment, neither the child, nor the parent, feels safe. Neither is responding in a flexible, best-interests manner in the present. Both are reacting in a rigid manner, reminiscent of previous unresolved events from their attachment histories.

Some parents are able to defend against their own affective states by responding to the child's intense affective with a more detached manner. They may well be able to focus on the child's behavior and possibly a consequence in a way that does not trigger an intense escalation. However, often these parents are able to defend against their affect by not responding to the child's affective experience of the immediate event. When that occurs, the parent is often unable to provide empathy for the child. Empathy requires that the parent resonate with the child's affective state and exist within the child's experiential world. This is a central way to co-regulate the child's affect. While such a defense is preferable to an escalation cycle, its inhibiting effect on empathy can take a toll on the child's need for parental support to regulate his intense affect. Also, the child is less likely to develop empathy for others unless he experiences empathy for his distress from his parents.

Parents do not need to establish defenses that inhibit both affective escalation and empathy when their own attachment histories are resolved. When the child's affect activates something from their own history, they are able to remain in the present in the child's experiential world rather than sinking into their own past. They may re-experience an aspect of their past, but this does not lead to dysregulation. They remain able to reflect on their past, observe similarities with their child, and then respond in a manner that is helpful to the present situation. It is crucial when one is attempting to raise a child like Katie that the parent is able to self-reflect about her own history in order to respond to her child. At times, psychotherapy for the parent may be necessary.

## PSYCHOTHERAPY

The psychological treatment of Katie, known as Dyadic Developmental Psychotherapy (Hughes, 2004; Becker-Weidman & Shell, 2005), involved providing her with a series of complex integrative affective and reflective experiences. The central features of her treatment involved intersubjective affective experiences of both attunement as well as shame reduction. By providing a setting in which both she and Jackie were closely attuned to Katie's affective states, Allison was providing a context of trust that approximated the setting in which attachment security occurs. Within this atmosphere of trust, Allison and Jackie employed empathy and curiosity, always grounded in acceptance, to explore with Katie various experiences of shame from her past and present life. Shame-reduction occurred by bringing the incident to Katie's awareness, actively communicating empathy for her distress, and then through co-creating the meaning of Katie's new affective and reflective states. This enabled her to integrate her fragmented self, increase her sense of self-worth, and enhance her ability to develop attachment security with Jackie.

When Allison sensed and was responsive to Katie's affective states, she provided her with primary and secondary intersubjective experiences. The experience was the most therapeutic when it occurred in a manner that involved eye contact, facial expressiveness, rich and varied voice modifications, and a wide range of gestures and movements. Allison's voice moved easily from loud to soft, rapid to slow, with periodic long latencies in which she and Katie were wondering about a problem and its solution. Allison giggled and laughed, moved her face close and pulled away, and she demonstrated empathic sadness, fear, or anger, closely attuned with Katie's affective state quite readily in her facial and vocal expressions. While exploring the immediate interaction as well as a recent or distant event, she sat close to Katie and frequently touched her. Such physical contact greatly facilitated the communication of shared affect. Physical contact was as effective as voice tone and facial gestures in co-regulating various emotional themes of joy, excitement, shame, anger, sadness, and anxiety.

Along with voice modifications, facial gestures, movements, and touch, Allison was able to maintain Katie's attention, attuned affect and intention to remain engaged through saying and doing the unexpected. This created an air of expectancy and Katie was likely to be quite responsive to the communicated affect. Allison might comment on Katie's posture, gestures, exclamation, or groan, often with empathy, humor, or curiosity. Such reflections helped to keep Katie involved in the affective/reflective dialogue. What is important in such interchanges is not the content, but the therapeutic *attitude* that Allison was conveying. Without using words, Allison was, in essence, saying:

> Katie, you are an interesting and delightful girl. I want to get to know you, play with you, and discover who you are. I want to know all about you, child. With me and your mom, there need be no shameful secrets that diminish you. *You* are welcome here, and that includes your rage, your fear, and your desire for warmth and joy. We will walk along with you and guide you on this journey. We will stay with you no matter where this journey takes us.

Therapy also helps children to increase their ability to reflect on the meaning of their behaviors. Rather than simply assuming that their behavior indicates that they are "bad," children need to develop curiosity about their own motives. When they understand the context of their behavior, they might feel appropriately guilty but they need not experience the behavior itself as shameful. Thus, Katie's anger could signify her interpretation of Jackie's discipline as apathy to Katie's "needs." Katie's threat to hurt the dog might represent her incomprehension at the family's unconditional love for the pet or a plea for her mother's extra supervision so that she would not hurt the family pet. When Katie became resistant in therapy, Allison would always accept her resistance and communicate to her that Katie was doing the best that she could and "of course" she would resist sometimes since the work was so hard. Allison frequently interpreted her resistance in therapy in a very positive manner, suggesting that Katie was wise to go slowly now. The *attitude* qualities of curiosity, playfulness, empathy, and acceptance each facilitated this manner of relating with Katie. Whenever there is a playful tone to the communication, it is crucial that there be no sarcasm.

Therapeutic suggestions integrate easily into these affectively rich and reciprocal conversations. Allison might have asked her if she would like to learn to reduce her anger first or become more relaxed first. If she accepted the limits of the choices available to her, she was going to make progress. Allison might have wondered if her progress would be fast or slow, if she would first show progress in an area that they had already explored or if she would choose to surprise them by making progress in something that they had never discussed.

Finally, Allison also used music at times to support the affective tone of a conversation with Katie. Playing music can set a calm and relaxed tone or it can offer a supportive atmosphere for Katie while she was dealing with shame-inducing experiences. Music facilitated nurturing experiences between Jackie and Katie. At times, Jackie and Katie, or the three of them, created their own music that reflected the tone of their immediate focus and interactions.

Along with providing affective attunement experiences, for therapy to be effective it needs to also provide shame-reduction experiences. Attachment sequences which involve intersubjectivity, emotional separations created by shame, anger or fear due to the themes being explored, and interactive repair of the relationship occur frequently throughout the therapy session. Katie's denial of an event was an effort to reduce the emotional pain of shame. Her pervasive sense of shame permeated her definition of self as being bad and left her in isolation and despair. Her only recourse was to deny the experience. This led to lies, excuses, distortions, and very often, to rage. By exploring the shame-based experience, in the context of the therapeutic *attitude* being conveyed by Allison and Jackie, Katie managed to reduce the shame and integrate the experience into her sense of self. She then became more receptive to greater intersubjectivity with Jackie throughout the day, since her sense of self as being more worthwhile could now integrate movements toward such a relationship. She needed not be so afraid of loving and being loved. For Katie, eventually, reciprocal enjoyment was not so frightening.

Throughout Katie's therapy, Allison spoke for Katie or gave her the words to say. She would often encourage Katie to look at her or Jackie while she spoke them. Allison also would speak with heightened affective expression in her voice and in her facial expressions and gestures. This is a very powerful intervention that often enabled Katie to find the words that described the harsh realities of her life so that she could gradually begin to integrate them into a more cohesive self. The words alone did not reach Katie's inner experience; they required a consort of meaningful, congruent, affective expressions. Shock, surprise, sadness, rage, excitement, joy, interest, and fear accompanied requests for Katie to express certain phrases as representing her own inner life.

When asking her to engage in these affective/reflective phrases, Allison remained attuned with Katie's affective states so that she would discard a phrase that did not match an aspect of her inner life. At times Katie might refuse to repeat a phrase even when Allison's statement did accurately reflect her thoughts and emotions. Allison simply accepted her refusal to speak for herself and spoke for her, and then waited to see if Katie was demonstrating an affective response to Allison's nonverbal and verbal communication. If Katie were to express her wish that Allison not speak for her, Allison would listen to her request and then explore with her the source of her reluctance. If Katie were to say that Allison's words did not reflect her own thoughts and feelings, Allison would always accept Katie's statement. Katie is the only one who can say what her subjective experience is.

Finally, it is important to note that the therapy provided to Katie was very difficult work for Katie, Jackie, and Allison. To facilitate the child's motivation to change, the therapist must recognize this difficulty and make it explicit in an early session.

The joint affective attunement experiences that are crucial to Katie's therapy are central to *Theraplay* (1999) by Jernberg and Booth. *Theraplay* emphasizes many qualities of the mother-child relationship during the first two years of life and stresses interactive parent-child play rather than symbolic play. Positive, here-and-now intersubjective—mostly nonverbal— experiences are the activities of the sessions. This approach emphasizes physical contact, eye contact, facial gestures, movement, and reciprocal enjoyment. The relationship between the therapist and child is the primary therapeutic focus. The therapist also provides training and consultation to the child's parents regarding ways to maximize the quality of their relationship at home. The "floor-time" of Stanley Greenspan (1992) also contains strong components of affective attunement and preverbal play with curiosity and acceptance.

The treatment of Katie contrasts with the above forms of therapy in stressing that children with attachment-related traumas often need to directly deal with their constant experience of pervasive shame. Intersubjective experiences need to precede, accompany, and follow any exploration of events that are associated with profound shame in order to reduce this shame and co-create new experiences of those events. Simply providing intersubjective experiences around positive events often does not reach into, explore, and integrate the "bad self" which so permeates the life of the child with trauma/attachment problems.

This model of psychotherapy employs principles derived from attachment and intersubjectivity theories and focuses on assisting children and youth to begin to rely on their present caregivers for an overall sense of safety, for developing a more positive and coherent sense of self-and-other, and for a safe haven from which to resolve past traumas. While attachment principles guide the therapeutic stance and the therapist's active use of self, the overall therapeutic interventions and characteristics are congruent with core features of process-experiential, psychodynamic, gestalt, Rogerian, and cognitive-behavioral therapy. These features include the therapy relationship, empathy, acceptance, and curiosity, as well as gradual exposure, parent consultation, and the development of self-soothing, coping, and communication skills.

Attachment security is certainly one of the central treatment goals in working with Katie and attachment and intersubjective theories and principles serve as guides for psychotherapeutic interventions. However, this treatment is not considered to be "attachment therapy" just as it is not considered to be "affect regulation" therapy or "shame-reduction" therapy, even though those are also frequent goals. This treatment is a blend of individual psychotherapy and family therapy. Katie's psychological treatment focused more on her functioning in the context of her new relationship with Jackie. Were Jackie to have significant psychological problems, the treatment would necessarily focus first on helping her to resolve her difficulties so that she would be in the position to facilitate attachment security with Katie.

I wish to differentiate this model of treatment from forms of "attachment therapy" and "holding therapy" that some have employed in the treatment of children with serious problems secondary to attachment disruption/disorganization and childhood trauma. Two better-known forms of such treatments are those of Martha Welch (1989) and Foster Cline (1992). Both models of therapy consider coercive holding of the child to be necessary to the treatment process. Dr. Welch only has the parent hold the child whereas Dr. Cline frequently has the therapist do the primary holding. Both models very actively confront the child about his serious behavioral problems, first elicit anger/rage, encourage the child to give release to his fear and despair, and then provide an opportunity for a resolution and comforting by the parent. Both treatments center on confrontation at the early stages. Neither emphasizes the acceptance, curiosity, and empathy that are present throughout Katie's treatment, at least they don't in the early stages of the interventions. My fear is that the confrontation that these models stress is likely to increase shame and lead to a bond that has components of an unhealthy dependency on an authority figure. Beverly James (1994) and others express similar concerns.

In contrast to Cline's work, rather than increasing shame in treatment, my stance in therapy and at home is to comprehensively work to reduce shame from the outset. In therapy, I will calmly and gently focus on a shame-inducing experience in the child's life, and the act of exploring it often precipitates a shame-full response. I then accept the response, manifest empathy for it, explore it, and enable the child to reduce and integrate it into his developing sense of self. I do not create shame in therapy by becoming angry with the child. I supportively bring out for resolution the hidden shame that was already present within him. This stance involves the belief that when shame decreases, the associated denial, excuses, and rage will also decrease. As shame decreases, the child becomes more receptive to entering into attachment-related behaviors with his parents through intersubjective experiences of both joy and excitement during happy events, and support and comfort following shame-related events. When this treatment is successful, the child's sense of self-worth develops together with his attachment security with his parents. Rather than coming to believe that his parents love him in spite of his being worthless, he begins to discover *at the same time* that both he and his parents are worthwhile and that the attachment follows naturally from this realization.

These children already experience habitual profound shame because of the countless traumas and deficiencies in their early attachment history during the first 18 months of their lives. A treatment stance that acknowledges and reduces their preexisting shame, rather than first increasing it, is likely to provide both safety as well as an openness to develop a healthier experience of self-and-other.

Some of these treatment approaches for children with significant problems secondary to intrafamilial trauma and attachment disorganization do not have a research base. However, I believe that the model of treatment presented here is congruent with principles that are congruent with attachment theory and research (Siegel, 2001). Allison's model of treatment is now being practiced by many therapists throughout the United States, the United Kingdom, and Canada. There have been some early efforts to develop an empirical foundation for this treatment. Dr. Arthur Becker-Weidman (2006) has authored an office-based research study in which he compares the results of this treatment model with a control group of children with similar histories and behavioral problems. Though the study is small, and it lacks the elaborate measures and controls of a research center, the results are very favorable regarding the efficacy of this model of treatment for children similar to Katie. A follow-up study by Dr. Becker-Weidman (in press) demonstrates that the treatment gains secondary to this model of intervention are stable for three years after treatment, whereas the children who received traditional treatment were actually functioning with more severe symptoms.

The work of Beverly James (1989, 1994) represents an important effort to increase the effectiveness of play therapy with children with trauma/attachment problems. Some of her interventions integrate easily into the therapeutic format suggested in this work. The same is true of the gestalt strategies and stance of Violet Oaklander (1978). Finally, narrative therapy developed for children by J. Freeman, D. Epston, and D. Lobovits (1997) demonstrates a manner of relating with a child about his problems that has similarity with the playful and relaxed manner that I have stressed. Its approach also externalizes the problem in a manner that might enable the child to address it with less shame.

Cognitive-Behavioral interventions are primarily verbal efforts to conceptualize the problem and provide the parent and child with specific cognitive and behavioral strategies to reduce the behaviors of concern and increase alternative, adaptive behaviors. The therapist is directive and recommends a similar directive, problem-solving strategy to the parent. In general, therapists who rely on a cognitive-behavioral framework do not emphasize the importance of establishing intersubjective experiences with children and their crucial importance in developing positive affective states of joy and excitement while reducing the negative states of shame or terror. Too often, this framework does not adequately recognize that, with children who have significant difficulty developing attachment security and a readiness for intersubjective experiences, the usual social reinforcers are not effective. Also the concrete reinforcers that are often provided to these children are not effective for any period of time and do not generalize to ongoing interpersonal behaviors. These children experience their greatest reinforcements in manipulating the reinforcement program and then causing emotional distress in their parents because of their inability to control them. However, as is the case with certain play-therapy interventions, cognitive-behavioral strategies can integrate in the framework suggested by Katie's treatment and are effective interventions once the participants accept the basic intersubjective process and begin to establish attachment security. Recent works recognize the need to integrate cognitive-behavioral interventions into a treatment that recognizes the need to build safety in relationships, integrate affective states, and facilitate relationship skills themselves (Cloitre et al., 2002; Saywitz et al., 2000).

Katie's treatment with Allison is quite similar to Accelerated Experiential Dynamic Psychotherapy developed by Diana Fosha (2000, 2003). Dr. Fosha's model of treatment for adults within an individual therapy format has striking similarities with the principles and interventions presented here. There are also similarities between this model and Emotionally Focused Therapy for individuals and couples (Greenberg, 2002; Johnson, 1996, 2002).

# References

Archer, Caroline. 1999a. *First Steps in Parenting the Child Who Hurts*. London: Jessica Kingsley.

———. 1999b. *Next Steps in Parenting the Child Who Hurts*. London: Jessica Kingsley.

Becker-Weidman, Arthur. 2006. "Treatment for Children with Trauma-Attachment Disorders: Dyadic Developmental Psychotherapy." *Child and Adolescent Social Work Journal* 13.

———. In press. "The Effective Treatment of Abused Children with Dyadic Developmental Psychotherapy." *Child Abuse and Its Impact*, ed. Frank Columbus. New York: Nova Science.

Becker-Weidman, Arthur & Deborah Shell. 2005. *Creating Capacity for Attachment*. Oklahoma City, OK: Wood 'N' Barnes.

Bohart, Arthur C., Robert Elliott, Leslie S. Greenberg, & Jeanne C. Watson. 2002. Empathy. Pp. 89–108 in *Psychotherapy Relationships that Work: Therapist Contributions and Responsiveness to Patients*, ed. J. C. Norcross. New York: Oxford University.

Cassidy, Jude & Phillip R. Shaver, ed. 1999. *Handbook of Attachment*. New York: Guilford.

Cicchetti, Dante. 1989. "How Research on Child Maltreatment Has Informed the Study of Child Development: Perspectives from Developmental Psychopathology." Pp. 377–431 in *Child Maltreatment*, ed. D. Cicchetti & V. Carlson. New York: Cambridge University.

Cline, Foster W. 1992. *Hope for High Risk and Rage Filled Children*. Evergreen, CO: EC Publications.

Cloitre, Marylee, Karestan C. Koenen, Lisa R. Cohen, & Hyemee Han. 2002. "Skills Training in Affective and Interpersonal Regulation Followed by Exposure: A Phase-Based Treatment for PTSD Related to Childhood Abuse." *Journal of Consulting and Clinical Psychology* 70, 1067–1074.

Dozier, Mary, K. Chase Stovall, Katy E. Albus, & Brady Bates. 2001. "Attachment for Infants in Foster Care: The Role of Caregiver State of Mind." *Child Development* 72, 1467–1477.

Egeland, Byron, & Martha F. Erickson. 1987. "Psychologically Unavailable Caregiving." Pp.110–120 in *Psychological Maltreatment of Children and Youth*, ed. M. R. Brassard, R. Germain, & S. N. Hart. New York: Pergamon.

Feiring, Candice, Lynn Taska, & Michael Lewis. 2002. "Adjustment Following Sexual Abuse Discovery: The Role of Shame and Attributional Style." *Developmental Psychology* 38, 79–92.

Field, Tiffany. 2002. *Touch*. Cambridge, MA: MIT.

Fosha, Dianna. 2000. *The Transforming Power of Affect*. New York: Basic Books.

——. 2003. "Dyadic Regulation and Experiential Work with Emotion and Relatedness in Trauma and Disorganized Attachment." Pp.221–281 in *Healing Trauma: Attachment, Mind, Body, and Brain*, ed. M. F. Solomon, & D. J. Siegel. New York: W. W. Norton.

Freeman, Jennifer, David Epston, & Dean Lobovits. 1997. *Playful Approaches to Serious Problems*. New York: W. W. Norton.

Greenberg, Leslie. 2002. *Emotion-Focused Therapy*. Washington, DC: APA.

Greenspan, Stanley I. 1992. *Infancy and Early Childhood*. Madison, CT: International Universities.

Greenspan, Stanley I., & Alicia F. Lieberman. 1988. "A Clinical Approach to Attachment." Pp. 387–424 in *Clinical Implications of Attachment*, ed. J. Belsky, & J. T. Nezworski. Hillsdale, NJ: Lawrence Erlbaum.

Hughes, Daniel. 2004. "An Attachment-Based Treatment of Maltreated Children and Young People." *Attachment and Human Development* 6, 263–278.

James, Beverly. 1989. *Treating Traumatized Children*. Lexington, MA: Lexington Books.

——. 1994. *Handbook for Treatment of Attachment-Trauma Problems in Children*. Lexington, MA: Lexington Books.

Jernberg, Ann, & Phyllis Booth. 1999. *Theraplay*. 2nd ed. San Francisco: Jossey-Bass.

Johnson, Susan M. 1996. *Creating Connections*. Lewittown, PA: Brunner/Mazel.

——. 2002. *Emotionally Focused Couple Therapy with Trauma Survivors: Strengthening Attachment Bonds*. New York: Guilford.

Kaufman, Gerald. 1996. *The Psychology of Shame*. 2nd ed. New York: Springer.

Kohn, Alfie. 2005. *Unconditional Parenting*. NY: Atria.

Lansky, Vicki. 1993. *Games Babies Play*. Deephaven, MN: The Book Peddlers.

Lyons-Ruth, Karlen, & Deborah Jacobvitz. 1999. "Attachment Disorganization: Unresolved Loss, Relational Violence, and Lapses in Behavioral and Attentional Strategies." Pp. 520–554 in *Handbook of Attachment*, ed. J. Cassidy, & P. Shaver. New York: Guilford.

Marvin, Robert, Glen Cooper, Kent Hoffman, & Bert Powell. 2002. "The Circle of Security Project: Attachment-Based Intervention with Caregiver-Pre-School Child Dyads." *Attachment & Human Development* 4, 107–124.

Morin, Virginia K. 1999. *Fun to Grow On*. Chicago: Magnolia Street Publishers.

Oaklander, Violet. 1978. *Windows to Our Children*. Moab, UT: Real People.

Pears, Katherine C., & P. A. Fisher. 2005. "Emotion Understanding and Theory of Mind among Maltreated Children in Foster Care: Evidence of Deficits." *Development and Psychopathology* 17, 47–65.

Saywitz, Karen J., Anthony P. Mannarino, Lucy Berliner, & Judith A. Cohen. 2000. "Treatment for Sexually Abused Children and Adolescents." *American Psychologist* 55, 1040–1049.

Schore, Allan N. 1994. *Affect Regulation and the Origin of the Self*. Hillsdale, NJ: Lawrence Erlbaum.

———. 2001. "Effects of a Secure Attachment on Right Brain Development, Affect Regulation, and Infant Mental Health." *Infant Mental Health Journal* 22, 7–67.

Siegel, Daniel J. 1999. *The Developing Mind*. New York: Guilford.

———. 2001. "Toward an Interpersonal Neurobiology of the Developing Mind: Attachment Relationships, 'Mindsight,' and Neural Integration." *Infant Mental Health Journal* 22, 67–94.

Sroufe, L. Alan. 1995. *Emotional Development: The Organization of Emotional Life in the Early Years*. New York: Cambridge University.

Steele, Miriam, Jill Hodge, Jeanne Kaniuk, Saul Hillman, & Kay Henderson. 2003. "Attachment Representations and Adoption: Associations between Maternal States of Mind and Emotion Narratives in Previously Maltreated Children." *Journal of Child Psychotherapy* 29, 187–205.

Stern, Daniel N. 1985. *The Interpersonal World of the Infant*. New York: Basic Books.

———. 2004. *The Present Moment in Psychotherapy and Everyday Life*. New York: W. W. Norton.

Tangney, June, & Ronda Dearing. 2002. *Shame and Guilt*. New York: Guilford.

Trevarthen, Colwyn. 2001. "Intrinsic Motivation for Companionship in Understanding: the Origin, Development, and Significance for Infant Mental Health." *Infant Mental Health Journal* 22, 95–131.

Trevarthen, Colwyn, & Kenneth J. Aitken. 2001. "Infant Intersubjectivity: Research, Theory, and Clinical Applications." *Journal of Child Psychology and Psychiatry* 42, 3–48.

Welch, Martha G. 1989. *Holding Time*. New York: Fireside Books.

Weininger, Otto. 2002. *Time-in Parenting*. Toronto, Ontario: Rinascente Books.

# About the Author

**Daniel A. Hughes**, Ph.D., is a clinical psychologist who specializes in child abuse and neglect, attachment, foster care, and adoption. He resides in Maine and actively trains other therapists in the model of treatment known as Dyadic Developmental Psychotherapy, both within the United States and in other countries.